AMERICAN STUDIES

Louis Menand

FARRAR, STRAUS AND GIROUX

NEW YORK

Farrar, Straus and Giroux
19 Union Square West, New York 10003

Copyright © 2002 by Louis Menand
All rights reserved
Distributed in Canada by Douglas & McIntyre Ltd.
Printed in the United States of America
Published in 2002 by Farrar, Straus and Giroux
First paperback edition, 2003

The Library of Congress has cataloged the hardcover edition as follows:
Menand, Louis.
    American studies / Louis Menand.— 1st ed.
        p.   cm.
    Includes bibliographical references.
    ISBN 0-374-10434-4 (hc : alk. paper)
        1. United States—Intellectual life—20th century.   2. United States—
Civilization—20th century.   I. Title.

E169.1 .M5457 2002
973.9—dc21

                                                             2002022813

                    Paperback ISBN 0-374-52900-0

                Designed by Cassandra J. Pappas

                        www.fsgbooks.com

            1   3   5   7   9   10   8   6   4   2

Louis Menand

AMERICAN STUDIES

Louis Menand is the Pulitzer Prize–winning author of *The Meta-physical Club,* Professor of English and American Literature and Language at Harvard, and a staff writer at the *New Yorker.*

ALSO BY LOUIS MENAND

The Metaphysical Club

AMERICAN STUDIES

To Lev and Joseph

with love and awe

Contents

Preface

The only reliable lesson the past teaches us is how locked we are in the present. People ask, Where are the great Hollywood movies, the great pop songs, the great television newsmen, the great Democratic presidents, the great public intellectuals, the Great Books?, as though these were all eternally available types. They are not. Their availability is a myth.

I wrote most of the essays contained in this book in an office that overlooked a block of Times Square during a period of frenetic redevelopment. Every day, I watched tall buildings being demolished so that even taller ones could be constructed on their sites. Everyone has had the experience of driving past work crews on the highway. You see five guys sipping coffee and watching one man with a pick while he hacks halfheartedly at some gravel. You suspect that in five minutes the man with the pick will also be on a coffee break. Six months later, there is a new road. Building demolition is like that. You can watch for hours while workers move a few planks on a temporary scaffolding. Maybe a man with a blowtorch is laboring with apparent futility on a huge steel beam. Nothing else is going on. Two days later, a floor has disappeared. At the end of three years, the derelict structure has been obliterated and a new tower, whose erection was similarly mysterious, shimmers in its place. I was a witness to this transformation several times, but somehow I never *saw* it.

History is the same. The critical massing of conditions that enables a particular way of life to come into being is almost impossible to detect while it is happening, and so is its deterioration. The world just rolls over, without anyone noticing exactly when, and a new set of circumstances is put in place. But the impulse to hold on to the past is very strong, and it is often hard to understand why things that worked once can't continue to work. A lot of energy and imagination are consumed trying to fit old systems to new settings, though the pegs keep getting squarer and the holes keep getting rounder. In the end, the only way to make the past usable is to misinterpret it, which means, strictly speaking, to lose it.

Not every culture is like this, but American culture has been like this since the late nineteenth century. It is the culture of modernity, where the highest praise one can receive after death is to be declared to have been "ahead of one's time"—which, in life, is pretty much the definition of unhappiness. Happiness is being *in* one's time, and the essays in this book are all, in one way or another, about efforts to cope with that fact under the conditions of modern life. The book begins with a story about a man who was the first American to invent a full-scale philosophy for modernity, William James; it ends with the story of a woman determined not to be put in the position of having to repeat her first success, Maya Lin.

The essays are exercises in historical criticism. Historical criticism is the business of putting things back into their contexts to see whether that makes a difference to the way we understand them. Beyond the commitment to historicizing, there is really no method to it. The hardest part (besides knowing that you are fated always to get the past wrong on its own terms) is suppressing the element of wishful thinking that infects all critical writing. "Cast a cold eye" is possibly too stern a directive, but a cool eye is desirable.

Still, the intention is to make sense, not to discredit. It's true that things aren't always what they seem, but what they seem is always part of what they are. The man on the subway platform looking at the woman with her nose in a book is a critic: he is trying to figure out whether she is really reading, and hasn't noticed him, or is just pretending to be reading, and, if she is just pretending to be reading, whether that is because she hopes he won't approach her or because she calculates that he will. If he does approach her, though, on the theory that she is just pretending to be reading, the first thing he will say is, "What are you reading?" Appearance, mystique, aura, reputation: these are all aspects of the things that interest us, and they are as real as anything else. It is good not to be fooled, but there is a difference between being disenthralled and being disillusioned. Criticism that denies the subject its surface appeal is unsuccessful criticism, and if something doesn't seem more interesting after it has been taken apart, then it wasn't worth taking apart. The last word—though only the last word—should be one of appreciation.

My own capacity for adjusting to change is no better than anyone else's. Probably it is worse, which could explain my need constantly to write about it. We look backward for clues because, the future being the other side of a closed door, we have no place else to look. But even in America, where people are supposed to have no sense of history, there is a persistent reluctance to play with the cards that are on the table. We want to play with yesterday's cards, but yesterday has already unraveled past reconstructing. Today is the only day we have.

AMERICAN STUDIES

William James and the
Case of the Epileptic Patient

I

I n 1901, when he was fifty-nine, William James delivered the Gifford Lectures at the University of Edinburgh. James was an international academic celebrity. *The Principles of Psychology*, which appeared in 1890 and which had taken him twelve years to write, had been quickly recognized as the leading summation of developments in a field transformed by the introduction of laboratory methods and by the evolutionary theories of Charles Darwin. An abridged edition for students, *Psychology: Briefer Course*, popularly known as "Jimmy," appeared in 1892; by the time of the Gifford Lectures, it had sold nearly fifty thousand copies.

The Gifford lectureship was a two-year appointment. James returned to Edinburgh for the second set of lectures in 1902, and that year the lectures were published as *The Varieties of Religious Experience*. The *Varieties* has probably been, over the years, James's most popular book, read even when his functionalist psychology had been superseded by Freudianism and behaviorism, and his pragmatist philosophy was in eclipse. It is composed primarily of case histories, collected from all around the world and organized by category—"Conversion," "Saintliness," "Mysticism," and so on. It looks, in other words, like a psychology textbook, and that is because it *is* a psychology textbook. The *Varieties* is not a study of religion; it is, as the subtitle states, "a study in human nature."

James regarded the investigation of religious experience as a branch of abnormal psychology. He did not think that by treating the subject in this manner he was debunking religion; he thought that by treating it in this manner he was taking religion seriously. His approach reflected the holistic empiricism of which he was possibly the greatest nineteenth-century exponent: people have religious experiences, just as people have the experience of seeing tables or feeling cold. We assume that having the experience of seeing tables has something to do with there being tables in the world, and that feeling cold has something to do with a change in the temperature. Not everyone has visions or receives mystical revelations; but some human beings do. Those experiences are as psychologically real as any other state of consciousness, and since consciousness has evolved for the purpose of helping us to cope with our environment—since consciousness is not epiphenomenal, but is an active player in life—there must be something in the universe to which the religious feeling "belongs." "God is real," as James put it, summing up what he took to be the common-sense intuition about religion, "since he produces real effects."[1]

When he published the lectures, James put the sixth and seventh together in a chapter called "The Sick Soul." "The Sick Soul" is an examination of morbidity—pessimism, disillusionment, anhedonia, and various types of melancholy, one of which James calls "panic fear," and as an illustration of which he offers the following case:

> Here is an excellent example, for permission to print which I have to thank the sufferer. The original is in French, and though the subject was evidently in a bad nervous condition at the time of which he writes, his case has otherwise the merit of extreme simplicity. I translate freely.

"Whilst in this state of philosophic pessimism and general depression of spirits about my prospects, I went one evening into a dressing-room in the twilight to procure some article that was there; when suddenly there fell upon me without any warning, just as if it came out of the darkness, a horrible fear of my own existence. Simultaneously there arose in my mind the image of an epileptic patient whom I had seen in the asylum, a black-haired youth with greenish skin, entirely idiotic, who used to sit all day on one of the benches, or rather shelves against the wall, with his knees drawn up against his chin, and the coarse gray undershirt, which was his only garment, drawn over them enclosing his entire figure. He sat there like a sort of sculptured Egyptian mummy, moving nothing but his black eyes and looking absolutely nonhuman. This image and my fear entered into a species of combination with each other. *That shape am I*, I felt, potentially. Nothing that I possess can defend me against that fate, if the hour for it should strike for me as it struck for him. There was such a horror of him, and such a perception of my own merely momentary discrepancy from him, that it was as if something hitherto solid within my breast gave way entirely, and I became a mass of quivering fear. After this the universe was changed for me altogether. I awoke morning after morning with a horrible dread at the pit of my stomach, and with a sense of the insecurity of life that I never knew before, and that I have never felt since. It was like a revelation; and although the immediate feelings passed away, the experience has made me sympathetic with the morbid feelings of others ever since. It gradually faded, but for months I was unable to go out into the dark alone.

"In general I dreaded to be left alone. I remember wondering how other people could live, how I myself had ever lived, so unconscious of that pit of insecurity beneath the surface of life. My mother in particular, a very cheerful person, seemed to me a perfect paradox in her unconsciousness of danger, which you may well believe I was very careful not to disturb by revelations of my own state of mind. I have always thought that this experience of melancholia of mine had a religious bearing."

On asking this correspondent to explain more fully what he
meant by these last words, the answer he wrote was this:

"I mean that the fear was so invasive and powerful that if I had
not clung to scripture-texts like 'The eternal God is my refuge,' etc.,
'Come unto me, all ye that labor and are heavy-laden,' etc., 'I am
the resurrection and the life,' etc., I think I should have grown really insane."[2]

As everyone now knows, the business about this being translated
from the French was a pretense. In 1904, the *Varieties* was itself
translated into French, and the translator, a man named Frank
Abauzit, wrote to James requesting, understandably, the original
text for this passage. "The document," James wrote back, ". . . is
my own case—acute neurasthenic attack with phobia. I naturally
disguised the *provenance*! So you may translate freely."[3] Abauzit was
a friend of the Swiss psychologist Théodore Flournoy, who was a
friend of James's: they shared an interest in psychic phenomena—
spiritualism, mediums, trances, and so on. James died in 1910; a
year later, Flournoy published a little book called *La Philosophie de
William James*, in which he quoted the passage in the *Varieties* about
the vision of the epileptic and cited James's letter to Abauzit con-
fessing the deception. And that is how it became known that the
story is autobiographical.

Edwin Holt, who had published *The Principles of Psychology*,
and William James, Jr., James's son, put out an English edition of
Flournoy's book in 1917, but they removed the material about the vision of the epileptic patient: neither the quotation from the *Varieties*
nor the reference to James's letter appears in it. In 1920, though, the
story was quoted and identified as James's own in *The Letters of
William James*, edited by his oldest son, Henry, and it has turned up
in virtually every account of James's life ever since. It has been the
cause of endless biographical mischief; for although the vision of
the epileptic has an important place in the story of James's thought,
it does not have an important place in the story of James's life.

This may seem counterintuitive. James called the story, in his
letter to Abauzit, "my own case," after all, and there is no reason to
believe that he made *that* up. It is the story of a kind of crisis, and

biographies tend conventionally to be structured as crisis-and-recovery narratives, in which the subject undergoes a period of disillusionment or adversity, and then has a "breakthrough" or arrives at a "turning point" (or, in the case of religious figures, undergoes a conversion experience) before going on to achieve distinction. The vision of the epileptic is an obvious candidate for such a crisis in James's life, and most biographers have elected it to the office. But that is the wrong place to put it.

In the standard narrative of James's life, the vision of the epileptic is paired with a second experience, which is made to represent James's recovery or breakthrough. This is what can be called the Renouvier episode. Information about it also first surfaced in the 1920 edition of James's *Letters*. In this case the source is a diary James kept from 1868, when he was twenty-six and studying in Germany, until 1873, when he accepted an offer to join the Harvard faculty. The entry for April 30, 1870, reads as follows. (The reference in the second sentence is to the second of the *Essais de critique générale*, entitled *L'Homme* [1859], by the French philosopher Charles Renouvier; "Bain," later on, is Alexander Bain, a British psychologist who was a friend and follower of John Stuart Mill.)

> I think that yesterday was a crisis in my life. I finished the first part of Renouvier's second "Essais" and see no reason why his definition of Free Will—"the sustaining of a thought *because I choose to* when I might have other thoughts"—need be the definition of an illusion. At any rate, I will assume for the present—until next year—that it is no illusion. My first act of free will shall be to believe in free will. For the remainder of the year, I will abstain from the mere speculation and contemplative *Grüblei* [in this context, "grubbing among subtleties"] in which my nature takes most delight, and voluntarily cultivate the feeling of moral freedom, by reading books favorable to it, as well as by acting. After the first of January, my callow skin being somewhat fledged, I may perhaps return to metaphysical study and skepticism without danger to my powers of action. For the present then remember: care little for speculation; much for the *form* of my action; recollect that only when habits of order are formed can we advance to really interesting fields of action—and

consequently accumulate grain on grain of willful choice like a very miser; never forgetting how one link dropped undoes an indefinite number. *Principiis obsta* ["Resist beginnings"]—Today has furnished the exceptionally passionate initiative which Bain posits as needful for the acquisition of habits. I will see to the sequel. Not in maxims, not in *Anschauungen* ["contemplations"], but in accumulated *acts* of thought lies salvation. *Passer outre* ["To go on"]. Hitherto, when I have felt like taking a free initiative, like daring to act originally, without carefully waiting for contemplation of the external world to determine all for me, suicide seemed the most manly form to put my daring into; now, I will go a step further with my will, not only act with it, but believe as well; believe in my individual reality and creative power. My belief, to be sure, *can't* be optimistic—but I will posit life (the real, the good) in the self-governing *resistance* of the ego to the world. Life shall [consist in? the page is torn here] doing and suffering and creating.[4]

The obvious temptation is to make the vision of the epileptic the crisis for which the reading of Renouvier was the cure. And this is just what James's son Henry did in his edition of the *Letters*: he suggested that the vision of the epileptic must have occurred in the winter of 1869–70, and that the diary entry for April 30, 1870, therefore marks the moment his father's "resolution and self-confidence appear to be reasserting themselves."[5] Ralph Barton Perry, James's former colleague in the Harvard philosophy department and his official biographer, linked them in the same way in his two-volume life, *The Thought and Character of William James* (1935): he called the Renouvier episode the "turning point" in James's "spiritual crisis," and dated the vision of the epileptic "probably in 1870, just prior to his conversion to Renouvier."[6] Most biographers have followed their practice.

Gay Wilson Allen, in *William James: A Biography* (1967), had it that James told his son Henry when the vision of the epileptic had occurred, but this assumption seems to have no basis. Henry apparently learned about the episode the same way everyone else did, from Flournoy's book, after his father's death. And this means that we have no idea when the original experience actually took place. Assuming—no small assumption—that the autobiographical details in the phony Frenchman's account are James's own, it can be inferred that it happened after James had visited an asylum, during a period of uncertainty about his career, and while he was living at home. This narrows the possibilities down to some date before 1878, which is the year that, at the age of thirty-six, James finally got married. James was continually changing his mind about his career (as, nearly until the wedding, he continually changed his mind about his marriage). And he was often inside asylums. Insanity was a particular interest of his, and he knew people who were patients in asylums, notably his cousin Kitty James (who married her psychiatrist, Morton Prince). James was a student at the Harvard Medical School from 1866 to 1869, and probably visited asylums as part of his training. Although the diary in which the Renouvier entry appears is complete from December 1869 through April 1870, there is no mention in it of a vision of an epileptic, or even of a visit to an asylum. Yet commentators can be remarkably certain about the timing. Jacques Barzun, in *A Stroll with William James*, informs us that the episode of the epileptic occurred "within the week before or after" March 8, 1870—that is, the month before the Renouvier episode.[7] He does not explain how he arrived at this determination.

In fact, there is nothing to exclude the possibility that the vision of the epileptic occurred *after* the Renouvier episode. Such a theory was proposed by the psychiatrist Howard M. Feinstein in an article published in 1981, which became the basis for his fascinating work of biographical speculation, *Becoming William James* (1984). Feinstein begins with the psychiatrist's standard presumption that whatever the etiology of a crisis, the patient's own account of it cannot possibly be the correct one. In his diary and letters beginning around 1867 and continuing into the early 1870s, James complains continually of a bad back, an inability to use his eyes, poor digestion, restlessness, pessimism, melancholy, misanthropy, general feelings of ineffectualness, and, a few times, suicidal impulses. Something, as Miss Clavel liked to say, was not right. Feinstein's diagnosis is family dynamics: he thinks that (among other things) Henry Sr. was driving his son nuts on the subject of his future career. The Renouvier episode, in Feinstein's view, was just another self-punishing effort by William during this period to take himself in hand and make something of his life—specifically, by denying himself (as the diary puts it) the "speculation and contemplative *Grüblei* in which my nature takes most delight." There does indeed seem to be a load of bad superego in that passage.

Feinstein quotes a letter from William to his brother Robertson, who had settled in Milwaukee (a reasonable distance from the indeed distracting Henry Sr.), which seems to support the contention that the Renouvier episode was a hollow epiphany. The Renouvier diary entry is dated April 30, 1870; on July 25, 1870, William informs Robertson that "my own symptoms of improvement 2 months ago have not amounted to anything." "As is so often the case with such self-treatment," observes Dr. Feinstein, "the 'cure' was part of the problem."[8]

But Feinstein did not wish to abandon the crisis-and-recovery narrative. He only wished to invert it. In his new chronology, the Renouvier episode becomes the crisis, and the vision of the epileptic marks the breakthrough. James had the vision, Feinstein argues, not in the winter of 1870, which is where Perry and most other commentators place it, but two and a half years later; and he offers as evidence another letter to Robertson, this one written in 1874, in which William reports that "I had a crisis just before and about the time of your last visit here." Robertson's "last visit" to the James family home in Cambridge took place in November 1872: he had just gotten married, and was introducing his new wife to the family. (She was approved, but only just: "She is in no way responsive; takes everything as her due, is a peer of all the world, and don't know the beginning of a life beyond sense," Henry Sr. reported serenely to his son the novelist.)[9] The vision of the epileptic, Feinstein concludes, must have happened in the fall of 1872, long after the Renouvier episode. Many people, including the editors of the marvelous twelve-volume edition of *The Correspondence of William James*, have accepted Feinstein's chronology.[10]

But it has a few holes. The July 25, 1870, letter to Robertson which Feinstein cites to show that the Renouvier "cure" had failed ("my own symptoms of improvement 2 months ago have not amounted to anything") was preceded by another letter from William to Robertson, dated April 17, 1870, in which William reports that "after 3 months prostration I begin to show signs of getting on my legs again."[11] This can't be an allusion to the Renouvier episode, because the diary for April 30 states that "yesterday was a crisis in my life"—that is, April 29. What James is referring to, in fact, is his bad back, which was almost always the leading item on his list of health problems, and which at times prevented him from walking even short distances without pain. "Getting on my legs" is not a metaphor. There is, in James's letters, always a strong correlation between the state of his back and the state of his spirits, as would be natural for someone with a chronic ailment. But he is not saying, in that July 25 letter, "Renouvier has failed me." He's saying that his back is bothering him again.

And the 1874 letter, also to Robertson, that Feinstein offers in support of his dating of the vision of the epileptic is at odds with his own theory. Feinstein cites the letter, but he does not quote it. Here is what it says:

> I had a crisis just before and about the time of your last visit here, which was more philosophical than theological perhaps, that is did not deal with my personal relations to God as yours seem to have done [Robertson had written to William about his own developing religious interests]—but it was accompanied with anxiety and despair &c—I worked through it into the faith in free-will and into the final reign of the Good conditional on the co-operation of each of us in the sphere—small enough often—in which it is allowed him to be operative. Why God waits on our cooperation is not to be fathomed—but as a fact of experience I believe it—and having that belief open to me, I have lost much of my former interest in speculative questions—I have taken up Physiology instead of Philosophy and go along on a much calmer sea with a more even keel.[12]

This is essentially the language of the Renouvier diary entry.

Whatever this "crisis" in the fall of 1872 entailed, therefore, it was not a renouncement of Renouvier. On November 2, 1872, James wrote a letter to Renouvier himself, in which he expressed "the admiration and gratitude that reading your essays has inspired in me. . . . Thanks to you, I possess for the first time an intelligible and rational conception of freedom."[13] Six weeks later, he wrote to Robertson, who was safely back in Wisconsin again, advising him that when feelings of depression come, "the only thing is to have faith and wait, and resolve whatever happens to be faithful 'in the outward act' (as a philosopher says) that is *do* as if the good were the law of being, even if one can't for the moment really believe it. The belief will come in its time."[14] And there is a letter from William's father to Henry the novelist (then living in Rome), apparently written in March 1873, in which he reports that William has been crowing recently about the improvement in his health and spirits since the previous spring: "I ventured to ask what especially in his opinion had produced the change. He said several things: the reading of Renouvier (particularly his vindication of the freedom of the will) and of Wordsworth."[15]

Finally, there is a piece of evidence that has not been mentioned before, but that brings us as close as we are likely to get to this mysterious crisis of 1872. It is on a single sheet of notepaper dated October 21, 1872, and it reads, in part:

> Tonight I feel full of *Lebensmut* [optimism] because of the unforeseen awakening in me within the past few days of dormant feelings and keen powers of thought. But this is an irrational ground of reconciliation with the Universe, being based on accidental particulars of experience, the which if they happened to be of an opposite quality wd. justify an opposite conclusion. The desideratum is a conception of the whole which, no matter what be the experience of the moment, will reconcile one to it. So far I see only the: "for the sake of—!" The evil is somehow mechanically continuous with the good. The latter is thus ever imminent, ever potential and for its sake I'll go the former.[16]

This does not correlate very well with the feelings aroused by the apparition of the epileptic patient described in *The Varieties of Religious Experience*.

What is significant about these notes and letters from 1872 and 1873 is that they indicate that James was still struggling to recover from some sort of breakdown two and a half years after recording in his diary the fresh start inspired by Renouvier. Feinstein is surely right to point out that an experience that does not produce results for almost three years can hardly be counted a breakthrough. The most we can say is that Renouvier's idea about free will was one of the things James preserved from a long period of ill health and poor spirits. It was neither the cause of a breakdown nor the cure.

2

What *was* the problem? In 1979, a graduate student felicitously named James William Anderson reported, in his dissertation, rumors that James had once been a patient at the McLean Asylum for the Insane, outside Boston. The same rumor has been reported since by the historian of science Robert J. Richards, who said it had been confirmed for him by "someone who had worked in the hospital in an official capacity"; by Feinstein, in *Becoming William James*; and by Alfred Kazin, who wrote in 1993 that "years ago the famous Harvard psychologist Henry A. Murray told me that at one point in his life James had put himself into McLean's."[17] In her biography of James, *Genuine Reality*, Linda Simon names a psychiatrist, Ruth Tiffany Barnhouse, who did her residency at McLean in the 1950s and who says that she saw James's patient records in the archives there.

This fresh wrinkle has had two effects. It has devalued somewhat the biographical significance of the Renouvier episode—since if James was hospitalized, it is not likely to have been for frustration with what is, after all, a fairly ancient philosophical puzzle about whether there is such a thing as free will. And it has redirected attention to the story about the epileptic patient. Hospitalization for a mental disorder not only seems to explain the shock of recognition in that story (*"That shape am I"*); it suggests that something more is possibly being masked than the nationality of "the sufferer." James may have had deeper reasons for not wishing to give himself away, reasons having to do with an incident in his life he wished to remain suppressed, when he recalled the vision in *The Varieties of Religious Experience*.

But is it so? The McLean Hospital (the name was changed in 1892) still exists. Robert Lowell was a patient there; so was Sylvia Plath. It is now located in Belmont, and is affiliated, as it has been since its founding, in 1811, with Massachusetts General Hospital and the Harvard Medical School. Scholars who have asked to see James's patient records there have been informed that hospital policy forbids the release of information about individual patients, including confirmation that someone was ever a patient.

I wrote to the archivist at McLean asking whether James might simply have been at the hospital in his capacity as a medical student, and met with this boilerplate rebuff. But when I approached the administration of the hospital, I got a different response, which is that requests for information about William James had been forwarded to the James family, which has refused to permit the information to be released.[18] Robertson James, in later life an alcoholic, was a patient at McLean;[19] so was William's cousin Kitty James Prince (he used to visit her there). And William James, Jr., James's son, may, as Linda Simon notes in her biography, also have been hospitalized at McLean for depression. So that the family's reluctance to send researchers into the archives looking for folders labeled "James"—or even "James, William"—might only be an effort to protect the privacy of some of its less celebrated members. On the other hand, if the celebrated one was never an inmate, a statement to that effect would have sufficed to shield the rest. In the absence of such a statement, we can probably assume that he was.

The next question is, When? What makes incomplete biographical information generally worse than no information at all is that speculation fills the gaps and eventually becomes indistinguishable from "the facts"—as has happened with the dating of the episode of the epileptic patient. In the case of James's hospitalization, the inclination is to insert the information into the period of his physical and mental distress—that is, sometime between 1867, when he began to complain regularly about his various symptoms, and late

1872, when, at the age of thirty, he finally got a job, as a part-time teacher at Harvard—and then to try to rewrite the crisis-and-recovery narrative around it.

The boldest venture in this direction so far is by Kim Townsend, in an original book called *Manhood at Harvard*, which is about the construction of a weirdly brittle culture of masculinity in late-nineteenth-century Cambridge. James is, quite appropriately, a leading character in the book, and Townsend has a long analysis of his breakdown. Townsend thinks that James's hospitalization occurred before 1870, and he offers a letter (until now unnoticed) that appears in the second volume of Henry James the novelist's autobiography, *Notes of a Son and Brother* (1914), as a possible smoking gun.

The letter is from Henry Sr. to Henry the novelist, written, according to the autobiography, in "the spring of '70." "Horatio Alger is writing a Life of Edwin Forrest," the father reports in this letter, and has recently paid a visit to the James home in Cambridge. (Forrest was a popular actor whom Henry Sr. had known when the family was living in New York City.) "Alger talks freely about his own late insanity," the letter continues, "—which he in fact appears to enjoy as a subject of conversation and in which he has somewhat interested William, who has talked with him a good deal of his experience at the Somerville Asylum."[20] "The Somerville Asylum" is McLean, which was originally located in Somerville. The "his" in that last clause is ambiguous: it can refer either to William's or to Alger's "experience at the Somerville Asylum." But Horatio Alger was never a patient in an asylum.

Townsend (following Feinstein) believes that the episode of the epileptic patient happened later, in 1872, but he also thinks that the passage recalling it contains a screen memory: he thinks that the patient ("a black-haired youth with greenish skin, entirely idiotic, who used to sit all day . . . with his knees drawn up against his chin, and the coarse gray undershirt, which was his only garment, drawn over them") is a man who has been driven insane by masturbation. Thus the shock of identification, and thus the "panic fear."

The notion that James had a "problem" with what one biographer rather quaintly calls "self-abuse"[21] predates the rumor about McLean. It seems to have been introduced to the world by the historian Cushing Strout, in an article published in 1968. Strout's idea is that the episode of the epileptic occurred sometime between 1866, when James returned from a scientific expedition to Brazil led by Louis Agassiz, and decided that he didn't want to become a naturalist, and 1869, when he received his medical degree, and decided that he didn't want to become a doctor. Strout thinks that James became convinced, after reading a work called *The Functions and Disorders of the Reproductive Organs*, by William Acton, that there is a linkage between introspection ("speculation and contemplative *Grüblei*") and masturbation, and between masturbation and insanity. So that, Strout concludes: "That hideous figure [of the epileptic] . . . objectified not only the self-punishing guilt in his own symptoms, but also his fear of being trapped in a medical career which seemed to be his only option after his disillusionment with natural history."[22]

This interpretation was amplified a little by Sander Gilman, in a book on *Disease and Representation*, who suggested that the source for James's vision of the epileptic patient might have been a work called *Des maladies mentales*, by Jean Etienne Dominique Esquirol, published in 1838 (and written, as Gilman points out, in the supposed language of James's "sufferer"). Esquirol's book contains full-length illustrations (drawings, obviously, not photographs) of mentally ill persons, one of which depicts a patient who looks uncannily like the epileptic described by James, and whom Esquirol identifies as an idiot and a masturbator. "James's fear of madness," Gilman concludes, ". . . was a direct fear of receding into madness as a result of his own behavior." And he quotes a passage from James's diary, dated February 1, 1870, which, he says, refers to James's masturbatory habit "in a direct manner": "Hitherto I have tried to fire myself with the moral interest, as an aid in the accomplishing of certain utilitarian ends of attaining certain salutary but difficult habits. I tried to associate the feeling of Moral degradation with failure. . . . But in all this I was cultivating the moral . . . only as a means and more or less humbugging myself."[23] We have moved some distance from the philosophy of Charles Renouvier.

The notion of William James as a compulsive masturbator (but are they, as the protagonist of the episode in the *Varieties* says of himself, afraid of the dark?) has a certain sensational appeal, so it is slightly disappointing to discover that every one of the leaves comes off this biographical onion. Townsend has, to begin with, made a mistake all students of the Jameses eventually learn to avoid, which is to rely on anything Henry James says in his autobiography. Henry freely changed dates, suppressed facts, and rewrote passages from other people's letters, and then often added injury to insult by destroying the originals. Horatio Alger didn't write a biography of Edwin Forrest. His cousin William Alger did. William Alger was a Unitarian clergyman who lived in Boston and was a friend of Emerson, which is how he would have known Henry James, Sr. Henry James, Jr., though, had probably never heard of him, or by 1914 had forgotten him if he had, so in transcribing this letter, he very likely either added the first name or changed it to Horatio on the assumption that his ditsy father had got it wrong.

Horatio Alger, too, had been a Unitarian minister, in Brewster, on Cape Cod, but he had been obliged to resign his ministry in 1866 following accusations (which he did not contest) of pederasty with members of his congregation. He fled to New York City, and soon after began his career as the author of the famous books for boys. He continued to cultivate friendships with eligible boys, but he is supposed to have forsworn further sexual indulgence. Alger evidently felt a good deal of anguish about his "sin," but he is not likely to have volunteered to chat about it four years later with people he barely knew, and "insanity" (Henry Sr.'s term) seems, in any case, a couple of shades too strong.

William Alger, on the other hand, really had been insane. During a trip to Europe in 1871, he collapsed in Paris and was pronounced "hopelessly insane" by Charles Brown-Séquard, a renowned physiologist. (The diagnosis was reported in the Boston newspapers: so much for nineteenth-century notions of medical confidentiality.) Alger was brought back to Boston and immediately admitted into the McLean Asylum. He was released in the spring of 1872, and was able to return to his work.[24] His *Life of Edwin Forrest: The American Tragedian* was published in 1877.

Then when did William Alger have his conversation at the James family home about his (not William James's) experiences at McLean? In his autobiography, Henry says his father's letter reporting that conversation was written in "the spring of '70"—a year before William Alger's breakdown. But he is, as usual, making it up. Henry Sr.'s letter, changing topics, continues: "Everyone hopes that J. G. hasn't caught a Rosamund Vincy in Miss M." J. G. is John Chipman Gray, an intimate friend of Henry and of William's favorite cousin, Minny Temple (who died, of tuberculosis, in 1870, and who was the inspiration thirty years later for the character of Milly Theale in *The Wings of the Dove*). Miss M. is Nina Mason; she and John Gray were married on June 4, 1873. Rosamund Vincy, of course, is the woman who marries and then ruins the ambitious physician Tertius Lydgate in George Eliot's *Middlemarch*. That novel was published in December 1872. Henry's date was therefore three years off. His father's letter was written not in 1870, the year of the Renouvier diary entry, but in 1873. (The life of the Grays, by the way, did not imitate art. John Gray cofounded Ropes & Gray, the famous Boston law firm, and was a professor for forty years at the Harvard Law School. Nina Gray became, in later years, a confidant of her husband's old friend Justice Oliver Wendell Holmes.) The "Horatio Alger letter," in short, is a red herring.

Which leaves the self-abuse. There is no evidence that James ever read Acton on *The Functions and Disorders of the Reproductive Organs* or Esquirol on *Des maladies mentales*. But (as Townsend notes) he did read, and with some admiration, Henry Maudsley's *Body and Mind* (1870), a respected psychology text, which warns that "the development of puberty may lead indirectly to insanity by becoming the occasion of a vicious habit of self-abuse in men."[25] But the connection between masturbation and mental disorder was a commonplace of nineteenth-century neurology. James was a medical student with a special interest in nervous disorders; he would not have needed any particular book to pick up the idea.

Leaving psychoanalytic interpretations of the story of the epileptic patient aside for the moment, it is not easy to find evidence that James ever felt that he had a problem with masturbation himself. The passage from his diary that Gilman quotes—"Hitherto I have tried to fire myself with the moral interest, as an aid in . . . attaining certain salutary but difficult habits"—is suggestive, but only if we read "moral" and "habit" in a twentieth-century sense. James was taking those terms from Alexander Bain's *The Emotions and the Will* (1859), for decades a standard text in British psychology and a work James later relied on in key sections of his own *Principles of Psychology*. (This is the same Bain who turns up in the Renouvier entry three months later: "Today has furnished the exceptionally passionate initiative which Bain posits as needful for the acquisition of habits.") In a chapter called "Moral Habits," Bain uses, as an example of a situation in which such habits might be developed, what he describes as "one of the strongest of our fleshly indulgences": sleeping late. The passage is such a choice specimen of the Victorian rhetoric of moral hygiene that it is worth quoting the heroic climax:

> Some necessity that there is no escaping, compels a man from his early youth to be out of bed every morning at six o'clock. For weeks and months, and perhaps, years, the struggle and the suffering are acutely felt. Meanwhile, the hand of power is remorseless in the uniformity of its application. And now it is that there creeps a certain habitude of the system, modifying by imperceptible degrees the bitterness of that oft-repeated conflict. What the individual has had to act so many times in one way, brings on a current of nervous power, confirming the victorious, and sapping the vanquished, impulse. The force of determination that unites the decisive movement of jumping out of bed with the perception of the appointed hour, is invigorated slowly but surely. Iteration is softening down the harsh experience of the early riser, and bringing about, as time advances, an approach to the final condition of mechanical punctuality and entire indifference. Years may be wanted to arrive at this point, but sooner or later the plastic element in our constitution will succeed.[26]

If getting out of bed early is a "moral habit," pretty much anything can be a moral habit. Nothing in his diary requires us to assume that James was talking about masturbation.

The only evidence that remains is the passage about the epileptic patient. But the crucial thing to notice about that passage is that the epileptic is epileptic. He is a person with an organic disorder, not a person who has made himself idiotic by "unhealthy habits." "Nothing that I possess can defend me against that fate, if the hour for it should strike for me as it struck for him," says the Frenchman. The fear being expressed is the fear of unforeseen catastrophe. It is precisely not the fear of self-destruction.

The story of the epileptic is a story about what used to be called "the problem of evil"; that is why it appears in a book on religious experience. The epileptic patient represents the classic challenge to faith: innocent suffering. The realization that people can suffer as a result of their own actions does not cause a religious crisis. What causes a religious crisis is the realization that people can lead exemplary lives and suffer anyway. The Frenchman has been insulated by the assumption that in a rational universe, bad things cannot happen to good people. The blow to his ego, when the image of the patient is suddenly before him, comes from his recognition that moral worth does not immunize us against disaster. "The eternal God is my refuge" is the lesson of the vision: there is nothing we can do to protect ourselves against undeserved suffering. The only salvation is faith. Evil, in James's time, was a motiveless malignancy. We think of evils as *caused* by something—by greed, or genes, or sexual abuse—and miss the point of James's story.

3

The biggest impediment to getting a coherent crisis-and-recovery narrative out of the materials of William James's life between 1867 and 1873 is that large portions of the record are simply missing. James was never a daily diarist, but the entries in the notebook he used for a diary are fairly regular from April 1868, when it begins, to February 1869. Then twenty-one pages (as much as forty-two pages of writing) have been cut out, apparently with scissors. The next dated entry is for December 21, 1869. Most of James's diary for 1869, in other words, has disappeared.

Those pages were probably destroyed either by James himself or by his widow, Alice, who winnowed her husband's papers with meticulous care, sitting in front of a fireplace, and who had (like her brother-in-law Henry) small tolerance for the embarrassing detail. It is, of course, stimulating to imagine the sort of revelation that might have led James, or his heirs, to consign these pages to the flames. And people who want to place the vision of the epileptic or the McLean hospitalization in 1869 will naturally look upon the missing pages as the dog that does not bark.

The reason letters and diaries are usually destroyed, though, is that they contain references to other people. And there is one tiny clue that points in this direction. James graduated from medical school in June 1869 and spent the summer—the period the missing pages presumably cover—in Pomfret, Connecticut, on vacation with his family. He was, by his mother's account in her letters to her son Henry, in fairly miserable shape. Two sheets of notepaper are preserved among his papers in an envelope labeled "Pomfret 1869." James seems to have been trying to work out, on these pages, some sort of philosophy of conduct, and is weighing the alternative postures of sympathy (an "expansive embracing tendency") and defensiveness, or what he calls "self-sufficingness"—and in the course of this he writes: "My feeling towards B.W. (e.g.) comes from too partial a sympathy; so does the optimist's each sympathizing with opposite sides of her being." And later on: "sympathy gives pain (B.W.) Shd. sympathy go so far as to dictate suicide?"[27] The wording is cryptic, but James seems to be referring to his feelings for a woman.

Certain identification of *la belle B.W. sans merci* is impossible. One candidate is Bessie Ward, the sister of Tom Ward, one of James's best friends. Her father was the James family banker; her mother, the former Anna Hazard Barker, was a famous beauty. "The adorable Miss Bessy," Henry later called the daughter after running into her in Rome; ". . .—pretty, intelligent, gracious and elegant—a most noble and delightful maiden."[28] "Sympathy gives pain" suggests that if William had a crush on Bessie Ward (and she certainly sounds like a person compatible with crushes), it was not reciprocated. (William seems to have nursed a number of fruitless passions in his youth. He appears to have gotten involved, while he was in Germany, with an American woman, Catherine Havens, who was even more neurotic than he was; he was smitten by Fanny Dixwell, who married Oliver Wendell Holmes, and by Clover Hooper, who married Henry Adams. Bessie Ward, much to the amusement of William's sister, Alice, eventually married a Saxon baron named Schönberg.) If William had committed his feelings about her (or some other B.W.) to paper, this might later have constituted a reason for destroying that portion of his diary. In any case, there is no hint of the asylum here.

And the excised pages from 1869 form the *small* gap in the record. After the extant diary resumes on December 21, 1869, there are regular entries up to the Renouvier episode, on April 30, 1870. But the next page is dated February 10, 1873—more than three and a half years later. There is one more entry, for April 10, 1873, and the diary ends. The silence of the diary would matter less if we had enough letters. But we don't. Though James was ordinarily a prolific correspondent, between the July 25, 1870, letter to Robertson James, already quoted, and a letter dated May 30, 1872—a period of nearly two years—only four letters survive. If James wrote other letters besides these four, they were presumably destroyed along with the diary pages. Between August 1871 and May 1872, ten months, nothing remains at all.[29] And third-person information about William's activities during this period—for example, in letters written by other family members—is sparse. All kinds of things may have happened to James between 1869 and 1872. We know only a few.

Was the period for which there are neither letters nor diaries the period in which James was a patient at the McLean Asylum? Apparently not. Although Linda Simon was, of course, denied access to James's medical records at McLean, she did arrange to examine the patient logs from 1866 through 1872 with the names blacked out. She found nothing in the remaining information about age, sex, occupation, and time of stay that matches up with William James. Given the fragmentary nature of our knowledge of James's life in the early 1870s, it seems fair to conclude that the story of the epileptic patient is biographical flotsam. It is unmoored to any known event in James's life. It can be interpreted as a precipitating crisis, as a psychological breakthrough, as simply one among many crises, most of which are now unrecoverable—or as a partial invention, a little work of faction.

Even considered as a discrete event, unembedded in some larger structure of negation and transcendence, the story of the epileptic is not exactly raw data. Simon registers some skepticism about the verisimilitude of the account in *The Varieties of Religious Experience*, and she is right to do so. The passage feels mildly precooked; the coda, in particular, about clinging to "scripture texts" in order to avoid insanity does not sound very much like William James (or, for that matter, like a Frenchman). The passage is designed, after all, to mimic a medical case history and to fit into a book about religious experiences. The Frenchman's testimony is cross-referenced to Bunyan's *Pilgrim's Progress* and to a well-known story James's father wrote about his own spiritual crisis, which led to his conversion to Swedenborgianism, and remarkable similarities are pointed out by James. As Oscar Wilde once said of Wordsworth: He found under the stones the sermons he had already placed there. One reason for disguising the source must have been to license some opportunistic revisions of the original experience—whatever it was.

The literary self-consciousness of the passage, in particular the way in which it resembles Henry Sr.'s account of *his* crisis—which involved the apparition of "some damnèd shape squatting invisible to me . . . and raying out from his fetid personality influences fatal to life"[30]—has been remarked on by a number of commentators. But even the perception that the boundary separating the epileptic from the "normal" person is paper-thin was probably not as spontaneous as the passage makes it appear. Charles Brown-Séquard, the man who diagnosed poor William Alger in Paris in 1871, had been William James's teacher at the Harvard Medical School five years earlier. Diseases of the brain were his specialty, and he taught, according to William's own lecture notes, that there is "a not[able] tendency in every man to some of the features of epilepsy." He mentioned coitus and the involuntary jerking of muscles when being tickled or in sleep: "Thus degree by degree we are led to look on epilepsy as an incr^d. degree of the normal reflex excitability of *certain parts* of nervous centres."[31]

This notion, much amplified, grew to occupy a central place in James's own psychology. "His thought was that there is no sharp line to be drawn between 'healthy' and 'unhealthy' minds, that all have something of both," James's former student Dickinson Miller recalled. "Once when we were returning from visits to two insane asylums at one of which we had seen a dangerous, almost naked maniac, I remember his saying, 'President Eliot [Charles William Eliot, the president of Harvard] would not like to admit that no sharp line could be drawn between himself and the men we have just seen, but it is true.' "[32] The epileptic patient had performed his heuristic role before.

4

Without suggesting that anything that might significantly transform our understanding of William James has been suppressed, we are entitled to note that the version of his early breakdown in his son Henry's 1920 edition of the *Letters* and his protégé Perry's 1935 biography is very much the authorized version. Two pieces of evidence—the story of the epileptic patient and the response to Renouvier—were plucked from a fragmentary record and erected into the narrative emblems of a breakdown and recovery. For the story of a philosophical-spiritual crisis overcome by "the will to believe" is conveniently symmetrical with James's writings in *The Will to Believe* (1897) and *Pragmatism* (1907), books that exhort us to act "as if" in the face of uncertainty—to believe that if we take a risk, the universe will meet us halfway. The biography is made to lend authenticity to the philosophy: James, too, knew pessimism and despair, and this is how he willed himself to overcome them.

Except that he never overcame them. Simon's biography emphasizes, more fully than any earlier one, the persistence of James's ill health. For James was depressive *all his life*. And this may be the diagnosis that explains the insufficiency of all other diagnoses. Commentators prefer to assume that James was despondent in the years after his graduation from medical school because of some problem—a family problem, a sexual problem, a career problem, an identity problem, a philosophical problem. But depression is not a problem; it's a weather pattern. Under its cloud, *everything else* is a problem. When the weather changes, these problems disappear, or become "opportunities," or "challenges"—until dark skies return.

Throughout James's life, evidence in letters or diaries that he has recovered his health and spirits is always followed, sooner or later, by evidence that he has had a relapse. The letter from James's father in the spring of 1873 announcing William's new robustness is followed by a letter in the summer from his mother (never the tenderest analyst of her oldest child's troubles) to Henry Jr. (her favorite), complaining that William "has such a morbid sympathy with every form of trouble and privation. . . . He is very despondent about himself." In March 1874, she complains, again to Henry, that "the trouble with [William] is that he *must express* every fluctuation of feeling, and especially every unfavorable symptom." And the following July: "His temperament is a morbidly hopeless one." In the summer of 1880, Henry, after seeing his brother in London, confides to his mother that "I can't get rid of the feeling that he takes himself, and his nerves, and his physical condition too hard and too consciously."[33]

William did take those things rather consciously. "If you knew my life," he wrote to Renouvier in 1882, when he was forty, "you would confess that my little stream of work runs on under great disadvantages."[34] He was not referring to external pressures. He seems to have undergone what he called an "annual collapse" every February. He agonized for two years about his courtship of Alice Gibbens until their marriage in 1878—a period when he behaved, as he confessed to her later, like "a man morally utterly diseased."[35] He complained of depression in 1893 ("I . . . know now a new kind of melancholy").[36] In 1899, when he was supposed to be writing *The Varieties of Religious Experience*, a heart ailment brought on a depression that lasted nearly two years. He was incapacitated again by severe depression in 1909, the year before his heart disease finally killed him. "The fact is," he wrote in 1901 to his brother Henry (who, despite his wish that William would display a little more fortitude, was subject to serious depressions himself), "that my nervous system is utter trash, and always was so. It has been a hard burden to bear all these years, the more so as I have seemed to others perfectly well; and now it is on top and 'I' am under."[37]

William experimented with pretty much every cure available for his various psychosomatic symptoms: chloroform, electric shock (intended to stimulate the nerves), weight-lifting, diet, hypnotism, drugs, travel, Christian Science, "mind cure" treatments (during which the practitioner "disentangled" his mind while he slept), and the "talking cure" (a primitive form of psychotherapy). So it would hardly be surprising if he had also checked himself into the McLean Hospital. Some of the rumors that have been reported indicate that he was being treated there for depression later in life. This seems plausible. It is worth noting that McLean did not accept voluntary admissions until 1881.

Still, the events used to frame the standard biographical narrative—the Renouvier diary entry and the story of the epileptic patient—are plainly relevant to our understanding of James's thought. The question is, How? The texts themselves are a good deal less clear on this point than has generally been assumed. In the story of the epileptic patient, the Frenchman's sudden perception that he might end up in the same condition induces a fear of going out in the dark and of being left alone, which is allayed by recalling tags from the Bible. In the Renouvier episode, a feeling of inanition caused by excessive philosophical speculation is addressed by a decision to assume a more active role in life. In the first case the problem is fear of catastrophe, and the remedy is religious consolation. In the second, the problem is intellectual paralysis, and the remedy is a belief in the efficacy of self-assertion. The two episodes do not seem to be related as crisis and recovery, or negation and transcendence, or down and up. They seem to be experiences of different kinds of distress alleviated by different kinds of self-therapy. The mistake has not been singling these passages out as emblematic of

Jamesian insights. The mistake has been stringing them together as the endpoints of a single crisis.

In fact, for James the two experiences represented eternally opposed responses to life. He made himself clear on the matter in an odd corner of his work—in the introduction he wrote to his father's *Literary Remains*, a memorial anthology which was published in 1884 and promptly sank without a trace. Most people who believe in God, William says there, are really pluralists. God for them is just one force in the universe, "a concrete being whom it does not take a scholar to love and make sacrifices and die for." It is hard to feel affection for an omnipotent God, a God defined as Universal Substance, or as First Principle. And pluralism, says James, is anyway "a view to which we all practically incline when in the full and successful exercise of our moral energy." For when we feel healthy, our will seems a match for the forces we confront; life, as James put it elsewhere, "feels like a real fight," whose outcome is still in doubt.

But, he continues, there are also times when life feels like a mechanical and predetermined process whose outcome we are powerless to change; and at these times, trying to buck ourselves up with the thought that we, too, can make a difference, that we get a vote, is futile. In his description of this fatalistic state of mind, he evokes the epileptic:

> To suggest personal will and effort to one "all sicklied o'er" with the sense of weakness, of helpless failure, and of fear, is to suggest the most horrible of things to him. What he craves is to be consoled in his very impotence, to feel that the Powers of the Universe recognize and secure him, all passive and failing as he is. Well, we are all *potentially* such sick men. The sanest and best of us are of one clay with lunatics and prison-inmates. And whenever we feel this, such a sense of the vanity of our voluntary career comes over us, that all our morality appears but a plaster hiding a sore it can never cure, and all our well-doing as the hollowest substitute for that well-*being* that our lives ought to be grounded in, but, alas! are not. This well-being is the object of the *religious* demand,—a demand so penetrating and unassuageable that no consciousness of such oc-

casional and outward well-doing as befalls the human lot can ever
give it satisfaction. On the other hand, to satisfy the religious demand is to deny the demands of the moralist. . . . So that of religion
and moralism, the morbid and the healthy view, it may be said that
what is meat to the one is the other's poison. Any absolute moralism is a pluralism; any absolute religion is a monism. . . . The ac-
cord of moralism and religion is superficial, their discord radical.
Only the deepest thinkers on both sides see that one must go.[38]

James was a moralist who gave a great deal of his time and intellectual energy to the business of trying to understand religion. But
although he believed in the legitimacy of the religious response to
the universe, he was never able to attain its consolation for himself.
All his efforts to make contact with God, or to enter into what he
could regard as a spiritual state of mind, were unsuccessful. "My
personal position is simple," he wrote two years after the publication of *The Varieties of Religious Experience* to one of the book's critics. "I have no living sense of commerce with God." And then, in an
understatement: "I envy those who have, for I know that the addi-
tion of such a sense would help me greatly."[39]

This is why treating the Renouvier episode as a response to a
spiritual crisis is a disservice to James. James thought that philosophy could never be an adequate response to despair, because he
thought that philosophy begins and ends with the recognition of its
own inadequacy. Philosophy is a moralism: it is for people who feel
strong enough to face the universe on its own terms, knowing that
there is, in the end, nothing to back them up, nothing to *guarantee*
that their vote will be counted. "A philosopher has publicly re-
nounced the privilege of trusting *blindly* which every simple man
owns as a right," James wrote in 1873, in the final entry in his diary,
"—and my sight is not always clear enough for such constant
duty."[40] He went on, of course, to write a great deal of philosophy,
but he could do it only when he felt healthy enough to face the
abyss, and he always expressed pleasure when he could take a break
from it. Gertrude Stein's anecdote about the final exam she took in
James's course when she was his student at Harvard is well known.

"Dear Professor James," she claims she wrote on the exam, "I am so sorry but I really do not feel a bit like an examination paper in philosophy to-day." The next day, she says, she received a note from James. "Dear Miss Stein," he wrote, "I understand perfectly how you feel I often feel like that myself," and he gave her the highest mark in the course.[41] Gertrude Stein was not above autobiographical embellishment, but this story is probably truer than it seems. She *had* understood the lesson. James knew that philosophy was not enough. But it was all he had.

James was a beloved figure—not just a man whose writings other people found inspiring, but someone more personally affecting than that. He was adored even by people, such as Bertrand Russell, who detested his philosophical views. After James's death, many of these people, both the inspired and the uninspired, struggled to explain what it was about James that had made him such a genuine and irresistible character. For there was a side of James that is not captured in his writing, as colloquial and highly inflected with personality as it is.

In his work, James can sometimes seem to be expounding, with too much bravado, a kind of can-do, self-help attitude toward life, to be suggesting that the answer to most of our problems is just to drop our philosophical worry-bones and get on with the business of making and doing. Many readers since James's time have complained that the pragmatism and pluralism he promoted are not enough, that life confronts us with some situations that call for a different sort of response. But no one knew this better than James. It is the poignancy of his life that he never found, for himself, that other sort of response. He created a philosophy of hope expressly premised on the understanding that there is, finally, no *reason* for hope. This is why reading Renouvier was not a cure, and it is why the experience with the epileptic patient is attributed to someone else. James was too wise to believe that true melancholy can ever be overcome by a theory, and he was too honest to pretend to a spiritual satisfaction he was never able to feel.

John Jay Chapman was one of the readers whom James's writings failed to inspire, but he loved James anyway, and in his memoir he put into words the quality others searched for: "There was, in spite of his playfulness, a deep sadness about James. You felt that he had just stepped out of this sadness in order to meet you, and was to go back in the moment you left him."[42] What lends authenticity to his philosophy is not its triumph over the unhappiness in his own life, but its failure.

The Principles of
Oliver Wendell Holmes

I

"Talks too much" was the comment on the first report card of Oliver Wendell Holmes, Jr., the future Supreme Court justice and founder of the constitutional law of free speech.[1] Wendy Holmes (as he was known to his intimates) was six. He lived for another eighty-seven years, and no one ever accused him of keeping his views to himself. He opined regularly to dozens of correspondents, among them the English jurist Sir Frederick Pollock (their letters are collected in two volumes), the political theorist Harold Laski (two volumes), the Washington lawyer Felix Frankfurter (one volume), the diplomat Lewis Einstein (one volume), the Irish priest Patrick Augustine Sheehan (one volume), the progressive journalist and eccentric Franklin Ford (one volume), the philosopher Morris R. Cohen, the Chinese jurist John Wu, the Japanese nobleman Kentaro Kaneko, and a stable of female confidants that included Nina Gray, Alice Stopford Green, Baroness Charlotte Moncheur, and Holmes's Anglo-Irish paramour, Lady Clare Castletown, of Granston Manor, Upper Ossory, Ireland.

When Holmes's brothers on the bench—he served for twenty years on the Supreme Judicial Court of Massachusetts and for thirty years, beginning in 1902, on the Supreme Court of the United States—fell behind in the production of opinions, he begged his chiefs to reassign their cases to him. In the end, he wrote over two thousand opinions, believed to be a record for judges sitting in courts of last resort. It was his habit, every few years, to refresh himself by traveling to England, leaving his wife behind, where he sought out the company of the leading philosophical and literary lights of the land and where he flirted aggressively with most of the women he met, once going so far in his banter with the twelve-year-old daughter of one of his hosts, Tom Hughes, the author of *Tom Brown's School Days*, that Hughes sent a letter afterward demanding to know Holmes's intentions. He had none, except to experience once again the pleasure of his own flamboyance. "He would catch a subject, toss it in the air, make it dance and play a hundred tricks, and bring it to solid earth again," an English acquaintance described his social manner. "He liked to have the ball caught and tossed back to him, so that he could send it spinning away again with a fresh twist."[2]

Holmes's father, Dr. Oliver Wendell Holmes, Sr., a pioneer of the germ theory of disease, the author of the patriotic poem "Old Ironsides," cofounder of the *Atlantic Monthly* (whose name he came up with), coiner of the term "Boston Brahmin," the first person to refer to Boston as "the Hub of the Solar System," and dean of the Harvard Medical School, was said to have been the greatest talker of his day. He thought the talent worth acquiring, and made it a rule that any child who uttered a clever remark at the dinner table be given extra marmalade. Holmes Sr. was five feet three and round; his son, fully grown, was six-three and lean, and their relations were notoriously fractious. But this was one trait that got passed along.

The law provided Holmes with a steady supply of occasions to exercise his gift for turning a phrase, but he did not allow the engine to idle. Early in his career, when he was in practice in Boston, he would walk into the office in the morning and announce to one of his firm's junior associates, "Mr. Evans, I am ready to contradict any statement you will make."[3] Mr. Evans evidently felt it his duty, each morning, to oblige. Fifty years later, Holmes liked to tell his colleagues on the Supreme Court, when they were conferring about a case, that he would admit any general principle of law they proposed, and then use it to decide the case under discussion either way. It was not persiflage, or it was not only persiflage. Holmes had a profound appreciation for the malleability of words, and that appreciation is the demon that sits at the bottom of his thought. His challenge to his fellow justices was not an excuse to show off his forensic dexterity; he was making a point about the nature of language. There have been hundreds of efforts since Holmes published *The Common Law*, in 1881, when he was thirty-nine, to sew a political label on him. Commentators have tried to prove that he was a progressive, a liberal, a civil libertarian, a democrat, an aristocrat, a reactionary, a Social Darwinist, and a fascist. But none of these efforts has gotten to the core of what Holmes did, because all of them have mistaken the implications for the premises. They have focused on the accidents of his thought.

Calling Holmes a progressive or a reactionary is like calling, say, Wittgenstein a progressive or a reactionary. It assumes that he was interested in the political consequences of his ideas. But one thing that can be said with certainty about Holmes as a judge is that he almost never cared, in the cases he decided, about outcomes. He didn't read the newspaper, and he was utterly, sometimes fantastically, indifferent to the real-world effects of his decisions. He saw the law as a series of minutely varied, frequently boring, but sometimes delightfully nasty intellectual problems. These took the form, in his view, of concrete conflicts, each with some slight but potentially crucial point of difference from the rest, submitted for resolution by the ultimately absurd process of reasoning out a result from abstract principles. From the very beginning of his career, Holmes regarded the reasoning part as factitious and, in its relation to the result, logically ex post facto. "It is the merit of the common law that it decides the case first and determines the principle afterwards,"[4] is the first sentence of the first legal article he ever published, "Codes, and the Arrangement of the Law" (1870), and he spent the next sixty-two years as a jurist and a judge trying to be faithful to this insight. That it was an impossible task by definition—as though one were to make it a principle never to rely on principles—seems only to have whetted his sense of sport.

Holmes repeated his view of the relation between reasons and results in the opinion that, after his opinions in the free speech cases, is his most celebrated, the dissent in *Lochner v. New York* (1905): "General propositions," he said there, "do not decide concrete cases."[5] This is a radical assertion; for it leaves us with the question, If principles don't decide cases, what does? Holmes's effort to answer that question led him, after many years, and very improbably, to the free speech opinions which capped his career, and on which his reputation now rests.

2

In 1995, the University of Chicago Press published the first three volumes of *The Collected Works of Justice Holmes*, which include all the nonjudicial writings, and is the first such comprehensive edition. It was edited by Sheldon M. Novick, whose *Honorable Justice* (1989) was the first full-length biography of Holmes to make use of all the archival material—a fact that is testimony chiefly to the speed with which Novick was able to take advantage of the opening, in 1984, of the Holmes Papers to biographers after fifty years of failed attempts to get an official life completed. Mark DeWolfe Howe, a professor at Harvard Law School who had once served as Holmes's secretary, managed to finish two detailed and elegant volumes, *The Shaping Years* (1957) and *The Proving Years* (1963); but these take the story only to 1882, the mere brink of Holmes's fifty-year career as a judge, and Howe died in 1967. Novick's biography, though serviceable as a narrative of Holmes's life, was notable for its relegation of virtually all discussion of Holmes's jurisprudential work to the footnotes, which sometimes assumed a rather disputatious tone. In his main text, Novick suggested that Holmes espoused "a kind of fascist ideology"; he described Holmes as "a violent, combative, womanizing aristocrat whose contribution to the development of law was surprisingly difficult to define"; and he announced it to be his conclusion that Holmes was, in his thought, a structuralist—a judgment that can be called, among the many that have been offered about Holmes's work, unique.[6]

How this came to be the person chosen to put together the official edition of Holmes's writings by the trustees of the Holmes Devise (the fund established from Holmes's bequest of a portion of his estate to the government of the United States) is a mystery, as is the decision of the University of Chicago Press to publish the volumes in the form in which they appear. The first volume contains 333 pages of text; 198 are by Oliver Wendell Holmes, and 135 are by Sheldon M. Novick. Most of these are devoted to a disquisition on "Holmes's Philosophy and Jurisprudence," with an ensuing "Critical Appraisal." This is a subject which has received continuous attention, at a pretty high level of critical inquiry, since about 1914. A bibliography of Holmes scholarship (none is provided) might have served the purpose more economically and, in what is presented as a memorial edition, more tastefully. Still, though it took sixty years, this is how the job was done.[7]

Novick's idea that Holmes was a structuralist belongs to a history that runs parallel to the history of efforts to define Holmes's politics. This is the history of efforts to define Holmes's philosophy. Holmes has been called a formalist, a positivist, a utilitarian, a realist, a historicist, and a pragmatist (not to mention a nihilist). Commentators who cleave to one of these terms usually find themselves spending a good deal of time explaining why commentators who favor one of the other terms cannot possibly be right. This is generally an easier business than defending the term they prefer; and the reason is that none of these terms can possibly be right, because each singles out one aspect of the law as the essential aspect, and it was Holmes's genius as a philosopher to see that the law has no essential aspect.

A case comes to court as a unique fact situation. It immediately enters a kind of vortex of discursive imperatives. There is the imperative to find the just result in the particular case. There is the imperative to find the result that will be consistent with results reached in analogous cases in the past. There is the imperative to find the result that, generalized across many similar cases, will be most beneficial to society as a whole—the result that will send the most useful behavioral message. There are also, though less explicitly acknowledged, the desire to secure the outcome most congenial to the judge's own politics; the desire to use the case to bend legal doctrine so that it will conform better with changes in social standards and conditions; and the desire to punish the wicked and excuse the good, and to redistribute costs from parties who can't afford them (like car accident victims) to parties who can (like car manufacturers and insurance companies). Hovering over this whole unpredictable weather pattern—all of which is already in motion, as it were, before the particular case at hand ever arises—is a single meta-imperative. This is the imperative not to let it appear as though any one of the lesser imperatives has decided the case at the blatant expense of the others. A result that seems just intuitively but is admittedly incompatible with legal precedent is taboo; so is a result that is formally consistent with precedent but appears unjust on its face. The court does not want to seem to excuse reckless behavior (like operating a railroad too close to a heavily populated area), but it does not want to raise too high a liability barrier to activities society wants to encourage (like building railroads). It wants the law to run in a politically desirable direction, but it does not want to be caught appearing to bend an anachronistic legal doctrine in order to compel a politically correct result.

There is also (to put the final spin on the system), within each of these competing imperatives, the problematic that Holmes's dictum about the nature of reasoning identified, which is the business of deciding what counts as relevant within that particular discourse and what does not. This series of problems begins with the question of what the legally relevant "facts" in the case really are; it runs through the questions of what counts as an analogous case, what counts as an applicable general legal principle, what counts as a benefit to society, and so on; and it ends with the question of what counts as a "just result." Holmes thought that there were no hard-and-fast distinctions in any of these areas; he believed that the answer always boils down to a matter of degree. And when he said that general propositions do not decide concrete cases, he was saying that even if we were to select one imperative to trump all the others in our approach to judicial decision-making, we would still find that the consequences for any particular case were indeterminate. "Cost-benefit analysis" is as malleable as "rights talk." When there are no bones, as T. S. Eliot once said, anybody can carve a goose.

There are bones, though. For cases get decided and verdicts get returned and opinions get written, and by a process that does not seem arbitrary or self-interested to the people who do the deciding, returning, and explaining. If the various discourses of fairness, policy, precedent, and so forth are simply being manipulated rather than applied, they are being manipulated to justify an outcome which has been reached in obedience to some standard. When Holmes said that the common law decided the result first and figured out a plausible account of how it got there afterward, the implication was not that the result was chosen randomly, but that it was dictated by something other than the formal legal rationale later adduced to support it. The purpose of *The Common Law* was to discover what that something was.

3

The book originated as a series of twelve lectures at the Lowell Institute, in Boston, which Holmes delivered, to a packed hall, extemporaneously. It was the product of prodigious research—Holmes was regarded by his contemporaries as a frighteningly disciplined worker—and it has seemed to many competent commentators a kind of thicket of contradictory approaches, all bristling with pedantic details of legal antiquarianism and technical analyses of legal doctrine.

The impression of methodological confusion arises from Holmes's unwillingness to see the law under just one aspect. He was suspicious of formalism—the extraction of abstract legal doctrines from the analysis of sequences of cases—which was the prevailing academic approach to the law at the time: he once referred to Christopher Columbus Langdell, the dean of the Harvard Law School and founder of the case method of legal instruction, as one of "the powers of darkness."[8] (Langdell was probably in the audience for the Lowell Lectures, and he offered Holmes a job afterward anyway.) But Holmes had, in fact, praised Langdell's casebooks, and he used the case method himself when he taught at Harvard; and if there are formalist elements in *The Common Law*, it is because there are formalist elements in the law. Doctrinal continuity, after all, is something highly valued by judges; it is, at a minimum, the best hedge against reversal. At the same time, Holmes believed that the law was susceptible to a utilitarian analysis, since the law is also an instrument of social policy; a moral analysis, since the law is a record of the conduct a society sees fit to penalize; and a historical analysis, since the law has historical roots and evolves in response to changing social conditions.

Thus the celebrated sentence in the opening paragraph of *The Common Law*, "The life of the law has not been logic; it has been experience,"[9] does not say that there is no logic in the law. It only says that logic is not responsible for what is living in the law. The active ingredient in the compound, what puts the bones in the goose, is the thing called "experience." Holmes was using that word in a particular sense. He meant it as the name for everything that arises out of the interaction of the human organism with its environment: beliefs, sentiments, customs, values, policies, prejudices—what he called "the felt necessities of the time."[10] Our word for it (in many ways less satisfactory) is "culture."

Understanding Holmes's conception of "experience" is the key to understanding almost everything that is distinctive about his view of the law. Three features seem especially significant. The first is that experience is not, in Holmes's view, reducible to propositions, even though human beings spend a lot of time so reducing it. "All the pleasure of life is in general ideas," Holmes wrote to a correspondent in 1899. "But all the use of life is in specific solutions—

which cannot be reached through generalities any more than a picture can be painted by knowing some rules of method. They are reached by insight, tact and specific knowledge."[11] Even people who think their thinking is guided by general principles, in other words, even people who think thought is deductive, actually think the way everyone else does—by the seat of their pants. First they decide, then they deduce.

This is obviously the idea that stands behind the assertion, in *Lochner* and many other places in Holmes's writing, that general propositions do not decide concrete cases. Logical reasoning from a prioris is just not the way people make practical choices. Holmes thought that learning the abstract legal doctrines on which judicial decisions are expressly based—what used to be called "black letter law"—was therefore poor training for a lawyer. Judges do invoke these doctrines when they are explaining their decision, but (as Holmes was pointing out when he volunteered to use the same principle to decide a given case either way) the doctrines are never sufficient to account for the result reached. The hole always has a different shape from the arrow sticking out of it. So that anything that might operate as a motive for a judge's decision—a moral conviction, a political preference, even (as he put it) "the blandishments of the emperor's wife"[12]—was, according to Holmes, legally material if it helped lawyers guess the result correctly.

This is the essence of the so-called prediction theory of the law, expressed in Holmes's most famous essay, "The Path of the Law" (1897), by the sentence: "The prophecies of what the courts will do in fact, and nothing more pretentious, are what I mean by the law."[13] Holmes was fifty-six when he wrote "The Path of the Law," and the starkness of its realism, the thoroughness with which it dismisses the notion that the law can be understood by reference to some higher system of morality or rationality, has seemed to some scholars—notably Morton Horwitz—to represent a loss of faith, on Holmes's part, in the moral cohesion, what Horwitz calls "the power of custom,"[14] of late-nineteenth-century American society. But the prediction theory, at least, was not new to Holmes in 1897. It appears in one of his earliest essays, published in the *American Law*

Review in 1872, where Holmes argued that it is not the law that determines the outcome in a particular case, but what judges *say* is the law. For "a precedent may not be followed; a statute may be emptied of its contents by construction. . . . The only question for the lawyer is, how will the judges act?"[15] From the very beginning, Holmes's view of the law was premised on the assumption that law is simply and empirically judicial behavior. A rule may be written down, it may express the will of the sovereign, it may be justified by logic or approved by custom; but if courts will not enforce it, it is not the law, and lawyers who bet their cases on it will lose.

A second distinctive feature of Holmes's conception of experience is that it is not individual and internal but collective and consensual; it is social, not psychological. This is the feature responsible for his most important contribution to the civil law, which is the invention of the reasonable man. The reasonable man is the fictional protagonist of modern liability theory. If you are injured as a result of an act of mine, what triggers civil liability? There are, traditionally, three ways to answer this question. The first is to say that it is enough merely to prove causation: I act at my peril, and I am therefore liable for any costs my actions incur, whether I could have foreseen them or not. The legal term for this is "strict liability." The second way of answering it is to say that I am liable for your injury if I wickedly intended it, but I cannot fairly be held liable for injuries I never contemplated. This is the theory of *mens rea*—"the guilty mind." And the third is to say that even if I neither wished for nor anticipated the possibility of your injury, I am liable to you anyway if my act was careless or imprudent. When I act without exercising due care, then I do act at my peril. This is the theory of negligence.

Holmes treated the problem of liability for injury in a series of dense and intense texts: "The Theory of Torts" (1873), "Trespass and Negligence" (1880), Lectures III and IV of *The Common Law* (1881), and "Privilege, Malice, and Intent" (1894), which is possibly his most brilliant essay. Just what Holmes is saying in these discussions is a matter of apparently endless dispute.[16] The subject seems fraught in part because it is often hard to distinguish, in Holmes's writing, between the descriptive and the prescriptive—between what Holmes believed the law was in practice and what he thought the law ought to be. Holmes didn't do a lot to help his readers make this distinction, but the reason is that his favorite method of argument was to show that what the law ought to be is what it pretty much already is, only under a wrong description. In the case of tort law (the common law governing civil liability for an injury not arising out of a contract), for example, Holmes argued for answer three—liability ought to be triggered by a finding of negligence—but he did so by attempting to demonstrate that negligence was already, and more or less always had been, the rough basis for tort liability. He argued, in other words, that if in our analysis of tort cases we dropped terms like "guilt" and "fault" and replaced them with terms like "carelessness" and "recklessness," we would find that we generally got the same results. The advantage of replacing the moral language of sin with the economic language of risk was not to punish a different class of wrongdoers or a different category of wrongs. It was simply to make explicit what moral language tends to disguise, which is that (in the words of *The Common Law*): "The substance of the law at any given time pretty nearly corresponds, so far as it goes, with what is then understood to be convenient"[17]—a sentence in which, as the context makes clear, we are meant to understand "convenient" in the widest possible sense.

The problem for Holmes wasn't, therefore, what the basis for tort liability ought to be. The problem was what the basis for deciding that a particular act was negligent ought to be. Assuming that we want to make persons who act carelessly pay the cost of cleaning up their tortious messes, how do we determine what sort of behavior counts as careless? How do we distinguish a tort from an accident, or from the permissible by-product of a socially desirable activity? One way of doing this would be to devise a series of general rules for conduct, violation of which would ipso facto constitute negligence; but this solution was obviously ruled out for Holmes by his contempt for the malleability of general rules. His alternative proposal was that we should do judicially what we all do anyway when we are confronted with a judgment call, which is to evaluate the conduct at issue by the lessons of experience. "Experience is the test," as he put it in *The Common Law*, "by which it is decided whether the degree of danger attending given conduct under certain known circumstances is sufficient to throw the risk upon the party pursuing it."[18]

Whose experience? The experience, Holmes said, of "an intelligent and prudent member of the community."[19] He didn't mean by this a *particularly* intelligent and prudent person—a judge, for instance. He meant, precisely, a person who is neither particularly prudent nor particularly imprudent, an "average member of the community"—in other words, a jury. "When men live in society," he explained in *The Common Law*, "a certain average of conduct, a sacrifice of individual peculiarities going beyond a certain point, is necessary to the general welfare. If . . . a man is born hasty and awkward, is always having accidents and hurting himself or his neighbors . . . his slips are no less troublesome to his neighbors than if they spring from guilty neglect. His neighbors accordingly require him, at his proper peril, to come up to their standard, and the courts which they establish decline to take his personal equation into account."[20] Putting it this way made blameworthiness, Holmes thought, into what he approvingly called "an external standard," a standard before which the defendant's state of mind (a legal imponderable anyway) becomes irrelevant. "A man may have as bad a heart as he chooses," as he put it in "Trespass and Negligence," "if his conduct is within the rules."[21]

"The reasonable man" is the phrase commonly associated with this theory of liability. Holmes didn't coin it—it began appearing in American and English opinions around 1850—but, along with his English friend Frederick Pollock, he probably did as much as anyone to define and establish it. What makes the concept work (on Holmes's theory) is that it represents a composite. It is a collective noun, a statistical fiction, an averaging out across the whole population. The "reasonable man" knows, because "experience" tells him, that a given behavior in a given circumstance—say, taking target practice in a populated area—carries the risk of injuring another person. Of course, any action in any circumstance carries some risk, however remote, of injuring another person; and reasonable people know this. But this knowledge is not what reasonableness consists in. What reasonableness consists in is the knowledge of the greater or lesser *probability* of an injury being caused by such and such an action in such and such circumstances. "Even in the domain of knowledge," as Holmes put it, "the law applies its principle of averages."[22]

By putting negligence at the center of tort liability, Holmes got accused, by some twentieth-century commentators, of making it easier for industry to escape liability for injuries, to workers or customers, incidental to its enterprise—injuries for which it would have had to pay under a theory of strict liability. But Holmes did accept a principle of strict liability for what he called "extra-hazardous" activity. Under this principle, a company that uses dynamite in the normal course of its business, for example, can be held accountable for any injuries it causes, even if it has taken reasonable precautions to avoid them. But Holmes didn't regard strict liability as inconsistent with the concept of reasonableness, or even with the concept of negligence; for the activities society labels extra-hazardous are just activities experience has led the reasonable man to believe to be risky per se. "Negligence" is infected a little by the kind of moral coloration Holmes deprecated in legal language: it suggests a personal failing on the part of the defendant. But all Holmes meant by it was acting in the face of foreseeable risk. We may have perfectly honorable reasons for doing so, but we also have to be willing to take our legal chances.

When Holmes remarked, therefore, in "The Path of the Law," that although "for the rational study of the law the black-letter man may be the man of the present . . . the man of the future is the man of statistics and the master of economics,"[23] he meant that the more it became obvious that legal liability can be thought of as a function of the probability of injury, and that courts will weigh the cost of avoiding such injuries against the social benefit of the activity in question, the more irrelevant a knowledge of formal legal doctrine would be to the ability to predict what courts will do. In his theory of torts, Holmes did what Charles Darwin did in his theory of evolution by chance variation and James Clerk Maxwell did in his kinetic theory of gases: he applied the great discovery of nineteenth-century science, which was that the indeterminacy of individual behavior could be regularized by considering groups statistically at the level of the mass, to his own special field.

The advantage of the "reasonable man" standard (in Holmes's view) is that it regularizes the business of evaluating conduct without locking courts into the application of codified principles guaranteed to break down whenever they are confronted with a hard case, or with a mutation in social custom. The disadvantage is that in practice, juries are not always consistent. This group of twelve may regard as reasonable what that group of twelve regards as careless. Holmes did think that since in many tort cases the facts, legally speaking, are essentially the same, judges, having seen the way juries generally dispose of such cases, should be able to determine liability as a matter of law. And in his own career as a judge, he did occasionally try to establish such common law rules, usually with disastrous results. The most famous of these is the Supreme Court case of *Baltimore & Ohio Railroad v. Goodman* (1927), which arose out of the death of a motorist at a railroad crossing where his view of the track was obstructed. Holmes overturned a decision for the plaintiff on the principle (newly laid down by him) that a motorist arriving at a railroad crossing has a duty to stop the car, get out, and look up and down the track before proceeding. "It is true," Holmes explained, "that the question of due care very generally is left to the jury. But we are dealing with a standard of conduct, and when the standard is clear it should be laid down once for all by the courts."[24] Holmes did not drive. After his death, the rule was thrown out by Benjamin Cardozo.

Holmes was wrong in *Baltimore & Ohio v. Goodman*, but he was wrong on his own theoretical ground. It just happens not to be the custom to get out of the car at railroad crossings, and therefore it was almost certainly not (as Holmes probably suspected) sympathy for the widow Goodman that dictated the lower-court result, but, precisely, the application of the community standard of what it is reasonable to do at a railroad crossing. Holmes did not mean to contradict his own argument against reliance on abstract principles in

Goodman; he only meant to increase the degree of predictability in tort law. And this emphasis on predictability is tied to the third significant element in Holmes's idea of "experience," which is what might be called the imprecision factor.

"The loss of certainty" is a phrase many intellectual historians have used to characterize the period in which Holmes lived. But the phrase has it backward. It was not the loss of certainty that stimulated the late-nineteenth-century thinkers with whom Holmes associated; it was the discovery of uncertainty. Holmes was, in many respects, a materialist. He believed, as he put it, that "the law of the grub . . . is also the law for man."[25] And concerning the hope of social betterment, he was something worse than a pessimist. "I despise," he said, "the upward and onward."[26] But he was not entirely a determinist, because he did not think that the course of human events was fixed—or that if it was fixed, we could reliably know anything about it. Complete certainty was an illusion; of that he was certain. There were only greater and lesser degrees of certainty, and that was enough. It was, in fact, better than enough; for although we always want to reduce the degree of uncertainty in our lives, we never want it to disappear entirely, since uncertainty is what puts the play in the joints. Imprecision, the sportiveness, as it were, of the quanta, is what makes life interesting and change possible. Holmes liked to call himself a "bettabilitarian": we cannot know what consequences the universe will attach to our choices, but we can bet on them, and we do it every day.

For although Holmes believed that experience is the only basis we have for guiding our affairs, he also believed that experience is too amorphous, or too multiple, ever to dictate a single line of conduct. Experience makes everything blurry at the edges; it reduces knowledge to a prediction of what should be the case most of the time, and we treat a prediction as an absolute at our peril. We start, in the law, with a principle or a concept that seems to help us decide the great mass of cases, and we therefore begin to assume this concept as fundamental. But as we move out toward the marginal cases, we begin to find that the concept actually rests on a whole submerged structure of other concepts, policies, intuitions, practices, and assumptions, and at a certain point we discover that it has become emptied of predictive force.

Sic utere tuo ut alienum non laedas, for instance, is an old common law maxim generally interpreted to mean that people are required to use their property in a way that will not injure the property of another. This certainly sounds unexceptionable, in law and in morals. But it is a principle, Holmes argued in "Privilege, Malice, and Intent," that "teaches nothing but a benevolent yearning."[27] If I burn down the mom-and-pop candy store around the corner, it is true that I will be held liable for the damage. But (to use one of Holmes's favorite examples) if I set up my own candy store right next door and, by deliberately underselling them, bring mom and pop to heartache and financial ruin, ultimately driving them homeless into the night, the law, although the consequences of my behavior are effectively the same, will be indifferent.

Holmes's perception here was not that we are hypocritical in punishing the first behavior and countenancing (not to say encouraging) the second. His perception was that we cannot make our way by universalizing our principles: it is always the underlying context that gives them force, and it is in the nature of contexts to shift. Nearly all of Holmes's greatest moments as a judge arose from this perception. It is at the bottom of his most famous opinions, the dissents in the free speech cases of *Abrams v. United States* (1919) and *Gitlow v. New York* (1925)—although there is something else interesting about those opinions, too, which is that in order to write them, Holmes had to overcome an innate resistance to the very idea of a right to free speech, a resistance which was based on a principle of his own.

4

That principle was actually a kind of an antiprinciple. Holmes was a lifelong enemy of the concept of natural law—the notion that individuals retain certain rights, against the state, simply by virtue of being human. There are, Holmes thought, no such immutable and universal rights. What we take to be rights are simply customs that have become settled enough to seem inevitable. "As an arbitrary fact people wish to live," he wrote in "Natural Law" (1918),

> and we say with various degrees of certainty that they can do so only on certain conditions. . . . But that seems to me the whole of the matter. I see no *a priori* duty to live with others and in that way, but simply a statement of what I must do if I wish to remain alive. If I do live with others they tell me that I must do and abstain from doing various things or they will put the screws on to me. I believe that they will, and being of the same mind as to their conduct I not only accept the rules but come in time to accept them with sympathy and emotional affirmation and begin to talk about duties and rights. But for legal purposes a right is only the hypostasis of a prophecy—the imagination of a substance supporting the fact that the public force will be brought to bear upon those who do things said to contravene it—just as we talk of the force of gravitation accounting for the conduct of bodies in space. One phrase adds no more than the other to what we know without it.[28]

In 1918, this was the creed of a liberal. For the rights Holmes had in mind were "the right to property" and "liberty of contract," rights which courts had, in the view of political progressives, invented in order to declare unconstitutional legislation intended to regulate the economic life. In *Lochner* (1905), for example, the Court had voided an act of the New York State legislature that limited, on grounds of public health, the number of hours employees could work in a bakery—a decision the majority based on the putative right, constructed out of the Fourteenth Amendment, to liberty of contract. Holmes, in his dissent, had argued not merely that the Fourteenth Amendment did not enact the liberty of contract, but that reading liberty of contract into the language of the Fourteenth Amendment short-circuited the very thing the law was supposed to allow for, which was the flexibility to adapt to circumstances as circumstances change. "A constitution is not intended to embody a particular economic theory," as he put it, "whether of paternalism and the organic relation of the citizen to the state or of laissez faire.

It is made for people of fundamentally differing views, and the accident of our finding certain opinions natural and familiar or novel and even shocking ought not to conclude our judgment upon the question whether statutes embodying them conflict with the Constitution of the United States."[29]

This belief—that the Constitution is designed to allow the majority to experiment, at the expense of the interests of individuals, with different social theories and arrangements—made it easy for Holmes, in 1919, the year after his essay on "Natural Law" appeared, to write three opinions for the Court sustaining convictions under the Espionage Act. The convictions (one was a ten-year sentence for Eugene Debs) were for expressing opinions calculated to encourage others to interfere with the American war effort—for example, by resisting the draft. They were cases, in other words, in which speech had been judged to constitute an incitement to a criminal act. It was in these opinions that Holmes formulated what has come to be known as the "clear and present danger" test for the prosecution of speech: "The question in every case is whether the words used are used in such circumstances and are of such a nature as to create a clear and present danger that they will bring about the substantive evils that Congress has a right to prevent," he wrote, in *Schenck v. United States.* "It is a question of proximity and degree."[30]

The "clear and present danger" test has received a good deal of criticism from commentators who find it insufficiently protective of speech—for example, Gerald Gunther, in his great biography *Learned Hand: The Man and the Judge* (1994). In 1919, Hand was at the beginning of his long career as a judge. His regard for Holmes was virtually unadulterated: he considered Holmes, he once said, "the epitome of all a judge should be."[31] But Hand thought that Holmes's formulation in *Schenck* was too broad. Two years earlier, Hand had written an opinion, in *Masses Publishing Co. v. Patten,* enjoining the New York postmaster from refusing to circulate, because of its antiwar sentiments, Max Eastman's journal the *Masses,* arguing that speech can constitutionally be suppressed or punished only when the words used explicitly counsel a violation of the law. The *Masses,* he believed, was being persecuted for its politics under cover of what would otherwise be an acceptable state effort to prevent interference with the war effort. "To assimilate agitation, legitimate as such, with direct incitement to violent resistance," Hand said, "is to disregard the tolerance of all methods of political agitation which in normal times is a safeguard of free government."[32] (His decision was quickly overturned.)

Hand believed that his construction provided narrower and more "objective" grounds for the prosecution of speech than Holmes's did; and in conversations and letters, he tried to convince Holmes to adopt it.[33] Holmes was persuaded (by Hand and others) to regard some prosecutions under the Espionage Act as unconstitutional, as he did the following term in the *Abrams* case; but he was never persuaded to adopt Hand's formula, and he even claimed not to see Hand's point. "I don't know what the matter is, or how we differ,"[34] he complained in a reply to one of Hand's letters. The matter was that under Holmes's rule, liability hinges on the probability that the evils Congress wishes to prevent will happen as a consequence of the speech in question, and this probability cannot be merely a function of the "objective" meaning of the words uttered. It is not strictly a matter of meaning, in Holmes's formulation; it is a matter of proximity and degree. I may counsel resistance to the draft in the shower as explicitly as I like (as Hand, of course, would have conceded). But out of the shower and before an audience of potential conscripts, I may communicate the same advice in language that never quite reaches the level of explicitness Hand's test requires, but that has the intended effect nonetheless. There are many ways to skin, linguistically, a cat. Gunther is correct to claim that Hand's formula is much more speech-protective than Holmes's. But Holmes's is much more language-sensitive. Holmes's theory of free speech rests on the assumption that informed Holmes's whole approach to liability generally, which is that the community can, given the facts, judge when speech crosses the line of expression and becomes incitement. Whether this is an attractive theory or not from a civil libertarian point of view, it is consistent with Holmes's belief that experience conditions language (and everything else) in unpredictable ways. We don't know in advance what words will constitute

an illegal incitement and what words will not. We have to measure
the intent of the speech by Holmes's usual standards: by context
and experience.

The trouble is that by those standards, every expression is potentially harmful; it is, as Holmes said, only a question of degree.
"Every idea is an incitement," as he admitted in the dissent in *Gitlow*. "It offers itself for belief and if believed is acted on unless some
other belief outweighs it or some failure of energy stifles the movement at its birth. The only difference between the expression of an
opinion and an incitement in the narrower sense is the speaker's enthusiasm for the result. Eloquence may set fire to reason."[35] It is almost the language of an enemy of free speech, for it makes it clear
that when we ask a court to weigh the probable effect of the speech
in question by experience, we are taking a chance that mere offen-
siveness will be excuse enough to find liability, which is just what
Hand feared. But Holmes thought that dominant opinion would
contrive a way to suppress what it regarded as evil no matter what
the legal foundation. And he liked the idea of risk. And, of course,
he was not an enemy of free speech. His opinion in *Schenck* and his
dissents in *Abrams* and *Gitlow* were fundamental to the establishment of First Amendment law. Holmes was able to write those opinions, though, not because he was suddenly convinced of the
inalienability of the right to freedom of expression, but because he
saw in those cases a corollary to his principled aversion to faith in
principles. He managed to articulate a rationale that had the effect
of making free speech a basic right without ever invoking the idea of
natural law.

His most celebrated opinion is probably the dissent in *Abrams*.
He argued there that the speech being punished under the Espionage Act (up to twenty-year sentences to Bolshevik sympathizers
for throwing pamphlets from a building in Manhattan) could not
plausibly be claimed, under the circumstances, to constitute an im-
minent danger to the war effort. The defendants, he thought, were
being punished simply for holding views offensive to the majority.
The danger represented by their prosecution was analogous to the
danger he had identified in *Lochner*: the danger of mistaking a gen-

eral sentiment for a truth. It read into the way we happen to live a certainty about the way people ought to live. It was, in a word, unbettabilitarian. Even the Constitution, Holmes said, is a bet we may lose. "It is an experiment, as all life is an experiment. Every year if not every day we have to wager our salvation upon some prophecy based upon imperfect knowledge."[36] It is the motto of a man who thought that there is no final word, only another way of putting it.

5

Holmes's disinterestedness has its unappealing side. He (like many turn-of-the-century progressives) was a believer in eugenics—a belief that underwrites his most notorious decision, the majority opinion (there was only one dissent) in *Buck v. Bell* (1927) upholding the constitutionality of a Virginia law permitting involuntary sterilization of the "feebleminded." "I felt I was getting near to the first principle of real reform," he told Laski after writing the opinion.[37] The immediate basis for Holmes's enthusiasm was the work of Thomas Malthus, which he read with what was, for him, an unusual degree of assent. But the belief had its roots in his experience in the Civil War, where he had been wounded three times, and where he believed that he had seen human nature in its elemental state: a war of pure aggression, in which one group of people made its view prevail by murdering those who disagreed. (This belief is why Edmund Wilson, who held exactly the same opinion, made Holmes the hero of *Patriotic Gore*, his book on the literature of the Civil War.) He never stopped regarding naked force—the will to power, to give it a nineteenth-century name—as the brute actuality at the bottom of all human transactions. "Every society rests on the death of men," he liked to say.[38] He thus could not see why if society, in order to make its view prevail, could call on its best citizens to sacrifice their lives (as the North had done in the Civil War), it could not also "call upon those who already sap the strength of the State"—in this case, the woman sterilized under the Virginia law, Carrie Buck—to suffer "lesser sacrifices,"[39] such as sterilization.

The legal error seems plain today: Carrie Buck's involuntary ster-

ilization violates an individual right of privacy which we have generally agreed to recognize, and which expresses the same respect for
other people that informs our understanding of the principle of free
speech. But Holmes did not think of the principle of free speech as
an acknowledgment of the rights of individuals, and the notion of a
right to privacy had barely been articulated—it was certainly no part
of constitutional law—when he wrote his opinion in *Buck v. Bell*.
The philosophical error in Holmes's decision is easy to see, though.
It arises from the belief that the way of the universe must necessarily be the way of the human world—the idea that what people do,
once all the mystification and self-deception have been stripped
away, is only a fancy version of what amoebas do. This is the classic
reductive philosophy of the late-Victorian secular mind, which is, of
course, the kind of mind Holmes had. It replaces the believer's su-
pernatural picture of the universe with a materialist picture that is,
in its own way, equally fantastic.

Few people maintain such a view without cheating on it a little
in order to go about the ordinary business of life; but Holmes made
it a point never to cheat, and he erected his fidelity into an ideal of
conduct and of thought. He felt strongly, for instance, that his old
companion William James's sympathetic interest in religious experience had prevented him from facing up to the way things are. "His
wishes led him to turn down the lights so as to give miracle a
chance," he complained to a friend in 1910, the year of James's
death.[40]

The austerity of this vision helps to explain the impression of
dazzling superficiality which Holmes's writing, almost always mag-
nificently lucid and aphoristic, leaves us with. He read, all his life
and in every field: he read *Das Kapital*; he read Casanova's memoirs
(twice); he read *The Sun Also Rises*. He approached each new book
with the same persistent curiosity, and even when he was disappointed or bored (as he was when, late in life, he reread Hegel), he
finished almost everything he started. (*Lady Chatterley's Lover* was,
he claimed, a rare exception.) His correspondence is filled with his
remarkably acute reactions to what he read, and one experiences
the same perfect openness of mind in the uncluttered prose and intellectual tolerance of his most celebrated judicial opinions.

But it all amounted, for Holmes, to an endless, fascinating, beautifully empty diversion, since at the bottom of every passionate belief and noble expression he saw the same armies of the night, fighting the same eternal war. There are, one comes to feel, only two spheres in Holmes's thought: the glittering toy store of art and ideas, and the darkling plain of Fredericksburg and Antietam. Most of us spend our lives in a middle world, in which beliefs matter to us for reasons better than the fact that they happen to be ours. This is the world that William and Henry James tried to write about. Holmes lived in that world, too, of course, and he must, each day, have felt its reality urgently enough. But it seems for him to have been largely inarticulable. The inner life was one of the few things about which Holmes had nothing to say.

T. S. Eliot and the Jews

I

The question of T. S. Eliot's attitude toward Jews provokes defensiveness whenever it is raised. For many people, to believe that Eliot was an anti-Semite is to discredit his poetry. What was striking about Anthony Julius's *T. S. Eliot, Anti-Semitism, and Literary Form*, when it came out in 1995, was that although Julius deplored, bitterly, the anti-Semitism in Eliot's poetry, he refused to regard it as a blemish on the poems. Julius thought that Eliot's anti-Semitism was integral to his poetry, and that there is nothing in the nature of poetry that renders the anti-Semitism less anti-Semitic for being expressed in the form of poetry or that renders the poetry less poetical for including anti-Semitic expressions. "Anti-Semitism," he wrote, "did not disfigure Eliot's work; it animated it. It was, on occasion, both his refuge and his inspiration, and his exploitation of its literary potential was virtuose."[1] There is, to put it another way, no artistic difference between Bleistein (in "Burbank with a Baedeker: Bleistein with a Cigar") and the hyacinth girl (in *The Waste Land*). The one is as poetically realized as the other. Exposure to anti-Semitism is simply part of the experience of reading Eliot. When we bracket the prejudice, Julius thought, we miss the experience.

This was presented as an argument against Eliot criticism in general, but it was most pointedly an argument against Christopher Ricks, who had considered the problem of Eliot and anti-Semitism in a chapter of *T. S. Eliot and Prejudice* (1988). Julius regarded Ricks's effort as an honorable failure, on the grounds that (to put it technically) Ricks tried to thematize the anti-Semitism in Eliot's poems. A literary critic "thematizes" an expression when he or she weaves it back, so to speak, into the fabric of the poem, so that instead of being an instance of what the poem "says," it becomes an instance of what the poem "is about." In Eliot's poem "Sweeney among the Nightingales," for example, we find the line "Rachel *née* Rabinovitch." We can read this as the expression of a prejudice against Jews who change their last names to un-Jewish-sounding ones; but whose prejudice is it? In merely noting the change of name, the line does not ridicule or condemn the practice. We cannot even say with certainty whether Rachel is Jewish, or what her new name might be; it might also be Jewish-sounding. And when we place the line in the context of the rest of the poem, we see that it is one instance of a general paranoia, which takes in a "lady in a cape," a "silent vertebrate in brown," a "man with heavy eyes," a "someone indistinct"—all descriptions that sound ominous but are perfectly innocent in themselves. Being heavy-eyed does not condemn a man to wickedness; your grandmother may possibly have affected a cape on occasion; we are all vertebrates; and so forth. At this point, the anti-Semitism has been thematized by being turned into an example of the general topic of "prejudice." "Sweeney among the Nightingales" becomes a work "about" perception, or representation, or some other morally safe abstraction.

Julius was quite willing to concede that "Rachel *née* Rabinovitch" may mock the paranoia of certain anti-Semites. But he refused to assimilate this prejudice against Jews to other types of prejudice in the poem (the "prejudice" against ladies in capes, for example). And he refused to acquit Eliot of anti-Semitism in this case merely because the poet has managed to be superior to the bigotry his poem evokes. "Sweeney among the Nightingales" is not, Julius pointed out, a dramatic monologue; it has no fictional "speaker," and critics who (like Ricks) attribute its anti-Semitism to a character are inventing literary entities for the purpose of getting Eliot off the hook. It is Eliot who summons up the traditions of the particular anti-Semitic slurs his lines evoke—even as he implies that the perniciousness of the Jews is not nearly as consequential as vulgar anti-Semites imagine:

> The silent vertebrate in brown
> Contracts and concentrates, withdraws;
> Rachel *née* Rabinovitch
> Tears at the grapes with murderous paws;
>
> She and the lady in the cape
> Are suspect, thought to be in league;
> Therefore the man with heavy eyes
> Declines the gambit, shows fatigue,
>
> Leaves the room and reappears
> Outside the window, leaning in,
> Branches of wistaria
> Circumscribe a golden grin.

The mouth full of gold-capped teeth, Julius pointed out, is a staple of anti-Semitic caricature. So are the "heavy eyes."

Julius judged four poems besides "Sweeney among the Nightingales" to be anti-Semitic: "Gerontion," which includes the line "the jew squats on the window sill"; "A Cooking Egg," which refers to the Jewish financier Alfred Mond; "Burbank with a Baedeker: Bleistein with a Cigar," which contains a figure of evidently dubious pedigree named Sir Ferdinand Klein, a caricatural description of Bleistein (with a "protrusive eye"), and the line "The jew is underneath the lot"; and "Dirge," a suppressed fragment in the original draft of *The Waste Land*, which is a lurid image of Bleistein drowned and which includes yet another association of Jews with exophthalmos in the line "Graves' Disease in a dead jew's eyes!"[2] Julius's procedure in each case was, first, to demonstrate that the references to Jews draw on specific traditions of anti-Semitic representation—bulging eyeballs, gold-capped teeth, leprous skin, rootlessness, parasitism, animality ("murderous paws"), and so forth—and, second, to show how intimately these insinuations and allusions matter to the sense of the poem as a whole.

All five poems were composed in the same brief period. Four are in the volume entitled *Ara Vos Prec* (the American edition is called *Poems*), published in 1920; and the fifth, the discarded "Dirge," was probably written in 1920 or 1921, the years in which Eliot was trying, with much difficulty, to write *The Waste Land*, which he completed and published in 1922. There are very few references to Jews in Eliot's poetry after 1922: the probable Jewishness of the vulgarians Klipstein and Krumpacker in the uncompleted drama *Sweeney Agonistes* (1926–27) is not especially salient, and the figure of Simeon, in "A Song for Simeon" (1928), is treated respectfully, in the tradition of Christian condescension toward the virtuous heathen.

But Eliot did discuss the Jews a number of times in his prose after 1922—most notoriously in a passage in *After Strange Gods* (1934) proposing that "reasons of race and religion combine to make any large number of free-thinking Jews undesirable"[3] in the ideal community, but also in a number of less obviously inflammatory contexts. Julius considered these cases in a separate chapter, and he closes with a survey of the results of invitations to Eliot to "amend" his earlier remarks about Jews. He judged Eliot's responses on these occasions to be confused, unconvincing, or inadequate. Julius took a more consistently hard line than Ricks did on the anti-Semitism in Eliot's prose, but their assessments are roughly in agreement.[4]

Julius frankly described his criticism as "adversarial," and he was clearly determined to make, in the juridical sense, a case. His writing retains the flavor of the courtroom: there are long lists of citations (many drawn from Leon Poliakov's four-volume *History of Anti-Semitism*), there is a considerable amount of arguing in the alternative, and sometimes, after the author has run through the law and the facts, he pounds the table. Julius described his book as "a work of resistance as well as respect."[5] This is an admirable approach, but there is something a little forensic about the way it was carried out—as though the law being the law, Julius felt he had a kind of professional duty to demolish every possible line of defense. Still, "the Spirit killeth, but the Letter giveth life." It was Eliot himself who said that; so there is some poetic justice in the proceedings. There is critical justice, as well.

What was missing in Julius's analysis is the etiology of Eliot's anti-Semitism. Julius was not terribly interested in the reasons *why* Eliot wrote the things he did about Jews, or where he learned them—reasons why having an exculpatory tendency. The problem with leaving the history of Eliot's opinions out of the account is that it implies the view that the anti-anti-Semites among Eliot's readers seem to hold, which is that anti-Semitism is a trait some people are just born with, like dishonesty or a fear of high places—a kind of closeted wickedness. But the significant thing about Eliot's anti-Semitism is that it was probably not primal or visceral; it was learned and, largely, theoretical. Julius was certainly right about *what* Eliot wrote, and right as well in the claim that Eliot's general conception of the Jews, intellectually half-baked and morally negligent though it was, formed an integral and frequently neglected aspect of his thought. I think it was a relatively minor aspect: part of the reason it was so half-baked even as anti-Semitism was that Eliot didn't give much attention to it, and in most of the poetry and almost all of the literary criticism it fades into insignificance. But it cannot be edited out of the general picture; and if the story of Eliot and the anti-Semites had been as well known as the story of Eliot and the *symbolistes*, if people had heard as much about Eliot and Charles Maurras as they heard about Eliot and Jules Laforgue, Eliot's reputation in the decades following the Second World War, when his influence in the literary world was most powerful, would have been very different. Or at least (as Jake said to Brett) it's pretty to think so.

2

The story of Eliot and the *symbolistes* goes like this. Eliot was in the Harvard Union one day in 1908, his senior year in college, when he happened to pick up a copy of *The Symbolist Movement in Literature*, by the English critic Arthur Symons. The book was, he said later, "a revelation."[6] It exposed him for the first time to the poetry of Verlaine, Rimbaud, de Nerval, and Laforgue. He ordered an edition of Laforgue's poems, and his own poetic style was transformed almost overnight from an imitation of Tennyson, as read through the prism of Rossetti and FitzGerald, to the mordant, discordant, imagistic style of Laforgue. Eliot's first modernist poems, a series of urban landscape pieces culminating in the "Preludes," date from this period.

Symons was a man of the nineties, a friend of Yeats (to whom *The Symbolist Movement in Literature*, first published in 1899, is dedicated) and a disciple of Walter Pater. It was not an accident that Eliot gave his earliest modernist efforts a musical title; for musicality was the epitome of the Paterian aesthetic, and Symons essentially invented the symbolist movement (the term "symbolist" was his own idea, with some assistance from Yeats) by imposing Pater onto nineteenth-century French literature.

Symons defined symbolism as the evocation of an unseen world beyond the world known to ordinary sense. Eliot accepted the definition and (characteristically) undercut it at the same time; thus, for example, the calculated dissonance of the fourth "Prelude":

> I am moved by fancies that are curled
> Around these images, and cling:
> The notion of some infinitely gentle
> Infinitely suffering thing.
>
> Wipe your hand across your mouth, and laugh;
> The worlds revolve like ancient women
> Gathering fuel in vacant lots.

In 1909–10 Eliot earned a master's degree in literature from Harvard, and then spent the next year on his own in Paris, where he became close friends with a young Frenchman named Jean Verdenal, who would die in the war and to whom Eliot later dedicated his first book of poems. The intellectual celebrity of the day in Paris was

Henri Bergson; Eliot attended his lectures in philosophy at the Collège de France, and underwent, in his own words, "a temporary conversion to Bergsonism."[7] Bergsonism was entirely compatible with
Symons's Paterized notion of *symbolisme*. It taught the existence of
an interior life of feeling, radically different from the world known
to the intellect, which we have access to only through "intuition."
And the key that opened the door to this inner experience was the
image. "Many diverse images," Bergson explained in *"Introduction à
la Métaphysique"* (1903), "borrowed from very different orders of
things, may, by the convergence of their action, direct consciousness to the precise point where there is a certain intuition to be
seized."[8] Eliot's fourth "Prelude" was completed in Paris; "fancies
that are curled / Around these images" is a Bergsonian idea in
Bergsonian language.

It also during this year abroad, in the summer of 1911, that Eliot
finished "The Love Song of J. Alfred Prufrock"—a poem which he
wrote, he later claimed, as a Bergsonian. He returned to Harvard in
the fall and began the graduate studies in philosophy that led to his
dissertation on the British philosopher F. H. Bradley. In 1914, he
went to England on a Harvard fellowship, and it was there that he
met Ezra Pound, to whom he showed "Prufrock." Pound was
stunned. (Eliot was unable to return the compliment. He regarded
Pound's verse, he told his friend Conrad Aiken, as "touchingly in-
competent.")[9]

Pound was not a Bergsonian, but he had been heavily influenced
by Bergson's leading disciple in England, the journalist-philosopher
T. E. Hulme. Hulme had translated the *"Introduction à la Métaphysique"* into English in 1913, and he had been busy for a number
of years before that trying to derive from Bergsonism a theory of poetry—a theory in which experience might be represented by the
equivalent of what Hulme called "a language of intuition."[10] It is always a little hard to know with Pound just what the intellectual
bases for his enthusiasms are, but he must have recognized in
"Prufrock" an extremely witty exercise in the sort of poetry Hulme
had been talking about. Pound had already been peddling his own
knock-off of Hulme's theory, which he called "imagism," and he was
quick to make Eliot a protégé by undertaking to promote his work.

This favor Eliot did return; he seems to have gotten over his indifference to Pound's poetry rather quickly.

Eliot finished his dissertation in 1916, but he had already decided on a literary career rather than an academic one. He remained in England, becoming an assistant editor at the little magazine the *Egoist*, which Pound had made into the flagship of the imagist movement. He and Pound continued to collaborate, experimenting with different metrical forms. In 1921, Eliot wrote the famous essay in which he praised the metaphysical poets of the seventeenth century—Donne, Herbert, Marvell, and so on—for "trying to find the verbal equivalent for states of mind and feeling,"[11] and in which he proposed that the only modern equivalent to their poetry was the poetry of the French *symbolistes* Corbière and Laforgue. The next year, with Pound's editorial help, he published *The Waste Land*, a poem organized in the five-part string-quartet structure he would later use for *Four Quartets*, and in which his own favorite passage was the thrush's water-dripping song, in Part V—a passage of sheer verbal musicality.

This is roughly the account of Eliot's development that informed the first major critical treatments of his work—in I. A. Richards's *Principles of Literary Criticism* (1924), Edmund Wilson's *Axel's Castle* (1931), F. R. Leavis's *New Bearings in English Poetry* (1932), and F. O. Matthiessen's *The Achievement of T. S. Eliot* (1935). The story is useful for explaining what all those critics were almost exclusively interested in explaining, which is how poems like "Prufrock" and *The Waste Land*, which seemed to set conventional literary decorum on its head, could be read and appreciated. The story is not useful for explaining what, beyond a general despair about modern life, Eliot's poetry might be expressing, because it takes into account only the aesthetic influences and leaves most of the intellectual influences out.

3

The intellectual story begins in 1909, the year that Eliot, starting work toward his master's degree at Harvard, registered for a course taught by Irving Babbitt on "Literary Criticism in France." Babbitt was the author of *Literature and the American College* (1908), an attack on what he called "humanitarianism" and a defense of what he called "humanism." Casting his argument in terms so apparently indistinguishable was possibly not the cleverest idea Babbitt ever had; what he meant by humanitarianism was, on the one hand, a brute scientism he associated with Bacon and, on the other, a fuzzy sentimentalism he associated with Rousseau—in other words, naturalism and emotivism. What he meant by humanism was, essentially, classicism—reason and restraint. He thought colleges were promoting the former when they should be instilling the latter.

Babbitt had recently returned from a sabbatical year in Paris (1907–08), where he had read and was greatly influenced by a book called *Le Romantisme français* (1907), by Pierre Lasserre. *Le Romantisme français* is an attack on French cultural decadence, which Lasserre blamed on nineteenth-century romanticism and the cult of the individual, and, in particular, on Rousseau; and it is a recommendation for a return to the spirit of classicism. Much of the book had first appeared in the *Revue de l'action française*, of which Lasserre was the editor; for the attack on romanticism, conceived in those terms, was one aspect of the "counterrevolutionary" program of the leader of the Action Française, Charles Maurras.

Maurras was one of the great enemies of the Third Republic, and the Action Française was his lifelong political party. He had made his name as a journalist by defending Hubert Henry, the colonel who had forged the documents used to convict Alfred Dreyfus. The Action Française arose out of the anti-Dreyfusard movement; Babbitt had, in fact, attended some lectures sponsored by the group on an earlier visit to Paris in the late 1890s. Anti-Semitism was therefore central to its program. Maurras later cited Edouard Drumont's rabidly anti-Semitic *La France juive* (1886) (a best-seller) as the intellectual landmark of his youth. He believed, as he argued in *Trois idées politiques* (1898) and on innumerable occasions thereafter, that the Jews were responsible for the poison of individualism; he blamed the Jews, in fact, for Protestantism. And he called, in the name of a return to order, for monarchism, Catholicism, and extreme economic and cultural nationalism. Babbitt admired Lasserre's critique of romanticism—he would eventually produce his own tome on the subject, *Rousseau and Romanticism* (1919)—although he regretted the extremism of the political movement the book was associated with. He helped to persuade Eliot to take his year abroad, and he encouraged him, when he got to Paris, to get a copy of Maurras's own attack on French cultural decadence, *L'Avenir de l'intelligence* (1905). Eliot took the advice. He bought the book in 1911, and it became one of the touchstones of his thought.

L'Avenir de l'intelligence has four parts, only two of which are likely to have interested Eliot: the first, which is an analysis of modern French history as a struggle between "Blood and Gold . . . the Usurer and the Prince, Finance and the Sword";[12] and the third, which is an attack on *"Le Romantisme féminin."* A crucial element in both discussions is the claim that the corrupting influences—the obsession with money, in the first case, and feminine solipsism, in the second—were not French. They were the products of what Maurras called the *"métèques"*—foreigners who adopt French ways. He habitually referred to Rousseau (and to the concepts of liberty, fraternity, and equality themselves) as "Swiss"; he described Madame de Staël as "a Swiss of Prussian origin."[13] There is no explicit attack on the Jews in *L'Avenir de l'intelligence*, but any reader of Drumont, who had argued that Jews had taken over France by controlling its finances, would have had no trouble identifying the alien representatives of finance and usury as Maurras described them.

Maurras's argument in *"Le Romantisme féminin"* is that the romantic imagination is inherently feminine. It spawns self-absorption, perversity, emotional anarchy—a general attitude of, as he put it, *"je souffre, donc je suis."*[14] To say that French culture was blighted by romanticism was to say that it had been feminized. Two years later, Lasserre, in *Le Romantisme français*, included a chapter on *"Le Sacerdoce de la femme,"* which recommends Maurras's *"Le Romantisme féminin"* as the best treatment of the subject. "Romanticism," Lasserre explained, "when one considers its impact on ideas, sentiments, manners, literature, or art, manifests everywhere the instincts and the travail of the self-indulgent woman."[15]

Eliot finished "The Love Song of J. Alfred Prufrock" shortly after he read *L'Avenir de l'intelligence*. Ricks, in *T. S. Eliot and Prejudice*, has a great deal of fun with the many critics, from John Crowe Ransom to Helen Gardner, who have simply assumed that the women in the lines "In the room the women come and go / Talking of Michelangelo" must be prating silliness. "The absurdity of discussing his giant art, in high-pitched feminine voices, drifting through a drawing room, adds merely extra irony to the underlying sense of the lines,"[16] as Helen Gardner once put it. It's true, as Ricks points out, that the poem says not a word about the intellectual quality, or, for that matter, about the pitch, of the talking these women are engaged in. But it is a little hard, after reading what Eliot had been reading with admiration just before turning his attention to this poem, not to believe that Dame Helen spoke truer than she knew, and that the intention of the lines is to depict a condition of cultural debilitation, and precisely for the reason that the talkers are identified as women and not men. Historical scholarship must be good for something.

Eliot's personal meeting with Maurras, in 1910 or 1911, was probably arranged by Jean Verdenal, who is reported to have had a literary and political interest in the Action Française.[17] Reactionary politics were common among young male Parisians at the time, and Maurras had a gang of followers, who were known as *les camelots du roi*, "the hawkers of the king," since they sold the movement's newspaper, *L'Action française*, on the sidewalks. They also engaged in harassment of the movement's enemies—which is to say, liberals and Jews, whom they chased through the streets and sometimes beat. In April 1911, for example, during Eliot's stay, the Comédie Française put on a play, called *Après moi*, by Henri Bernstein. Bernstein, who was Jewish, was an established playwright who had, in his youth, deserted briefly during his military service, an episode apparently largely forgotten by 1911. But on opening night, the *camelots* plastered the theater with stickers denouncing *"Le Juif Déserteur"*; they drowned out every performance with catcalls and disturbances. After two weeks, and a discreet official request, the play was withdrawn. The incident attracted considerable attention, and Maurras, to accompany the protests, published daily attacks on Jews on the front page of *L'Action française*.[18]

In March, the paper had published an article by Lasserre (who had become its literary critic in 1908) on *"La Philosophie de Bergson."* The article identified Bergson with romanticism, condemned his philosophy for its emphasis on individuality, sensation, and the irrational, and attacked him for being a Jew. (Maurras would later protest Bergson's election to the Académie Française because Bergson was Jewish; he protested on the same grounds after hearing that Albert Einstein might come to the Collège de France after fleeing Germany in 1933.) Whether Eliot read Lasserre's essay is not known; but T. E. Hulme read it—he had already taken an interest in Maurras and the politics of the Action Française—and it marked the beginning of a complete transformation in his theory of art.

Hulme was killed in the war, in 1917, and his writings have come down to us in the form of a collection called *Speculations*, edited in 1924 by Herbert Read, at the time Eliot's assistant at the *Criterion*. For years critics tried to treat the pieces in *Speculations* as though they were somehow intellectually consistent, until Michael Levenson pointed out, in *A Genealogy of Modernism* (1984), that about half the pieces—those written before 1912—are Bergsonian and the other half—those written after 1912—are anti-Bergsonian. Hulme completely changed his mind in 1912, going from a late-romantic subjectivism largely derived from Bergson to a profoundly antihumanist objectivism largely derived from the German aesthetician Wilhelm Worringer. Lasserre's article, Levenson suggests, was probably the reason.[19] So that by the time Eliot met him, Pound, influenced partly by this turn of Hulme's and partly by the self-promotional success of the Italian futurists, had dropped imagism for a "harder" aesthetic theory, something he called (in collaboration with Wyndham Lewis) "vorticism." Pound had become suspicious of the emotionalism and subjectivism implicit in the sort of impressionistic free verse he had once encouraged; when Eliot showed up at his door, his views were in the process of a severe hardening.

Two years after that meeting, in the fall of 1916, Eliot, having decided to remain in England and needing money, taught a course in the Oxford University Extension program on "Modern French Literature." His syllabus was essentially an outline of French antiromanticism: the reading list included *L'Avenir de l'intelligence, Le Romantisme français*, and Babbitt's *Masters of Modern French Criticism* (1912), which contains Babbitt's own attack on Bergson.[20] The following year marked the beginning of Eliot's closest collaboration with Pound, which was inaugurated by a joint decision to react against what Pound called the "emotional slither" and subjectivism of free verse and imagism. This was the decision that produced the anti-Semitic poems of *Ara Vos Prec*, with their strict metrical patterning and their "impersonal" voice.

These poems—"Sweeney among the Nightingales," "Burbank with a Baedeker: Bleistein with a Cigar," and the rest—are not dramatic monologues, because they are programmatically antagonistic to the very idea of self-expression as a literary value. They were written in deliberate reaction against "romantic individualism" and all its evils. Given the association of individualism, sensation, and "emotional slither" with women and Jews in the French criticism Eliot had been reading and teaching since 1910, it is not surprising to find the poems populated by figures like Rachel and Bleistein, Princess Volupine and Sir Ferdinand Klein, and the shadowy *étrangers* of "Gerontion": Mr. Silvero of the "caressing hands"; Hakagawa, "bowing among the Titians"; Fräulein von Kulp. For these are the *"métèques"*—in Eliot's mind, the representatives of the very dissolution for which the ostentatious formal regularity of the poems in which they appear is the symbolic antidote. They are literally what the poems are trying to "contain." When Eliot undertook this exercise in "classical" poetic form, the alleged lubricity of Jews and women must have come to him as his natural subject matter.

> A lustreless protrusive eye
>   Stares from the protozoic slime
> At a perspective of Canaletto.
>   The smoky candle end of time
>
> Declines. On the Rialto once.
>   The rats are underneath the piles.
> The jew is underneath the lot.

In 1920, Pound, on a visit to Paris, picked up a book by Julien Benda called *Belphegor*. He admired it, and mailed a copy to Eliot in London. Pound must have recognized the book immediately as the equivalent in prose of the poems Eliot had just published in *Ara Vos Prec*. For *Belphegor* (1918) is an attack on cultural decadence in the familiar Maurrasian and Lasserrean mode. "Contemporary French Society demands that all works of art shall arouse emotion and sensation,"[21] it complained; and it recited the familiar list of Rousseauian toxins: emotionalism, self-indulgence, and the craving for newness and originality.

Benda suggested several candidates as possible sources of cultural debility, among them the Jews. There are, he explained, two types: "the severe, moralistic Jew, and the Jew who is always greedy for sensation—speaking symbolically, the Hebrew and the Carthaginian, Jehovah and Belphegor [one of the biblical names for Baal], Spinoza and Bergson."[22] But the Jewish influence, he says, does not explain enough; for although French society has proved susceptible to the corrupting effect of the second type of Jew, it must have been corrupted already, or it would not have been susceptible. It is the classic anti-Semitic form of anti-anti-Semitism: the influence of the Jews has been exaggerated.

Benda therefore goes on to consider several anterior causes, including "the entrance into French society of people of a different class, whose minds are in a state of nature (parvenus of trade, industry and finance, etc.)."[23] But the crucial reason for the debasement of French culture, he says, "lies in the fact *that it is entirely created by women*":[24] "All the literary attributes exalted by contemporary aesthetics are those with which women are most highly endowed, and which form a kind of monopoly of their sex; absence of general ideas, cult of the concrete and circumstantial, swift and entirely intuitive perception, receptiveness to sentiment alone, interest centered on the self. . . . Men . . . try to imitate the literature of their rivals. Alas! . . . There is a degree of unintellectuality and shamelessness to which they will never attain."[25]

Pound knew his man. Eliot responded enthusiastically, and asked for more Benda. A month later, he told Scofield Thayer, editor of the American literary magazine the *Dial*, that "Benda's book is ripping,"[26] and recommended that the *Dial* serialize the whole thing. (It did.) In 1922, when Eliot was starting up the *Criterion*, he eagerly solicited something from Benda. Benda eventually gave him a short essay, which Eliot ran in 1923 with a note calling *Belphegor* "one of the most remarkable essays in criticism of our time."[27] He later reviewed (unfavorably) the book for which Benda is now famous, *La Trahison des clercs* (1927), and took the opportunity to describe *Belphegor* as "an almost final statement of the attitude of contemporary society to art and the artist."[28] When Eliot went to work at Faber and Faber, he published an English translation of *Belphegor*, with an introduction by his old teacher Irving Babbitt. And in 1926, he announced in the *Criterion* the existence of a "classical" tendency, which the magazine would henceforth endeavor to represent, and recommended six books as exemplary: Babbitt's *Democracy and Leadership*, Georges Sorel's *Réflexions sur la violence*, Jacques Maritain's *Réflexions sur l'intelligence*, Hulme's *Speculations*, Maurras's *L'Avenir de l'intelligence*, and *Belphegor*. With the exception of Benda and the equivocal exception of Babbitt, every one of these writers had at one time or another been associated with the Action Française.

The following year, Eliot underwent his conversion to Anglicanism—a secret first unveiled, for most of his readers, in the famous preface to the essay collection *For Lancelot Andrewes* (1928), where he explains that his "general point of view may be described as classicist in literature, royalist in politics, and anglo-catholic in religion."[29] The unusual trio (as several commentators have noted) is almost certainly an echo of a 1913 article on Maurras in the *Nouvelle revue française*, entitled "*L'Esthétique des trois traditions*," in which Maurras's views are described as "*classique, catholique, monarchique.*"[30] (The formula was current among admirers of the Action Française before the *NRF* article: Hulme used a version of it in 1912 in "A Tory Philosophy," which begins: "It is my aim to explain . . . why I believe in original sin, why I can't stand romanticism, and why I am a certain kind of Tory.)"[31] The allusion is fitting because, as Eliot told Paul Elmer More privately, Maurras had been a principal reason for his conversion.[32] Eliot made public acknowledgment of the influence as well, though the wording was elliptical: responding, in 1928, to the charge that Maurras's influence "is to pervert his disciples and students away from Christianity," Eliot testified that "upon me he has had exactly the opposite effect."[33]

But the influence was of a peculiar kind, for Maurras was not himself a believer. Eliot felt called upon to defend him in 1928, in fact, because two years earlier the pope had condemned the Action Française and placed many of Maurras's works (including *L'Avenir de l'intelligence*) on the Index of forbidden writings. Maurras's promotion of Catholicism was inspired entirely by his enthusiasm for the prospect of greater order and authority he thought it afforded. Eliot, of course, was a genuine believer. But having been persuaded into his faith by the arguments of a man for whom religion was an instrument not of personal salvation but of national cohesion, he proceeded to treat Christianity as the basis for social, economic, educational, and political reform. Thus the bizarre spectacle of Eliot's religious writings, in which twentieth-century Anglicanism, a faith not exactly noted for its proselytizing or millenarian spirit, becomes the foundation for a theocratic political vision.

The Jews therefore figured, in Eliot's sociology, as the vestigial remainder of a phase that Christendom had left behind. What is almost as startling as the direct reference to the undesirability of Jews in *After Strange Gods* (1934) is the general indifference displayed in *The Idea of a Christian Society* (1939) and *Notes Towards the Definition of Culture* (1948) to the problem of what to do with *any* group not assimilable to a homogeneous Christian order. Eliot does not seem, in those writings, antipathetic to the Jews, only indifferent. Their fate (short of conversion) simply did not matter to him. "The World is trying the experiment of attempting to form a civilized but non-Christian mentality," he wrote in 1931. "The experiment will fail; but we must be very patient awaiting its collapse; meanwhile redeeming the time: so that the Faith may be preserved alive through the dark ages before us; to renew and rebuild civilization, and save the World from suicide."[34] Non-Christians can feel glad at least for the recommendation of patience.

4

The great mistake in trying to make sense of Eliot is the assumption that he had a very consistent idea of what he was doing. The mistake is easy to fall into because of the sense of authority Eliot's writing has always conveyed. It was an extremely precocious authority: by the time he was thirty-two, he had written three of the most influential essays in twentieth-century criticism in English—"Hamlet and His Problems," "Tradition and the Individual Talent," and "The Metaphysical Poets." But a knack for sagaciousness is readily exploited, and Eliot sometimes used his capacity for sounding official as a mask for a temperament that was genuinely ad hoc. He was always announcing projects, movements, doctrines, tendencies; but as soon as anyone tried to climb up on the platform with him, he pushed him off. I. A. Richards, Herbert Read, and even Babbitt were subjected to public chastisement by Eliot for what they must have assumed were views Eliot would approve of. That the posthumous *Speculations* of T. E. Hulme was a hopelessly muddled collection hardly bothered Eliot—when the book appeared, he hailed Hulme as "the forerunner of a new attitude of mind, which should be the twentieth-century mind, if the twentieth century is to have a mind of its own"[35]—because the muddle so closely matched his own. He was, as a poet, Bergsonian and anti-Bergsonian, romantic and antiromantic, for his entire career. "Burbank with a Baedeker: Bleistein with a Cigar" is a reaction against symbolism; it is also, in its willful image-piling and narrative indeterminacy, a poem unimaginable without symbolism.

Eliot's was, remarkably, a mind of bits and pieces. His sources are easily traced, but what matters in his writing always comes from something untraceable. The influence of various aesthetic theories on his poetry can all be mapped and measured, and in the end they fail to account for what he actually wrote. There is nothing in imagism or Bergson or Pater that prepares one for "When the evening is spread out against the sky / Like a patient etherised upon a table" or for "April is the cruellest month."

Eliot picked up things he encountered and turned them to uses no one had quite imagined. The famous definition of the "objective correlative" in the essay on *Hamlet*—"The only way of expressing emotion in the form of art is by finding an 'objective correlative'; in other words, a set of objects, a situation, a chain of events which shall be the formula of that *particular* emotion; such that when the external facts, which must terminate in sensory experience, are given, the emotion is immediately evoked"[36]—is lifted straight out of a review by Pound's great friend Ford Madox Ford, in which Ford wrote: "poetry consists in so rendering concrete objects that the emotions produced by the objects shall arise in the reader."[37] But critics spent decades pondering Eliot's essay, and no one remembers Ford's. And having introduced the term to literary criticism, Eliot never used it again.

This creates difficulties when critics try to nail Eliot down to one set of influences or ideas. Kenneth Asher's *T. S. Eliot and Ideology* (1995), for example, made a significant contribution to our understanding of the importance Maurras had for Eliot, but it got hung up by looking for signposts where there are only many, many signs. "From beginning to end," Asher proposed, "Eliot's work, including both the poetry and the prose, was shaped by a political vision inherited from French reactionary thinkers, especially from Charles Maurras."[38] No doubt it was, and in ways Asher did a lot to illuminate; but Eliot's work was shaped by a dozen other influences as well, some consistent and some inconsistent with Maurrasian philosophy. Richard Wollheim once suggested that Eliot "was progressively led to substitute in his mind, on the one hand, ideas of less content for ideas of more content, and, on the other hand, poorer or softer ideas for better and stronger ideas."[39]

Two things are distressing about the political and sociological writings Eliot produced in the 1930s. One is the deeply antimodern animus, the high-minded intolerance, that informs them. The other is the comfort they seem so blithely to give to people and doctrines whose potential for evil must have been perfectly manifest. Some of these cases involve the fate of the European Jews. Julius went over many of them carefully and critically, noting, for example, that

Hitler had already come to power when Eliot made his remarks about the undesirability of "free-thinking Jews," and had been in power for a year when those remarks were finally published. That Eliot was indifferent to the threat posed by Nazism to German Jews is chillingly suggested by an unsigned book notice which appeared in the *Criterion* in 1936. The book was *The Yellow Spot: The Extermination of the Jews in Germany*; it carries an introduction by the Bishop of Durham. Julius, following several other scholars, including Ricks, believed the writing is Eliot's own. It is not; the review was by Montgomery Belgion, a writer Eliot often published on French subjects. The style, though, is plainly imitative of the style of the master. This is the review Eliot ran:

> There should be someone to point out that this book, although enjoying a cathedratic blessing, is an attempt to arouse moral indignation by means of sensationalism. Needless to say, it does not touch on how we might alleviate the situation of those whose misfortunes it describes, still less on why they, among all the unfortunates of the world, have a first claim on our compassion and help. Certainly no English man or woman would wish to be a German Jew in Germany today; but not only is our title to the moral dictatorship of the world open to question, there is not the least prospect of our being able to exercise it. More particularly, it is noticeable that the jacket of the book speaks of the "extermination" of the Jews in Germany, whereas the title-page refers only to their "persecution"; and as the title-page is to the jacket, so are the contents to the title-page, especially in the chapter devoted to the ill-treatment of Jews in German concentration camps.[40]

Eliot did not write this. He did, however, assign, edit, and publish it. For he seems to have thought it a brilliant strategy to use the spread of fascism in Europe as a stick to beat the British liberals with. So, for example, in his "Commentary" in the *Criterion* for October 1938—after Mussolini's Ethiopian war, after the *Anchluss*, after Munich—we find Eliot attacking "the heirs of liberalism, who find an emotional outlet in denouncing the iniquity of something called 'fascism.' " "The irresponsible 'anti-fascist,' " he complains, "is a danger in several ways. His activities . . . distract attention from the true evils of his own society. What some of these are may be learned by reading Viscount Lymington's *Famine in England*"[41]—which he goes on, at some length, though in vague terms, to praise.

Now, Viscount Lymington, later the Earl of Portsmouth, was a man named Gerard Wallop. He was a friend of Eliot's; they had met some years earlier at a private dinner in the House of Commons. *Famine in England* is a warning against war with Germany, a war the British are being driven to, Wallop advises, by Communist propaganda and by those who would benefit from the chaos war would bring. What England needs instead, he argues, is a renewal of its agricultural and its human stock: "It is blood and soil which rule at last."[42] It seems that the real danger is within:

> Foreign invasion of England has not happened in war time. It has happened in the last hundred years. Anyone who has been able to notice with his own eyes the foreign invasion of London should read Colonel Lane's *The Alien Menace* to see the extent to which it has been carried on. . . . These immigrants have invaded the slums and the high places as well. It should not be forgotten that those aliens who now appear to have a stake in this country have a stake also in many others. But most of them, who are obscure, have a definite stake in revolution and no instinct for or interest in English life and tradition. One by one they have "muscled in" on the Englishman's livelihood till they are everywhere in key positions. With them has come corruption and disrespect for the ancient decencies.[43]

Arthur Lane's *The Alien Menace* is a work of classic paranoid anti-Semitism, in the tradition of Nesta Webster, a writer Lane repeatedly cites. Two sentences are adequate to give the flavor of his book: "It is unsound and inconsistent of our Government to spend large sums of money in emigrating our best people instead of expelling and repatriating the scourings of the earth, whose natural climate and country is the East. Why not settle this evil horde in Palestine and the Euphrates Valley."[44] Following the publication of *Famine in England*, Wallop was invited to Berlin. He went for a week in 1939, meeting with Hitler (he had also had an audience with him earlier in the decade) and "being," as he put it in his autobiography, "wined and dined, seeing youth work camps, bride schools, and a very great many of the good things Hitler was doing."[45]

Eliot's inability to dissociate himself from men whose anti-Semitism was virulent and overt was lifelong. Such a man was Ezra Pound, long before he met Major Douglas or heard of Mussolini. In a series entitled "Patria Mia," in the British *New Age* in 1912, he praised the ethnic diversity of New York, but found it necessary to add, "The Jew alone can retain his detestable qualities."[46] Such a man was John Quinn, the New York lawyer who was the patron of Pound, Joyce, and Eliot. Quinn had written to Eliot in 1919 concerning some trouble with the publisher Horace Liveright (who was Jewish), and expressing his satisfaction on hearing news of Polish pogroms and his keen desire to start a pogrom in New York—so that Eliot must have thought it a useful piece of stroking when, writing to Quinn several years later to complain again about Liveright, he commented that he was sick of what he called Jew publishers and asked whether Quinn couldn't find a decent Christian one.[47] And such a man was Charles Maurras, who shouted *"C'est la revanche de Dreyfus!"* upon his conviction in 1945 by a French court for collaborating with the Nazi occupation. After the trial, the right-wing French newspaper *Aspects de la France et du Monde* published a special issue in homage to Maurras; Eliot contributed an essay in which he described Maurras as "a sort of Virgil who led us to the doors of the temple."[48]

As Julius argued, the poems in *Ara Vos Prec* are poetry, and they are anti-Semitic, and the two qualities are inseparable, for the poems have a place within a very specific tradition of anti-Semitic literary thought. Julius's claim that anti-Semitism casts a shadow on Eliot's writing after 1922 is right as well. And in the end, even his refusal to concede ground to exculpatory arguments seems just. For indifference is not a defense. There is no evidence that Eliot ever demonstrated personal hostility to a Jew. His anti-Semitism was certainly not, as some of his defenders claimed over the years, "genteel" (whatever it could mean to be a genteel bigot); but neither was it, except as a spur to writing, acted upon or intended to be acted upon. I don't think Eliot ever wished any harm to the Jews. But he took support from and gave support to many people who did. He was a traveler in that terrible fellowship.

For most of his career Eliot laid claim to a position outside the fray. It was his role, he seemed to feel, to be the one man who could think eschatologically while everyone around him was thinking merely politically and biologically. Asher has a nice phrase for the rhetorical gambit Eliot used when he assumed this stance: "the calling of a truce while he attacks from above."[49] But I don't think Eliot's personal associations with anti-Semitism were unworldly. I think they were all too worldly.

Richard Wright:

The Hammer and the Nail

I

Richard Wright was thirty-one when *Native Son* was published, in 1940. He was born in a sharecropper's cabin in Mississippi and grew up in extreme poverty: his father abandoned the family when Wright was five, and his mother was incapacitated by a stroke before he was ten. In 1927 he fled to Chicago and eventually found a job in the Post Office there, which enabled him (as he later said) to go to bed with a full stomach every night for the first time in his life. He became active in literary circles, and in 1933 he was elected executive secretary of the Chicago branch of the John Reed Club, a writers' organization associated with the Communist Party. In 1935 he finished a short novel called *Cesspool*, about a day in the life of a black postal worker. No one would publish it. He had better luck with a collection of short stories, *Uncle Tom's Children*, which appeared in 1938. The reviews were admiring, but they did not please Wright. "I found that I had written a book which even bankers' daughters could read and weep over and feel good about,"[1] he complained, and he vowed that his next book would be too hard for tears.

Native Son was that book, and it is not a novel for sentimentalists. It involves the asphyxiation, decapitation, and cremation of a white woman by a poor young black man from the South Side of Chicago. The man, Bigger Thomas, feels so invigorated by what he has done that he tries to extort money from the woman's wealthy parents. When that scheme fails, he murders his black girlfriend, and even after he has finally been captured and sentenced to death he refuses to repent. Nobody in America had ever before told a story like this and had it published. In three weeks the book sold 215,000 copies.

It will give an idea of the world into which *Native Son* made its uncouth appearance to recall that at almost the same moment that Wright's novel was entering the best-seller lists—the spring of 1940—Hattie McDaniel was being given an Academy Award for her performance as Mammy in *Gone with the Wind*. McDaniel was the first black person ever voted an Oscar, and she gave Hollywood (as Oscar winners ideally do) an occasion for self-congratulation. "Only in America, the Land of the Free, could such a thing have happened," the columnist Louella Parsons explained. "The Academy is apparently growing up and so is Hollywood. We are beginning to realize that art has no boundaries and that creed, race, or color must not interfere where credit is due." She did not go on to note that when McDaniel and her escort arrived at the Coconut Grove for the awards ceremony, they found that they had been seated at a special table at the rear of the room, near the kitchen.[2]

"The day *Native Son* appeared, American culture was changed forever,"[3] Irving Howe once wrote, and this remark has been quoted many times. What Howe meant was that after *Native Son* it was no longer possible to pretend, as Louella Parsons had pretended, that the history of racial oppression was a legacy from which Americans could emerge without suffering an enduring penalty. White Americans had attempted to dehumanize black Americans, and everyone carried the scars; it would take more than calling America "the Land of the Free" and really meaning it to make the country whole. If this is what, almost sixty years ago, Wright intended to say in *Native Son*, he isn't wrong yet. *Native Son* also stands at the beginning of a period in which novels (and, more recently, movies) by black Americans have treated the subject of race with a lack of gentility almost unimaginable before 1940. In this respect, too, Wright's novel casts a long shadow. But if we consider *Native Son* primarily in the company of works by other black artists, we'll miss what Wright was up to, and why he is such a remarkable figure.

Wright's intentions have been difficult to grasp, because many of his books were mangled or chopped up by various editors, and their publication was strewn over five decades. *Lawd Today!* (the retitled *Cesspool*) was not published until 1963, three years after Wright's death, and then it appeared in a bowdlerized edition. One of the stories in *Uncle Tom's Children* was rejected by its publisher and did not appear in the first edition of the book; it was added to a second edition after *Native Son* became a best-seller. *Native Son* itself was partly expurgated, and a significant episode was dropped, at the request of the Book-of-the-Month Club. Half of Wright's autobiography, *Black Boy* (published in 1945), was cut, also in order to please the Book-of-the-Month Club, and remained unpublished in book form until 1977, when it appeared under Wright's original title for the entire work, *American Hunger*. And the long novel *The Outsider* was heavily edited, and some pages were dropped without Wright's approval, when it was first published in 1953.

These five books were only restored to their original condition in 1991, by Arnold Rampersad, in the edition of Wright's work published by the Library of America. (Wright produced more work after *The Outsider* than the Library of America edition included: in the last seven years of his life he wrote two novels, a collection of stories, a play, several works of nonfiction, and some four thousand haiku.) The result gave readers the core of Wright's work not as it was first seen, but as it was first intended, and there turned out to be a difference.

Putting the expurgated material back in gives all three of the novels a grittier surface; and in the case of *Native Son* it also adds a dimension to the story. In the familiar version of the novel, a puzzling line appears during a scene, late in the book, in which the state's attorney tries to intimidate Bigger by letting him understand that he has information about other crimes and misdeeds Bigger has committed, including, he says, "that dirty trick you and your friend Jack pulled off in the Regal Theatre."[4] The reference is opaque. Bigger and his friend do go to the Regal Theatre, a movie house, early in the novel, but no dirty trick is described. In the original version, though, after Bigger and his friend enter the theater they masturbate (the state's attorney's comment is now revealed to include a pun) and are seen by a female patron and reported to the manager.

The Book-of-the-Month Club, Wright's editor informed him, objected to the scene, which, the editor thought Wright would agree, was "a bit on the raw side."[5] Wright obliged the club's sense of propriety by removing the "dirty trick." But he hadn't intended Bigger's public masturbation to be simply a redundant example of his general sociopathy. In Wright's original version, after Bigger and Jack masturbate they watch a newsreel featuring the woman Bigger will accidentally kill that night, Mary Dalton. She is shown on vacation on a beach in Florida, and Bigger and Jack decide (as the newsreel encourages them to) that she looks as if she might be "a hot kind of girl."[6] Wright cut this episode as well (he had Bigger watch a movie critical of political radicalism instead); and he also eliminated a few lines (apparently too steamy for the Book-of-the-Month Club) from Bigger's later encounter with the flesh-and-blood Mary which made it clear that Bigger is sexually aroused by her.

Restoring this material restores more than a couple of scenes. Bigger's sexuality has always been a puzzle. He hates Mary and is afraid of her, but she is attractive and is negligent about sexual decorum, and the combination ought to provoke some sort of sexual reaction; yet in the familiar edition it does not. Now we can see that, originally, it was meant to. The restoration of Bigger's sexuality also helps to make sense of his later treatment of his girlfriend, Bessie. He repeats intentionally with Bessie what he has done, for the most part unpremeditatedly, to Mary: he takes her upstairs in an abandoned building, kills her by crushing her skull with a brick, and disposes of her body by throwing it down an airshaft. But before Bigger

kills Bessie he rapes her, and if the scene is to carry its full power we
have to have felt that when Bigger was with Mary in her bedroom,
he had rape in his heart.

2

Wright was a writer of warring impulses. His rage at the injustice of
the world he knew made him impatient with the usual logic of literary expression. He was a gifted inventor of morally explosive situations, but once the situations in his stories actually explode he can
never seem to let the pieces fall where they will. His novels suffer
from an essentially antinovelistic condition: they are hostage to a
politics of outcomes. Wright tries to order events to fit his sense of
justice—or, more accurately, his sense of the impossibility of justice—and when the moral is not unambiguous enough, he inserts a
speech. At the same time, Wright loved literature intimately, as you
might love a person who has rescued you from misery or danger. Literature, he said, was the first place in which he found his inner
sense of the world reflected and ratified. Everything else, from the
laws and mores of Southern apartheid to the religious fanaticism of
his own family (he grew up mostly in the house of his maternal
grandmother, a devout Seventh-Day Adventist, who believed that
storytelling was a sin), he experienced as pure hostility.

After he moved to Chicago, he discovered in Marxism a second
corroboration of his convictions, and he joined the Communist
Party. But he believed that Marxist politics were compatible with a
commitment to literature—and the belief led, in 1942, to his break,
and subsequent feud, with the party. He had an appreciation not
only of those writers whose influence on his own work is most obvious—Dostoevsky and Dreiser and, later on, Camus and Sartre—
but also of Gertrude Stein, Henry James, T. S. Eliot, Turgenev, and
Proust. From the beginning of his literary career, in the John Reed
Club, until the end, in self-exile in France, he participated in writers' organizations and congresses, where he spoke as a champion of
artistic freedom; and he was a mentor for, among other young writers, James Baldwin, Ralph Ellison, and Gwendolyn Brooks.

It's true that Wright's convictions flatten out the "literary" qualities of his fiction, and lead him to sacrifice complexity for force. His novels tend to be prolix and didactic, and his style is often dogged. But force is a literary quality, too—and one that can make other limitations seem irrelevant. Wright's descriptions, for example, are almost all painted in primary colors straight out of the naturalist paintbox; but the flight of Bigger Thomas through the snow in *Native Son*—a black man seeking invisibility in a world of whiteness— is one of the most effective sequences in American fiction. The apparent indifference to artistry in Wright's work has seemed to some people a thing to be admired, a guarantee of literary honesty. It's the way a black man living in America should write, they feel. This interpretation is one of the ways Wright's race has been made the key to understanding him; and it's a position that, in various guises and more subtly argued, has turned up often in the long critical debate over Wright's work—a debate that has engaged, over the years, Baldwin, Ellison, Howe, and Eldridge Cleaver.

It is not a position that Wright would have accepted. His heroes were the major modern writers (nearly all of them white), and he wanted to serve art in the same spirit they had. He was frank about the models he relied on in making *Native Son*: "Association with white writers was the life preserver of my hope to depict Negro life in fiction," he wrote in the essay "How Bigger Was Born," "for my race possessed no fictional works dealing with such problems, had no background in such sharp and critical testing of experience, no novels that went with a deep and fearless will down to the dark roots of life."[7] He made it clear that his greatest satisfaction in writing *Native Son* came not from entering a protest against racism and injustice but from proving to himself (he didn't care, he said, what others thought) that he was indeed a maker of literature in the tradition of Poe, Hawthorne, and Henry James. In "the oppression of the Negro," he said, he had found a subject worthy of those writers' genius: "If Poe were alive, he would not have to invent horror; horror would invent him."[8]

What Wright took to be his good fortune was also his dilemma. Poe was, in a sense, the luckier writer. The moral outlines of

Wright's principal subject matter were so vivid when he wrote his books that efforts to complicate them would have seemed irresponsible and efforts to heighten them melodramatic. Some of the stories about black victims of Southern racism in *Uncle Tom's Children* have memorable touches of atmosphere and drama, and some are morality plays, but in all of them the action is determined entirely by the unmitigated viciousness of the white characters. When the subject is violent confrontation in a racially divided community—as it is in those stories and in *Native Son*—a "literary" imagination can seem superfluous. In the last section of *Native Son*, for example, Wright has Bigger read a long article about his case in a Chicago newspaper, in which he finds himself described in these terms:

> Though the Negro killer's body does not seem compactly built, he gives the impression of possessing abnormal physical strength. He is about five feet, nine inches tall and his skin is exceedingly black. His lower jaw protrudes obnoxiously, reminding one of a jungle beast.
>
> His arms are long, hanging in a dangling fashion to his knees. . . . His shoulders are huge and muscular, and he keeps them hunched, as if about to spring upon you at any moment. He looks at the world with a strange, sullen, fixed-from-under stare, as though defying all efforts of compassion.
>
> All in all, he seems a beast utterly untouched by the softening influences of modern civilization. In speech and manner he lacks the charm of the average, harmless, genial, grinning southern darky so beloved by the American people.[9]

The passage may strike readers today as a case of moral overloading—a caricature of attitudes whose virulence we already acknowledge. In fact, as one student of Wright's work, Keneth Kinnamon, has pointed out, Wright was using the exact language of articles in the *Chicago Tribune* about Robert Nixon, a black man who was executed in 1939 for the murder of a white woman.[10]

For the Wright who wanted to expose an evil that other writers had ignored, the starkness of his material made his job simpler; for the Wright who wanted to write novels, the same starkness made it harder. In *A Passage to India*, E. M. Forster took a situation very like the one Wright used in *Native Son*—impermissible sexual contact between a white woman and a man of color—and built around it a textured, essentially tragic novel about the limits of human goodness. Forster's sensibility was very different from Wright's, but he could work his material in the way he did in part because his "racists" were people who imagined themselves to be enlightened, and this allowed him to tell his story in a highly developed ironic voice. The kind of racism that figures in most of *Native Son*, though, is not tragic, and it is not an occasion for irony. It is simply criminal.

Wright seems to have recognized this difficulty partway through *Native Son* and to have responded by giving his work a sociological turn. In *Lawd Today!* (about a black man who is not only a victim of bigotry but a bigot himself), in *Uncle Tom's Children*, and in the first two parts of *Native Son*, he had tried to describe the conditions of life in a racist society; in the last part of *Native Son* he undertook to explain them. He therefore introduced into his novel a character who has never, I think, won a single admirer: Mr. Max, the Communist lawyer who volunteers to represent Bigger at his trial. Max's bombastic and seemingly interminable speech before the court (twenty-three pages in the Library of America edition), in which he proposes a theory of modern life meant to explain Bigger's conduct, is almost universally regarded as a mistake. The speech is surely a mistake, but the error is not merely a formal one—putting a long sociological or philosophical disquisition into the mouth of a character. Ivan Karamazov goes on at considerable length about the Grand Inquisitor, and few people object. The problem with Max's oration isn't that it's sociology; it's that it's boring. And it's boring because Wright didn't really believe it himself.

Max's thesis is that twentieth-century industrialism has created a "mass man," a creature who is bombarded with images of consumerist bliss by movies and advertisements, but has been given no means for genuine fulfillment. The consequence is an inner condition of fear and rage which everyone shares, and for which black men like Bigger are made the scapegoats. This fits neatly enough with much of the story for it to sound like Wright's last word. But it is not. Max's courtroom performance is followed by a final scene, in which Bigger talks with Max in his jail cell. They carry on a rather broken conversation, at the end of which Bigger cries out:

> "I didn't want to kill! . . . But what I killed for, I *am!* It must've been pretty deep in me to make me kill! I must have felt it awful hard to murder. . . ."
>
> Max lifted his hand to touch Bigger, but did not.
>
> "No; no; no . . . Bigger, not that . . ." Max pleaded despairingly.
>
> "What I killed for must've been good!" Bigger's voice was full of frenzied anguish. "It must've been good! When a man kills, it's for something. . . . I didn't know I was really alive in this world until I felt things hard enough to kill for 'em. . . . It's the truth, Mr. Max. I can say it now, 'cause I'm going to die. I know what I'm saying real good and I know how it sounds. But I'm all right. I feel all right when I look at it that way. . . ."
>
> Max's eyes were full of terror. Several times his body moved nervously, as though he were about to go to Bigger; but he stood still.
>
> "I'm all right, Mr. Max. Just go and tell Ma I was all right and not to worry none, see? Tell her I was all right and wasn't crying none. . . ."
>
> Max's eyes were wet. Slowly, he extended his hand. Bigger shook it.
>
> "Good-bye, Bigger," he said quietly.
>
> "Good-bye, Mr. Max."[11]

That Bigger should have the book's last word and that what he has to say should terrify, and apparently baffle, Max has seemed to some critics to be Wright's way of saying that not even the most sympathetic white person can hope to have a true understanding of a black person's experience—that the articulation of black experience requires a black voice. "Max's inability to respond and the fact that Bigger's words are left to stand alone without the mediation of authorial commentary serve as the signs that in this novel dedicated to the dramatization of a black man's consciousness the subject has finally found his own unqualified incontrovertible voice,"[12] is how one of these critics puts it. This academic excitement over a black character's saying something "unmediated" ought to be followed by some attention to what it is that the character is actually saying. For what Bigger says (and Max understands him perfectly well) has nothing to do with negritude. It is that he has discovered murder to be a form of self-realization—that it has been revealed to him that all the brave ideals of civilized life, including those of communist ideology, are sentimental delusions, and that the fundamental expression of the instinct of being is killing. Two years before Wright formally broke with the Communist Party, he had already turned in Marx for Nietzsche.

3

Now that Wright's books can be read in the sequence in which they were written, we can see more clearly the dominance that this belief came to have in Wright's thinking. It didn't replace his interest in the subject of race; it subsumed it. Wright intended *Black Boy*, for example, to have two parts—the first about his life in the South and the second about his experiences with the Communist Party. But the Book-of-the-Month Club refused to publish the second part. Wright was convinced that the Communists were behind the refusal (and it is hard to find another reason for it), but he agreed to the cut, and *Black Boy* became an indictment of Southern racism (and a best-seller). Wright managed to publish segments of the suppressed half of the book in various places during his lifetime—the most widely read excerpt is undoubtedly the one that appeared in Richard Crossman's postwar anthology *The God That Failed* (1950). When the autobiography is read as it was intended to be read, though, it is no longer a book about Jim Crow. It is a book about oppression in general, seen through three examples: the racism of Southern whites, the religious intolerance of Southern blacks, and the totalitarianism of the Communist Party.

The idea that there are no "better" forms of human community but only different kinds of domination—that, in the metaphor of *Native Son*'s famous opening scene, Bigger must kill the rat that has invaded his apartment not because Biggers are better than rats, but because if Bigger does not kill the rat, the rat will kill Bigger—is what gives *The Outsider*, the novel Wright published in 1953, its distinctly obsessive quality. The outsider is a black man, Cross Damon, who is presented with a chance to escape from an increasingly grim set of personal troubles when the subway train he is riding in crashes and one of the bodies is identified mistakenly as his. Cross has been, we learn, an avid reader of the existentialist philosophers, and he decides to assume a new identity and to see what it would be like to live in a world without moral meaning—to live "beyond good and evil." He quickly discovers that perfect moral freedom means the freedom to kill anyone whose existence he finds an inconvenience, and he murders four people and causes the suicide of a fifth before he is himself assassinated. (Wright was always drawn to composing lurid descriptions of physical violence. There are beatings and killings in nearly all his stories; his first published work, written when he was a schoolboy and now lost, was a short story called "The Voodoo of Hell's Half-Acre.")

The influence of Camus's *The Stranger* is easy to see, but Wright's book is even more explicitly a *roman à thèse*. Two of Cross's victims are Communists; a third is a fascist. Cross kills them, it is explained, because he recognizes in Communists and fascists the same capacity for murder and the same contempt for morality he has discovered in himself. The point (which Wright finds a number of occasions for Cross to spell out) is that Communism and fascism are particularly naked and cynical examples of the will to power. They accommodate two elemental desires: the desire of the strong to be masters and the desire of the weak to be slaves. Once, as Cross sees it, myths, religions, and the hard shell of social custom prevented people from acting on those desires directly; in the twentieth century, those restraining cultural influences have been stripped away, and in their absence totalitarian systems have emerged. Communism and fascism are, at bottom, identical expressions of the modern condition. And is racism as well? Race is only a minor theme in *The Outsider*, but there is no evidence in the book that Wright regards racism as a peculiar case, and *The Outsider* reads, without strain, as an extension of the idea he was developing

at the end of *Native Son*—that racial oppression is just another example of the pleasure the hammer takes in hitting the nail.

It's not completely clear how we're meant to understand this
analysis. Is the point supposed to be that twentieth-century society
is unique? Or only that it is uniquely barefaced? If it's the latter—if
the idea is that *all* societies are enactments of the impulses to dom-
inate and to submit, but that some have disguised their brutality
more cleverly than others—we have reached a dead end: every effort to conceive of a better way of life simply reduces to some new
hammer bashing away at some new nail. But if it's the former—if
Wright's idea is that modern industrial society, with its contempt for
life's traditional consolations, is a terrible mistake—then racism is
really an example that contradicts the thesis. For the South in
which slavery flourished was not an industrial economy; it was an
agricultural one, with a social system about two steps up the ladder
from feudalism. That civilization was destroyed by the Civil War,
but the racism survived, in the form that Wright himself described
so unsparingly in the first part of *Black Boy* and in the essay "The
Ethics of Living Jim Crow" (1937): as part of a deeply ingrained pattern of custom and belief. To the extent that the forces of modernity
are bent on wiping out tradition and superstition, institutionalized
racism is (like fascism) not their product, as Wright seems to be insisting, but a resistant cultural strain, an anachronism.

The evil of modern society isn't that it creates racism, but that it
creates conditions in which people who don't suffer from injustice
seem incapable of caring very much about people who do. Wright
knew this from his own experience. There is a passage in the restored half of *Black Boy* which is as fine as anything he wrote about
race in America, and which has an exactness and a poignancy often
missing from his fiction. Shortly after he arrived in Chicago, Wright
went to work as a dishwasher in a café.

One summer morning a white girl came late to work and rushed
into the pantry where I was busy. She went into the women's room
and changed her clothes; I heard the door open and a second later I
was surprised to hear her voice:

"Richard, quick! Tie my apron!"

She was standing with her back to me and the strings of her apron dangled loose. There was a moment of indecision on my part, then I took the two loose strings and carried them around her body and brought them again to her back and tied them in a clumsy knot.

"Thanks a million," she said grasping my hand for a split second, and was gone.

I continued my work, filled with all the possible meanings that that tiny, simple, human event could have meant to any Negro in the South where I had spent most of my hungry days.

I did not feel any admiration for the girls [who worked in the café], nor any hate. My attitude was one of abiding and friendly wonder. For the most part I was silent with them, though I knew that I had a firmer grasp of life than most of them. As I worked I listened to their talk and perceived its puzzled, wandering, superficial fumbling with the problems and facts of life. There were many things they wondered about that I could have explained to them, but I never dared. . . .

(I know that not race alone, not color alone, but the daily values that give meaning to life stood between me and those white girls with whom I worked. Their constant outward-looking, their mania for radios, cars, and a thousand other trinkets made them dream and fix their eyes upon the trash of life, made it impossible for them to learn a language which could have taught them to speak of what was in their or others' hearts. The words of their souls were the syllables of popular songs.)[13]

This feels much closer to the reality of human interaction than the simplified Nietzscheanism of *The Outsider*. But, having rejected first the religious culture in which he was brought up, then the American political culture that permitted his oppression, then communism, and, finally (as Cross's death symbolizes), the existential Marxism he encountered in postwar France, Wright seems, by 1953, to have found himself in a place beyond solutions. He was not driven there by an idiosyncratic logic, though; he was just following the path he had first chosen. Wright's experience, that of a Southern black man who became one of the best-known writers of his time, was unusual; his intellectual journey was not. The attraction of communism in the 1930s, the bitter split with the Party in the 1940s, the malaise resulting from "the failure of ideology" and from the emergence, after the war, of an American triumphalism—it's a familiar narrative. Wright's role as a writer was to take one of the literary forms most closely associated with that narrative, the naturalist novel, and to add race to its list of subject matter. What Upton Sinclair did for industrialism in *The Jungle*, what John Dos Passos did for materialism in *U.S.A.*, what Sinclair Lewis did for conformism in *Main Street* and *Babbitt*, Wright did for racism in *Native Son*: he made it part of the naturalist novel's critique of life in the capitalist era. And his strengths and weaknesses as a writer are, by and large, the strengths and weaknesses of the tradition in which he worked. He changed the way Americans thought about race, but he did not invent, because he did not need to invent, a new form to do it.

This helps to explain the Nietzschean element in *Native Son* and the nihilism of *The Outsider*: they are the characteristic symptoms of the exhaustion of the naturalist style. The young Norman Mailer, for example, used Dos Passos and James T. Farrell as his literary models in writing *The Naked and the Dead*, but added a dash of Nietzsche to the mixture, and then produced, in the early 1950s— like Wright, and with comparable results—a cloudy parable of ideological dead-endism, *Barbary Shore*.

Wright's most famous protégés, James Baldwin and Ralph Ellison, both eventually dissociated their work (Ellison more delicately than Baldwin) from his. They felt that Wright's books lacked a feeling for the richness of the culture of African-Americans—that those books were written as though black Americans were a people without resources. Someone reading *Native Son*, Baldwin complained, would think that "in Negro life there exists no tradition, no field of manners, no possibility of ritual or intercourse"[14] by which black Americans could sustain themselves in a hostile world. But that is what Wright did think. He believed that racism had succeeded in stripping black Americans of a genuine culture. There were, in his view, only two ways in which black Americans could respond actively to their condition: one was to adopt a theology of acceptance sustained by religious faith—a solution Wright had resisted violently as a boy—and the other was to become Biggers (or Crosses), and live outside the law until they were trapped and crushed. Otherwise, there was only the "cesspool" of daily life described in *Lawd Today!*—a perpetual cycle of demeaning drudgery and cheap thrills. It's not hard to understand why writers like Ellison and Baldwin resisted this vision of black experience, but it is a vision true to Wright's own particular history of deprivation. Ellison, by contrast, grew up in Oklahoma, a state that has no history of black slavery (though it certainly has a history of segregation), and he attended Tuskegee Institute, where he was introduced to, among other works, T. S. Eliot's *The Waste Land*, a poem whose influence on his novel *Invisible Man* is palpable—as is the influence of jazz and of the Southern black vernacular. Ellison had a different culture, in other words, because he had a different experience.

For culture is not something that just comes with one's race or gender. Culture comes *only* through experience; there isn't any other way to acquire it. And in the end everyone's culture is different, because everyone's experience is different. Some people are at home with the culture they encounter, as Ellison seems to have been. Some people borrow or adopt their culture, as Eliot did when he transformed himself into a British Anglo-Catholic. A few, extraordinary people have to steal it. Wright was living in Memphis when his serious immersion in literature began, but he could not get books from the public library. So he persuaded a sympathetic white man to lend him his library card, and he forged a note for himself to present to the librarian: "Dear Madam: Will you please let this nigger boy have some books by H. L. Mencken?"[15] He had discovered, on his own, a literary tradition in which no one had invited him to participate—from which, in fact, the world had conspired to exclude him. He saw in that tradition a way to express his own experience, his own sense of things, and through heroic persistence he made that experience part of the culture of other people.

The Long Shadow of
James B. Conant

I

J ames Bryant Conant was made president of Harvard in 1933,
when he was forty. He had been a professor of chemistry, and
was sufficiently untested as an administrator to have been
passed over, not long before, by his own high school, Roxbury
Latin, during its search for a new headmaster. But he proved an active and modernizing educator. Conant had supervised the production of a poison gas (never used) called lewisite during the First
World War, and shortly after the outbreak of the Second World War
he was invited to join a government body created to oversee scientific contributions to military research. In 1941 he was appointed
head of a subgroup known as S-1, which was the code name for the
atomic bomb, thus becoming the chief civilian administrator of
American nuclear research and, eventually, a principal figure in the
decision to drop the Hiroshima and Nagasaki bombs. He continued
to play a role in the articulation of nuclear policy after the war, and
in 1953 he left Harvard to become Eisenhower's high commissioner,

later ambassador, to Germany. After his return to the United States, in 1957, he undertook a series of widely circulated studies of public education, underwritten by the Carnegie Corporation. In 1965, his health began to fail, and he gradually withdrew from public life. *My Several Lives*, an autobiography notable for its reticence, appeared in 1970. He died in 1978.

It's a career that touches on many areas: science, government, education, the cold war, the national security state, the politics of the atom. Conant's biographer, James Hershberg, mostly concentrates on the story of Conant's role in nuclear policy from 1939 to 1950, and although the nuclear Conant is important, the educational Conant is equally important. This is not only because the changes in American higher education for which Conant was largely responsible affected two generations of professors and students—the generation that lived through those changes and the generation that lived through the backlash against them. The educational Conant is also important because Conant's educational philosophy—which, since it was the educational philosophy of the president of Harvard, once commanded a large and attentive audience—and Conant's political philosophy were reciprocal things. Conant believed that admissions policy was a weapon in the battle against communism; and he believed that the existence of a Communist state in possession of nuclear bombs was a factor in the formulation of admissions policy. For American educational doctrine in the postwar period was just as historically conditioned as American foreign policy. The educational views of people like Conant rose to prominence at the beginning of the cold war, and their authority only dissipated completely around the time of the cold war's demise. Those views had as much effect on life in the bipolar world as big defense contracts did. Conant helped to create the atomic bomb; he also helped to create the Scholastic Aptitude Test. Americans born after 1945 were raised in the shadow of both.

Conant was not an especially colorful character. He seems to have cultivated, even as a Harvard undergraduate, the personal style dictated by the first commandment of university presidency: Offend no one. He liked committees; he liked to chair committees;

and when he wasn't being invited to serve on or to chair someone else's committee, he was likely to be starting up a committee of his own. In a time when consensus was the official face of public policy, he was the consummate stage manager of consensus.

He was therefore much more successful as an administrator than as a politician: he preferred to work his will anonymously, and the prospect of public division invariably made him pull in his horns. If he was compelled to cast a vote on a controversial matter, he took every care to keep his ballot a secret one—a cautiousness that could sometimes be ridiculous. In 1961, the journalist Carl T. Rowan was nominated to join the very establishmentarian Cosmos Club, in Washington, D.C. Conant, as a longtime Washington insider, belonged to the Cosmos, and he agreed to write a letter on Rowan's behalf. Rowan would have been the club's first black member; when he was rejected by the admissions committee, in 1962, there was an embarrassing public scandal, in which some distinguished gentlemen threatened to resign and some equally distinguished gentlemen vowed to stay on and fight discrimination "from within." Conant was tormented by indecision: when the ambassador to India, John Kenneth Galbraith, and the governor of New York, Nelson Rockefeller, took opposing stands, what was the ex-president of Harvard to do? He was deeply relieved when the matter was resolved by a vote of the membership in favor of nondiscrimination, before he had to declare his own position. In 1962 Conant was no longer a Harvard official; he was no longer a public official; he believed in racial integration wholeheartedly. But the thought of breaking ranks made him miserable. This was not a man well equipped to face the 1960s.

The two-word ideological gloss on Conant is "liberal anticommunist," but he was a liberal anticommunist of a particular midcentury stripe—one of those high establishment figures for whom, at the deepest level, "liberal anticommunism" was an oxymoron. Liberalism is about the tolerance of ideas and practices; anticommunism, as Conant interpreted it, is about the intolerance of one idea and one practice. These views can coexist much of the time; but at certain moments the anticommunism asks the liberalism for a concession, and then a conflict comes into view, and the liberalism is in danger of being trumped, if ever so hesitantly and apologetically, by the anticommunism. Two of these conflicts in Conant's career are especially interesting.

The first has to do with the bomb. In 1945, Conant became a member of the Interim Committee ("so-named," as Hershberg explains, "to forestall congressional charges of executive usurpations of authority"),[1] which had been formed to advise Truman on atomic issues. On May 31, the issue was the use of the bomb against Japan. According to the minutes: "At the suggestion of Dr. Conant the Secretary [of War, Henry L. Stimson] agreed that the most desirable target would be a vital war plant employing a large number of workers and closely surrounded by workers' houses."[2] Conant's suggestion became, of course, atomic reality. Hiroshima was bombed on August 6, Nagasaki on August 9 (before Japanese officials had had time to inspect the damage from the Hiroshima explosion). There were 200,000 casualties. On August 14, Japan surrendered.

Conant seems never to have doubted that the destruction, without warning, of Hiroshima and Nagasaki was the wisest thing to do, and he never publicly expressed regret about it afterward (though Conant's grandchildren told his biographer that they remember him admitting privately, very late in life, that the Nagasaki bomb had been a "mistake"). Tactically, the decision involved a calculation, subsequently much disputed, about the number of lives it would have cost to win the war by conventional means (which would undoubtedly have included the continued firebombing of Japanese cities). But Conant's reasoning wasn't only tactical. He was given to geopolitical speculation anyway, and as one of the few people privy to knowledge about the bomb from the inception of the nuclear program, he had plenty of time to contemplate its usefulness in strategic terms.

The consideration that dominated his long-term thinking was the need for international control of atomic weapons. Conant believed that unless the American government was willing, after the war, to share nuclear information with the other powers, and to submit to the authority of an international atomic energy commission, it would sooner or later find itself engaged in a ruinous arms race. (Conant's friend J. Robert Oppenheimer believed the same thing; they were right about the arms race.) But Conant also believed that unless the American public was convinced, by some kind of demonstration, of the bomb's terrible power, it could never be persuaded to accede to international regulation, for it would be unable to imagine what an indiscriminate holocaust a nuclear war would inevitably be. He may have thought, too, although here the evidence is not so clear, that the Soviets, while still without a bomb of their own, required a similar demonstration to draw them to the arms control bargaining table. Was Conant's advice to bomb Hiroshima therefore influenced by a desire to show the world, by the instantaneous incineration of tens of thousands of Japanese citizens, how monstrous a weapon he had helped to produce? And was the decision of the administration as a whole dictated by a desire to impress the Soviets, with a view either to persuading them to agree to international regulation, or to chilling any postwar expansionist intentions they might have harbored?

The answer is difficult. Revisionist historians, such as Gar Alperovitz, have suggested that future relations with the Soviet Union were on the minds of the men who decided to use the bomb against Japan. There seems to be very little written evidence to support this claim, and it is clear that whatever other considerations it may have entertained, the Interim Committee's decision-making in 1945 was dominated by a desire to end the war as quickly as possible and with the least loss of life. In 1946, though, Conant thought he perceived the beginnings of a backlash against the bomb—something he feared, because he felt it could lead to atomic paralysis on the part of the American public, and therefore to an end to any strategic usefulness the bomb might have. If we couldn't bring ourselves to drop the bomb, what was the advantage of having it? John Hersey's "Hiroshima," which appeared in the New Yorker on August 31, 1946, is the best-known sign of this backlash, but there were rumblings elsewhere, as well, and Conant felt obliged to orchestrate a response. True to form, he kept his own role hidden.[3]

The response Conant conjured up was the famous article by

Stimson (by then retired) called "The Decision to Use the Atomic Bomb," which was published in *Harper's* in February 1947. Stimson introduced the article as "an exact description of our thoughts and actions as I find them in the records and in my clear recollection"; but it was, in fact, an exact description of some of the Truman administration's thoughts and actions, and a few of the recollections were Conant's. The piece was initiated entirely by Conant, who (as was his custom) got an intermediary, Harvey Bundy, to persuade Stimson to write it. In his letter to Bundy, Conant expressed dismay at the argument he saw being circulated that the decision to drop the bomb was immoral, and said he felt no cause to second-guess his reasoning as a member of the Interim Committee, which was that the use of the bomb was justified "on the grounds (1) that I believed it would shorten the war against Japan, and (2) that unless actually used in battle there was no chance of convincing the American public and the world that it should be controlled by international agreement."[4] There is ample evidence that Conant continued to use this ex post facto argument to defend the Interim Committee's decision; but the letter to Bundy seems to have been the only place in which he acknowledged that the desire to provide an admonitory example was a factor in his own thinking at the time. Still, it is a striking admission.

Stimson accepted his assignment reluctantly: "I have rarely been connected with a paper about which I have had so much doubt at the last moment," he complained to Felix Frankfurter.[5] The article was ghosted by Bundy's son McGeorge, who presented his drafts to Conant for editorial advice—which, according to Hershberg, was extensive, and which included the insertion of a passage written by Conant himself. Specifically, Conant was insistent that a discussion about modifying surrender terms to permit Japan to retain the emperor be deleted (it "diverts one's mind from the general line of argumentation," as he put it),[6] and that the article be couched not as an argument against nonmilitary alternatives, but as the neutral account of a decision dictated solely by military needs. And, in the end, it was: "No man, in our position," it concludes, "and subject to our responsibilities, holding in his hands a weapon of such possibility for accomplishing this purpose and saving those lives, could have failed to use it and afterwards looked his countrymen in the face."[7] There is no explanation for the second bomb; the Soviet Union, needless to say, is never mentioned.[8]

Henry Stimson had been secretary of war in the administration of William Howard Taft, secretary of state under Herbert Hoover, and secretary of war under Roosevelt and Truman. There was no more credible witness, and "The Decision to Use the Atomic Bomb" stood, as Hershberg says, "for almost two decades as the authoritative historical record of the events of 1945."[9] What is remarkable is not that a statesman should wish to fix the record to reflect most favorably on himself: that was, of course, exactly what Conant counted on when he approached Stimson and asked him to put his name on the piece. What is remarkable is that the president of the country's leading institution of liberal learning, having set in motion a process leading to the publication of the facts about an event, should intervene in order to censor details he judged it undesirable for the public to know.

The manner in which Conant handled the postwar issue of Communist Party members in the teaching profession is revealing, too, although the lesson can be misread. Harvard was celebrated at the time for its refusal to cooperate with McCarthy; but the university's reputation for resisting the intrusion of government loyalty hounds has been challenged since—for example, by Sigmund Diamond, in a book on the collaboration of universities and intelligence agencies in the early cold war period, *Compromised Campus*.[10] Diamond suggests that Conant may have acted, while president of Harvard, as a confidential informant for the FBI. How credible is the charge? It's true that Conant's position on loyalty issues was never exactly heroic. In 1935 he led a drive against a bill in the Massachusetts legislature mandating a loyalty oath for teachers, but when the bill was passed, he pledged Harvard's cooperation. His general view seems to have been that an administrative inquiry into a teacher's political beliefs was a violation of academic freedom, but that the state had a legitimate interest, which universities must respect, in exposing "subversives." His position on Communists, therefore, was that they should not be hired as teachers (since they were, in his view, subversives by definition), but that no effort should be made by universities to ferret out Communists already on the faculty. Ferreting, he felt, was the kind of thing the government ought to do. He also maintained that any faculty member who invoked the Fifth Amendment when asked about Communist Party associations was, ipso facto, disloyal, and should be fired. (Membership in the Communist Party, it's worth remembering, was not illegal.)

This sounds like a pretty hard line, but it seems clear that Conant's chief aim was to avoid having to follow it in any particular case. He conceded its inconsistency (it was, basically, a prototype of "don't ask, don't tell": political beliefs are irrelevant to academic merit, but teachers whose politics are discovered to be subversive should be fired), but he was not disposed to clarify it; for he had a presidential yearning to send a signal that would be comforting to everybody. He wanted his faculty to think that the university was committed to academic freedom, and would not pursue investigations into the politics of its members; and he wanted the government to think that Harvard was staunchly anticommunist, and would not act as a shield for teachers who were manifestly disloyal. It was a very shaky contraption, and fortunately for his reputation as a champion of academic freedom, Conant left for Germany before he was ever required to fly it.

So that when Diamond and Hershberg cite, as circumstantial evidence that Conant acted as an FBI informant, a memo to J. Edgar Hoover from the bureau's chief agent in Boston noting that Dr. Conant has "indicated his respect for the Bureau's work and his understanding for its many and varied interests,"[11] they are possibly eliding two points. The first is the innate desire of intelligence operatives everywhere to assure their masters that they enjoy access to the very highest levels of whatever it is they're supposed to be gathering intelligence about. ("Who? Oppenheimer? Oh, yes, he passed us lots of information. Most cooperative.") The second is the innate desire of men like Conant to express solidarity of purpose when there is nothing to be gained by appearing uncooperative. That he might have cooperated secretly seems contradicted by the fact that in 1953 Hoover (as Diamond himself reports) ordered a "thorough investigation as to character, loyalty, reputation, associates, and qualifications of Conant,"[12] and by the additional fact that McCarthy (as Hershberg says) was dissuaded from blocking Conant's nomination to be high commissioner to Germany only by the personal intercession of President Eisenhower.

Still, Conant's position wasn't all rhetorical balancing. It was substantive balancing as well. By the time of the Korean War, Conant's views on the Soviet Union had hardened permanently. He believed in the Communist juggernaut: he thought that the "Russian hordes,"[13] as he called them, were prepared to overrun Western Europe at the first opportunity, and that Communist propaganda was a threat to the free world from within. His response to the military threat was to advocate the rearming of Germany, the institution of a peacetime draft, the containment of Soviet expansion, and similar cold war policies. His response to Communist propaganda was liberal propaganda. He thought that the best defense free societies had against Communism was to advertise their freedoms. This is why he campaigned publicly for the principle of academic freedom, and why he was also (much less publicly) willing to countenance the exposure of American Communists and their expulsion from the academy. Communists were the exception that made the principles necessary.

It is the logic that governed his supervision of Stimson's article on the bomb, and it is a logic responsible for a great deal of folly, some of it criminal folly, in American political life in the cold war era: the belief that the survival of an open society depends upon concealment, and that the protection of rights in the general justifies their abrogation in the particular. Still, when Oppenheimer was hauled before a kangaroo court of the Atomic Energy Commission on security charges in 1954, Conant (though John Foster Dulles threatened to fire him for it) testified on his friend's behalf. The evidence against Oppenheimer was hopelessly inconclusive, but he lost his clearance anyway. He was a victim of the very national security mentality he and Conant had helped to create for the nuclear age.

Conant hated the atomic bomb. He had, he once said, "no sense of accomplishment"[14] about his own part in bringing it into existence, and although by the early 1950s he had come to believe, quite presciently, that if war could be avoided the Communist system would collapse of its own inefficiency sometime in the 1980s, he dreaded the interim. In concert with Oppenheimer, he opposed, unsuccessfully, the development of the hydrogen bomb, which he regarded as an instrument of genocide. He distrusted the military and barred classified research at Harvard. He despised right-wing anticommunists like McCarthy. But he thought the Communist threat was real, and that the public must never be permitted to relax its vigilance against it. He was even prepared to engage in deliberate hyperbole about the imminence of the danger to prevent this relaxation from happening.

There are many temptations to illiberalism implicit in this worldview: the sanctioning of secrecy, the willingness to engineer public opinion, the compromises entailed in presenting a united front with anticommunists of a less scrupulous stripe. Still, if the Communist threat could serve as a standing argument for the suppression of dissent, it could serve equally well as a standing argument for taking the principles of freedom and democracy seriously. The cold war obsession with communism helped make American society more conformist, but it also helped make it more liberal, and Conant was a representative figure in this development as well.

2

At the Harvard of his youth, Conant was a boy from the other side of the tracks. He was a townie, raised in Dorchester, and although his parents, by virtue of success in local business affairs, were reasonably well off, he took school very seriously—not only academically (he was, evidently, a gifted chemist), but as a way of bettering his lot in life. He was highly critical, even as an undergraduate, of anything suggestive of a class system in which wealth and position were handed on unearned. He believed in equality of opportunity and in the role of education in uncovering talent and bringing it to the fore; and this belief dictated his sense of the sort of people who ought to get to go to college, and the sort of people who ought to get to teach them.

The university Conant inherited in 1933 had been created largely by two men: Charles William Eliot, who became president in 1869 and transformed Harvard into a modern research university, and A. Lawrence Lowell, who succeeded Eliot in 1909 as the candidate of forces who thought that Eliot had gone too far. Conant essentially represented a return to the educational philosophy of Eliot (who was also, as it happens, a chemist—although, as Alfred North Whitehead noted in lamenting Conant's appointment, he was, at least, a very bad chemist). But Conant also reinforced the effect of certain innovations that had been instituted by Lowell.

Eliot revolutionized American higher education in two ways. He created the free elective system for undergraduates; and he established (on the model of Johns Hopkins, which got there first) the Harvard Graduate School of Arts and Sciences, which was designed to train and accredit the scholars who would teach the undergraduates. Eliot felt that the college experience should be nonutilitarian—that undergraduates should pursue their interests without vocational anxiety—but his notion of higher education as a whole was utilitarian, in the sense that he imagined a posttheological university whose students were being prepared for productive lives in a modern, industrialized society, and whose faculty were committed to research programs that kept social benefit in mind. Lowell rose to the presidency on a wave of reaction against the free elective system. His supporters wanted a return to the centrality of the liberal arts—to a less professional, less specialized, less vocational educational ideal. To limit the tendency to smattering inherent in the elective system, therefore, Lowell required undergraduates to choose a major and a minor field. The effect of this reform, though, was to place control over undergraduate course work in the hands of the specialists—the professors within the disciplines. Whatever Lowell's intentions, he actually ended up taking Harvard some further distance in the direction of academic professionalism.

Conant went the rest of the way. He did this by instituting an "up or out" tenure system, designed to ensure that Harvard departments were staffed by the most credentialed specialists available—that is, by professional scholars rather than by career teachers. Instead of promoting automatically from within, departments were expected to undertake national searches in filling tenured positions, and ad hoc committees were set up to monitor hiring and promotion. Conant himself intervened in several cases, a few of which became fractious, to let go junior faculty he considered academically underqualified. His preference was to farm out junior professors after their six-year stints and to make them earn their way back to Cambridge by scholarly toil subsidized by some lesser institution.

Conant thought that professors selected on merit ought to be teaching students selected the same way. One of his first acts as president was to assign two of his deans, William Bender and Henry Chauncey, to examine the newly created Scholastic Aptitude Test. Their favorable report led to Conant's campaign to introduce standardized testing into both the college and the graduate school admissions processes—a campaign that culminated in the establishment, in 1946, of the Educational Testing Service, with Chauncey at its head. To make the emphasis on aptitude meaningful at Harvard, Conant created a "National Scholarships" program, which provided financial assistance to students outside Harvard's traditional geographic and socioeconomic regions of recruitment.

Conant was, in short, as Nicholas Lemann has said, one of the founders of the modern American meritocracy.[15] The educational system he helped put into place remains the basis of the educational system we have today. In its ideal form, students are admitted to college on the basis of aptitude, where they are instructed in an academic specialty by experts who have been appointed on the basis of scholarly achievement. Successful performance in this arena, determined by grade point averages, commendations from teachers, and further standardized test scores, allows those with ability to proceed to graduate or professional school, where a final round of accreditation takes place. The reward for the student is a professional career that it is impossible to buy or to be born into. The reward for society is the enhancement in productivity that comes from matching talents more accurately with careers.

We now take the theory of this model virtually for granted. But it has governed the educational and socioeconomic reward system for only a few generations, and creating it involved a profound adjustment of traditional expectations. How profound this adjustment was is reflected in two striking articles Conant published during the war in the *Atlantic Monthly*: "Education for a Classless Society" (1940) and "Wanted: American Radicals" (1943). In a pure meritocracy, everyone must begin de novo: no one can be allowed an unearned head start, and this means, logically, that wealth should not be inheritable—which is, in fact, precisely what Conant believed. He felt, he complained in 1943, the need for a new American radicalism, which he defined as a commitment to the ideals of Jefferson, Emerson, Thoreau, and Whitman, and which he imagined as a stimulus to social and economic progress. "To prevent the growth of a caste system," he says, this imagined figure, "the American radical, will be resolute in his demand to confiscate (by constitutional methods) all property once a generation. He will demand really effective inheritance and gift taxes and the breaking up of trust funds and estates. And this point cannot be lightly pushed aside, for it is the kernel of his radical philosophy."[16] This was a fairly stunning thought to commit to print for the president of an institution heavily dependent on testamentary bequests, and the article actually inspired a brief but unsuccessful coup attempt, soon after it appeared, by members of the Harvard Corporation. Putting the idea in the mouth of a hypothetical "radical" gave Conant enough wiggle room to placate his trustees; but the idea was clearly his own.

The Second World War was the best thing that could have happened to the theory of meritocracy, for two reasons. The first was that large-scale social disruption had already taken place through mass conscription; so that there was (as Conant argued) a real-life opportunity to start everyone de novo by seeing to it that the eleven million American soldiers returning from the war were placed on the career ladders suited to each. This opportunity was cashed, in the end, by the GI Bill, which opened higher education to millions of men, and which helped to create the postwar middle class.

But the war was useful because it provided an immediate justification for egalitarianism and social mobility. A caste society is dangerous, Conant warned in "Wanted: American Radicals," in 1943, because a society stratified by class is exactly the kind of society in which communism takes root. This became the theme of all Conant's postwar educational writings, from *Education in a Divided World* (1948) to *Slums and Suburbs* (one of the Carnegie studies, published in 1961). "What can words like 'freedom,' 'liberty,' and 'equality of opportunity' mean for these young people?" Conant wrote of inner-city children in *Slums and Suburbs*. "With what kind of zeal and dedication can we expect them to withstand the relentless pressures of communism?"[17] Communism here is the license for liberalism.

The picture has one more piece. Equality of opportunity does not, as Conant conceived it, mean equality of result; and when the talented tenth goes off to law school, a gap opens between it and the nine other tenths, who are left behind to become office managers and civil servants and hamburger flippers. This is what is known as the problem of "general education": in a system designed to track students into the specialties appropriate to each, there must be some common core of learning appropriate to all, or social antagonisms will simply get reproduced in every generation. Shortly after the attack on Pearl Harbor, Conant convened a committee of twelve Harvard professors (which included I. A. Richards, Arthur Schlesinger, Sr., and George Wald) to address this issue. They labored for two years, and the book they produced, *General Education in a Free Society* (1945), commonly known as the Red Book, is one of the landmark documents in the general education movement. It's not a landmark because Conant's committee had anything especially original to say: "seldom has such an effort," as one educational historian has put it, "been devoted to reinventing the wheel."[18] The Harvard report is a landmark because it is the *Harvard* report, and it therefore constituted an influential endorsement of a solution that had already been adopted elsewhere, notably at the University of Chicago and Columbia.

The solution was a core curriculum, nonspecialized, in which classic texts of the Western tradition are read for what they have to say in themselves, rather than through some disciplinary matrix (as one would expect, for example, in an "Introduction to Literature" or an "Introduction to Political Science" course). These texts serve, in theory, as a vocabulary of ideas shared by all the members of an otherwise diverse and mobile society: social tradition, which stratifies and divides, is replaced by intellectual tradition, which provides what the report refers to as a "binding experience."[19] The belief that free societies are in danger from an external political threat is obviously a great argument on behalf of such a program: people with no common set of beliefs are vulnerable to ideologues peddling, if nothing else, coherence. It is not hard to see that the system is extraordinarily vulnerable on many points, and that it was probably fated, in certain respects, to become a victim of its own success. The greater the variety of people it accommodated, the greater the strain on the impersonal and abstract notions of "merit," "objectivity," and "greatness" which underwrite it. When nontraditional populations (that is, women and nonwhite students) began integrating American universities in substantial numbers after 1970, the backlash against the color-, race-, and gender-blind ideals of meritocratic theory, and of the "great books" solution, began. So did the backlash against the imposition of scientific standards of objectivity on the softer disciplines—the turn from paradigms of "knowledge" to paradigms of "interpretation." It took academic humanities departments more than twenty years to sort out the consequences.

And there is, in the end, something culturally tone-deaf about the system—as there was about Conant himself, a man who could never understand what the study of art and literature was doing at a research university, who attempted while president of Harvard to close Harvard University Press and to cut loose the Divinity School, and who confessed that the whole subject of higher education for women made him uneasy. The scientistic standards he imposed on the selection of students and faculty at Harvard (and, through that example, on much of the rest of the country's institutions of higher education) reflect a certain impercipience about the variety of forms that contributions to knowledge and to the cultural life can take. He largely drove imagination out of the university, and he helped to quantify talents—such as "verbal aptitude"—which it is meaningless to assess in purely quantitative terms. You don't have to be an enemy of logocentrism to have doubts about the system Conant helped to create. You only have to look around you at the people who have "made it."

The twelve authors of the Red Book were far more attuned to the holistic nature of intelligence and ability than the man who appointed them was. But a certain deafness persists. The report speaks continually of the "diversity" of the student population, but it never mentions differences of ethnic background, religious belief, or even gender. When the authors use the term, they mean only diversity of socioeconomic status; and the assumption that socioeconomic status correlates with some rank order of abstract aptitudes is still central to the meritocratic system the report presupposes.

This complaint about the Harvard report's definition of diversity is not anachronistic. The President's Commission on Higher Education for Democracy, headed by George Zook, whose report appeared just two years after Harvard's, in 1947, gives considerable attention to the inequalities in educational opportunities available to African-Americans. Yet the commission perceived the solution to the heterogeneity of the student population and the proliferation of specialized courses in the same terms the Harvard team did. "The failure to provide any core of unity in the essential diversity of higher education," it concluded,

> is a cause for grave concern. A society whose numbers lack a body of common experience and common knowledge is a society without a fundamental culture; it tends to disintegrate into a mere aggregation of individuals. Some community of values, ideas, and attitudes is essential as a cohesive force in this age of minute division of labor and intense conflicts of special interests. . . . Colleges must find a right relationship between specialized training on the one hand, aiming at a thousand different careers, and the transmission of a common cultural heritage toward a common citizenship on the other. . . . This purpose calls for a unity in the program of studies that a uniform system of courses cannot supply.[20]

As appealing as it understandably is to many people, the idea that a core curriculum of great books is the solution to the diversifi-

cation of ability and occupation among students and future citizens
in a democracy is surely the weakest point in the general education
program. For the "great books" don't, taken together, express anything like a coherent worldview. They don't even express a set of coherent individual worldviews. Skepticism about such coherence is
precisely one of the things in which, in many cases, their greatness
consists. It is probably enlightening for students to encounter this
kind of skepticism; but it is not (whatever the term is supposed to
mean) "binding." Still, the Harvard report's sensitivity to socioeconomic diversity (a subject rarely addressed in discussions of higher
education today) is the frankest and the most admirable thing about
it. It is the invocation of a homogenized conception of "culture" as
the palliative to class difference, and the belief (elaborated on at
length in the report) that educational institutions can replace the
family, the church, and the community as the means of accultura-
tion, that seem misconceived.

For there is great merit in the idea of "general education" when it
is not circumscribed by a "great books" program. American colleges
do fail to provide a common core of learning. Most students graduate without any exposure to knowledge about American political,
legal, and business institutions; they are no better equipped to peti-
tion a congressman, or to write a will, or to buy stock than they were
when they left high school. What they have received, for the most
part, is specialized training in a scholarly discipline—the consequence of the curriculum having been handed over to the departments, whose members are selected on the basis of professional
attainment rather than commitment to teaching or to "general"
learning. Despite the widespread call for it in Conant's time, general education has seldom been tried, even in the "great books" format. Where it has been, it has commonly taken the form of
"distribution requirements"—that is, mandatory smattering.

3

What happened to Conant's educational ideals? The three decades
after the Second World War, from 1945 to 1975, were a period

of enormous growth in American higher education. It is a period
known in the literature on higher education as the Golden Age. The
number of American undergraduates increased by almost 500 percent, the number of graduate students by nearly 900 percent.[21] In
the 1960s alone, enrollments more than doubled, from 3.5 million to
just under eight million; the number of doctorates awarded annu-
ally tripled; and more faculty were hired than had been hired in the
entire 325-year history of American higher education to that point.[22]
At the height of the expansion, between 1965 and 1972, new community college campuses were opening in the United States at the
rate of one every week.[23] This growth was fueled in part by the baby
boom, in part by the sustained high domestic economic growth rate
in the 1950s, and in part by cold war priorities. After the Second
World War, the national government began the practice of contract-
ing research out to universities, largely through the efforts of Conant and his government colleague Vannevar Bush, former vice
president and dean of engineering at MIT and director of the Office
of Scientific Research and Development during the war. After Sput-
nik, the National Defense Education Act of 1958 provided large
government grants to universities, directed principally at science
and foreign languages. In this expanding universe, the ideals of meritocracy, disinterested inquiry, and the general education curriculum centered on the "great books"—the ideals for which Conant
stood—were not often questioned. They were part of the culture of
assumptions in which higher education operated.

After 1975, though, the higher education system changed. Its
growth leveled off, and the economic value of a college degree began to fall. In the 1970s, the income differential between college
graduates and high school graduates dropped from 61 percent to 48
percent.[24] The percentage of students going on to college therefore
began to drop as well, and a system that had quintupled, and more,
in the span of a single generation suddenly found itself with empty
dormitory beds and a huge tenured faculty. One of the ways in
which colleges and universities responded to this crisis was by expanding the pool of candidates for admission, since there were
fewer white American males for selective schools to choose from.

After 1970, virtually every nonmilitary all-male college in the United States went coed. People had talked before 1970 about the educational desirability of coeducational and mixed-race student bodies, but in the end it was economic necessity that made them do it.[25] In 1947, 71 percent of college students in America were men; as late as 1965, 94 percent of college students in the United States were classified as white. By 1998, a minority of college students, 44 percent, were men, and 71 percent were classified as white.[26] Most of this diversification happened after 1975, and a single statistic makes the point. In the decade between 1984 and 1994, the total enrollment in American colleges and universities increased by two million, but not one of those two million new students was a white American-born man. They were all nonwhites, women, and foreign students. The absolute number of white American men in American higher education actually declined between 1984 and 1994.[27]

Faculty demographics changed in the same way, a reflection not so much of changes in hiring practices as of changes in the group that went to graduate school after 1975. Current full-time American faculty who were hired before 1985 are 28 percent female and about 11 percent nonwhite or Hispanic. Full-time faculty hired since 1985—that is, for the most part, faculty who entered graduate school after the Golden Age—are half again as female (40 percent) and more than half again as nonwhite (18 percent).[28] In 1997, there were 45,394 doctoral degrees conferred in the United States; 40 percent of the recipients were women (in the arts and humanities, just under 50 percent were women), and only 63 percent were classified as white American citizens. The other 37 percent were nonwhite Americans and foreign students.[29] The demographic mix in higher education, both students and faculty, completely changed in the span of about a generation.

As the new populations began to arrive in numbers in American universities after 1970, the meritocratic rationale was exploded. For it turned out that cultural differences were not only not so easy to bracket as men like Conant had imagined; those differences suddenly began to seem a lot more interesting than the similarities. This trend was made irreversible by Justice Lewis Powell's decision in *Regents of the University of California v. Bakke*, handed down by the U.S. Supreme Court in 1978.[30] Powell changed the language of college admissions by decreeing that if admissions committees wanted to stay on the safe side of the Constitution, they had to stop talking about quotas and start talking about diversity instead. Powell's opinion blew a hole in meritocratic theory, because he pointed out what should have been obvious from the beginning, which is that college admissions, even at places like Harvard, have never been purely meritocratic. Colleges have always taken nonstandardized and nonstandardizable attributes into account when selecting a class, from musical prodigies to football stars, alumni legacies, and the offspring of local bigwigs. If you admitted only students who got top scores on the SATs, you would have a very boring class. "Diversity" is the very word Powell used in the *Bakke* opinion, and there are probably very few college catalogues in the country today in which the word "diversity," or one of its cognates, does not appear.

In this radically more heterogeneous environment, the value of the SAT began to be questioned—in 2001 the University of California system announced it was dropping the test from its requirements for admission—and the curriculum began to undergo a series of changes. These changes have become visible in the recent emphasis on multiculturalism (meaning exposure to specifically ethnic perspectives and traditions) and values (the ethical implications of knowledge); in a renewed interest in service (manifested in the emergence of internship and off-campus social service programs) and in the idea of community; in what is called "education for citizenship"; and in a revival of a Deweyite conception of teaching as a collaborative process of learning and inquiry. The vocabulary of "disinterestedness," "objectivity," "reason," and "knowledge," and talk about things like "the scientific method," the canon of great books, and "the fact-value distinction," were replaced, in many fields, by talk about "interpretations" (rather than "facts"), "perspective" (rather than "objectivity"), and "understanding" (rather than "reason" or "analysis"). An emphasis on universalism and "greatness" was replaced by an emphasis on diversity and difference; the scientistic norms which once prevailed in many of the "soft" disciplines began to be viewed with skepticism; context and contingency were continually emphasized; attention to "objects" gave way to attention to "representations."[31] This transformation accompanied the change in the demographics of higher education; it was not caused by that change. For in many ways it was essentially a backlash against the excessive respect for scientistic norms that characterized the early cold war university. The transformation also demonstrates how historically specific the ideals of Conant and his generation of academic leaders, for all their patina of postideological universality, really were.

People like Conant did have a remarkable confidence in their beliefs; it's one of the things that make them seem a little remote to most Americans on this side of the cold war. Conant once asked the Harvard librarian to undertake secretly an appraisal of the costs of microfilming the printed record of Western civilization, which he proposed to bury in various places around the country, thus preserving it for survivors of a nuclear war. The librarian advised that the costs would probably be huge, and Conant dropped the project, having convinced himself that university libraries outside major cities would escape destruction in a nuclear exchange. But he stuck with the idea. "Perhaps the fated task of those of us now alive in this country," he wrote in *Education in a Divided World*, in 1948, "is to develop still further our civilization for the benefits of the survivors of World War III in other lands."[32] He had what seems today an almost naive faith in the virtues of the society for which he worked. It does not seem to have crossed his mind that the great works of a civilization that had ended in an act of self-destruction might not be the first thing the survivors of a nuclear holocaust would think it worthwhile to have.

The Last Emperor:
William S. Paley

I

William S. Paley became president of the Columbia Broadcasting System in 1928, when he was twenty-six, and he ran the company until 1983, when he retired and assumed the title of "founder chairman." Already a wealthy man when he and his family bought Columbia (the Paleys were cigar manufacturers), he was deeply attached to the style of living that enormous amounts of money make possible, and he cultivated a taste in fine art, fine furniture, fine clothing, and fine food. He married two striking and intelligent women—Dorothy Hart Hearst, whom he divorced in 1947, and Barbara Cushing Mortimer, called Babe, whom he married soon after his divorce and who died in 1978—in a time when it was expected of striking and intelligent women of a certain class that they would devote themselves to the comfort and adornment of their husbands' lives. He was, on social occasions and on most business occasions, a charming man who disliked unpleasantness and preferred to let others act as the agents of his disapproval, and as radio and then television grew to become the most influential and lucrative communications media in the history of the world, he had a personality equipped to extract a full measure of satisfaction from the power and prestige his position afforded him—something that was not lost on those who knew him. "He looks," Truman Capote once remarked, "like a man who has just swallowed an entire human being."

Sally Bedell Smith's biography of Paley, *In All His Glory*, came out in 1990, the year of Paley's death. The book epitomizes the reaction most people have to a life like Paley's: it is written for two audiences—one that would like a peek at the glamour of Paley's world, and another that would like to confirm its intuition that someone other people find so glamorous must actually be a person of rather limited accomplishment. For the first audience, the home furnishings, vacations, distinguished golfing partners, and romantic liaisons in Paley's life are carefully catalogued. One appendix lists the bequests, mostly of expensive jewelry, in Babe Paley's will; another gives the dollar value of Paley's holdings in CBS stock for each year of his life, beginning in 1928. (It increased.) For the audience that wants to see what the legend looks like with the varnish removed, there are stories of coldness to friends and to children, of bad business decisions and of credit stolen from others for good ones, and of personal mythmaking on an imperial scale. First we are asked to admire the cake, and then we get to eat it. This is a common enough form of celebrity biography, and satisfying in its mildly opportunistic way. It's nice to know how people who strike it rich spend their money, and it's also nice to feel that if we struck it rich ourselves we'd deserve it a little more and spend the money a little less selfishly. When we read of Babe Paley's being driven by her chauffeur to Kennedy Airport so that she can pick up the freshly shot game bird she has had flown in from Europe for her husband's dinner, our disappointment at being financially incapable of this sort of thing is exactly balanced by our satisfaction in feeling morally incapable of it as well.

Smith's chapters on Paley's personal life contain many stories like the story of the imported fowl, but the story of the fowl is about as exciting as most of them get. For Paley aspired merely to live well, and in what he understood to be the best possible taste; and although this aspiration led him, given his means, to excesses, it precluded any genuine folly. He was, with a few significant philanthropic exceptions, much too prudent to waste his money on anything but himself. His single traditional vice, apparently, was philandering, which is neither the most unusual vice for a very rich man to have nor the most interesting.

Smith's treatment of Paley's career as a broadcaster is somewhat less breathless than her treatment of his career as a devotee of the high life. Her pages on the business side of Paley's life are concerned mostly with debunking his reputation as a broadcasting genius. She does concede, as most commentators do, that Paley understood better and sooner than anyone else in broadcasting the importance of programming. (It seems odd that people in broadcasting ever doubted that the choice and quality of programs were important, but they did.) And she believes that he had a genuine instinct for guessing what most Americans wanted to hear and see. But she also points out that Paley went into radio not because he had a precocious sense of its potential, as he later claimed, but simply in order to get some executive training before returning to the cigar business; that he saw no money in television when it appeared, and discouraged efforts to move his company into it; and that during the years—from the late 1950s through the mid-1950s—when CBS assembled its television network and overtook NBC to become the dominant force in the industry, he was generally distracted by the enjoyment of his private life, and by a brief stint in public service, and it was really Frank Stanton, the president of the company (by then Paley had become chairman), who engineered CBS's triumph.

This part of the cake has been sliced by others, as well—in Robert Metz's *CBS: Reflections in a Bloodshot Eye* (1975) and in David Halberstam's *The Powers That Be* (1979), a work whose sections on CBS so irritated Paley when he read a version of them in the *Atlantic Monthly* in 1975 that he (and a large staff) composed his own memoir, *As It Happened*, and arranged to have it published a few weeks before Halberstam's book appeared. What distinguishes

Smith's book from those earlier efforts is all the stargazing attention it pays to Paley's personal life. But the stargazing makes a point of its own. For the way Paley lived—the homes, the art collection, even the wives—had as much to do with the success of CBS, and of network television generally, as his business decisions did. There was nothing foreordained about the dominance of network television; it was achieved in defiance of the normal mechanisms of the market and the normal tinkering instincts of politicians. Network television was an empire protected by an image, and it was Paley's real genius to understand why it was that every enhancement of his private life was also an investment in the continuing prosperity of the company he ran and the medium he helped to establish.

2

Americans who grew up in the postwar era are so accustomed to television as a fixture in their lives that its presence seems almost a dispensation of nature. Virtually everyone's memory of it is the same. If you had a set in 1955, it had twelve VHF (very high frequency) channels, all except three of which probably broadcast static—unless, by performing calisthenics with your aerial, you could pick up a network station from a distant city, the ghostly twin of a local channel. The picture was black and white, and if you switched on the set very early or very late in the day, you could contemplate an eerie piece of electronic arcana, now nearly forgotten—a test pattern. Ed Sullivan had already been on the air for seven years.

In 1970 your set had an extra dial, for UHF, the ultra-high frequency spectrum (Channels 14 to 83). This was a piece of machinery required by Congress on all televisions made after 1963, and it was somehow awkward to operate: you always seemed to be dialing past your station. On the VHF dial, there was now an "educational" channel: the Public Broadcasting System (PBS) had begun operating in 1969, the culmination of seventeen years of efforts to establish a national noncommercial network. You mostly watched the commercial networks, though, or an unaffiliated channel that,

when it wasn't showing sports or old movies, showed network re-
runs. The colors (color programming began in 1965) were so oversat-
urated that they seemed radioactive. Ed Sullivan was still on the air.

Today, even the Ed Sullivan impressionists are gone. You watch a
sleek cube fed by a cable, and, by keeping your thumb pressed to a
remote control, you can skim dozens of channels in a few seconds.
One channel plays music videos all day; one broadcasts world news;
one has a local talk show (a consequence of mandated "public access"); one or more, for a fee, show recent movies, uncensored; one
has a psychic you can call for on-the-air advice; one displays jewelry
you can shop for by phone. You can watch programs on which
pickup trucks with oversized tires are driven across rows of parked
cars, and programs on which naked people discuss sex in a manner
so unstimulating as to make you turn back to watch the pickup
trucks. There is always sport, and most of the local teams' games are
available. There are (since the arrival of Fox, in 1986) five "over the
air" networks, and one or more "superstations," beamed into the system by satellite. There is still, it's true, nothing to watch, but you
can turn to Channel 3 and put a rented movie in your videocassette
or DVD player.

Because we tend to think of technological development as analogous with biological development, we're likely to assume that
changes in our experience of television reflect changes in television
technology. It seems like a simple matter of evolution. We had to
have black-and-white pictures before we could have color; we had
to have twelve VHF channels before we could have seventy UHF
channels, and to have national over-the-air networks before we
could have cable, pay-per-view channels, and local programming.
We lived with broadcasting so that one day we could have narrow-
casting. In fact, the development of American television had almost
nothing to do with technology. Network television was no more natural or inevitable than any of the other empires that locked the cold
war world into place. It was no more accidental, either, but (like
those other empires) it considered itself extremely vulnerable to
accident, and understood eternal vigilance to be the price of its
survival.

One of the problems with scholarship on television is that a technological and corporate history of the medium often brings us no closer to understanding television as a cultural phenomenon— though it is a common assumption of mass-culture scholarship that such an approach must. An analysis of the economics of television still gives us no way to choose among the various slants on the medium people generally take: television is escapist, and television is propagandistic; television reflects what people are thinking, and television tells people what to think; television is too commercial, and the commercialism of television is inevitable; television is run by liberal elites, television is a pawn of politicians, and television is the tool of corporate America. There is also the tendency to express surprise at the obvious—for example, television's generally patriotic and consumerist biases. These are sometimes taken to have a brain-washing effect: scholars sometimes write as though they had forgotten that no one has ever been forced to watch a television show. It is pointless to blame everything that is wrong with television on capitalism, unless you are prepared to say that America has never produced any commercial culture worth caring about, which is something you would have to be culturally benumbed to believe. Still, where a biographer like Smith, in the interests of keeping her subject vividly before us, asks us to think of what we watched in the network years as largely a function of personality—"the flickering images on CBS represented the soul and sensibility of Bill Paley,"[1] as she puts it—technological and economic histories of the medium remind us that the style, the quality, the content, and even the color of network television programs were determined by forces much too strong for any personality, even an oversized one like Paley's, to have resisted.[2]

Television predates the Second World War. NBC started regular broadcasting in 1939, and although America's entry into the war delayed the development of national networks for several years, television technology had been quite fully explored by 1945. The return of the troops produced a massive potential audience and, for advertisers, massive consumer demand; and in 1948, when less than half of 1 percent of American households had television sets, national broadcasting made its real debut. Confronted with an industry poised to proliferate wildly and in need of elaborate technical coordination (standardization of signals and receivers, allocation of stations in the broadcast spectrum, and so on), the Federal Communications Commission (FCC) imposed a freeze on the licensing of new television stations in September 1948. The freeze turned out to be a kind of cultural Yalta; it lasted until 1952, by which time 33 percent of American homes had television sets, and NBC and CBS, the companies that had dominated radio broadcasting, and whose affiliates had secured most of the television licenses granted before the freeze, essentially controlled the field—which, along with the less powerful ABC (a company created in 1943 after the government ordered NBC to sell one of its two radio networks), they continued to do for more than thirty years.

The man who had the most to say about the way in which television was to enter the culture was not Paley but Paley's rival, NBC's David Sarnoff. NBC was the broadcasting arm of RCA, of which Sarnoff was the president. RCA also had a manufacturing arm, which produced television sets—sets engineered, as it happened, to receive twelve VHF channels and show a black-and-white picture. A color-picture technology had been developed by CBS in 1940; but Sarnoff, though he knew of this achievement, was not interested in color television. RCA had not pursued it, and CBS color technology was incompatible with RCA sets. In 1947, after Sarnoff promised that RCA was working on a color technology that could be used with its own sets, the FCC refused to approve the CBS—or any other—color system. (Several months after the decision was announced, the FCC's chairman left to become a vice president of RCA.) By 1953, when the commission lifted the ban on the manufacture of color sets, RCA, which had evidently *not* been working on a color picture, had flooded the market: there were twenty-three million black-and-white sets already in use.

The licensing freeze left the UHF market permanently underdeveloped. The networks' programs were designed to be broadcast on VHF, since their affiliates were VHF stations; and most sets could not receive UHF signals (which, incidentally, transmit color pictures better than VHF signals do). In 1953 the FCC began licensing UHF stations, but television manufacturers were reluctant to equip their sets to receive the signal—as late as 1960, only 7 percent of the sets in the country had UHF reception—for the simple reason that many set manufacturers owned VHF broadcasting stations (which might possibly explain why the UHF dial was such a nuisance to use). And cable, far from being a recent refinement, is a technology that predates broadcasting itself: transmitting electronic signals through wires is more rudimentary than transmitting them through the air (or through the ether, as the pioneers of radio imagined it). There were subscriber-supported cable systems for radio as early as 1923, and television networks have always used coaxial cable, leased from phone companies, to transmit their pictures to broadcasting stations.

In short, almost the only technologies used by television in the 1990s which could *not* have been used in the 1950s were satellite transmission and the VCR, and even those were not recent inventions. Video recorders went on the market in 1957 (though they were expensive, and did not use cassettes), and Telstar, the first television satellite, was launched in 1962. (The networks undertook to control development in those areas, too, for obvious reasons.) What we might have had for the last forty years is what, almost everywhere, we have had only since around 1990: a mixture of local and national programming and commercial-free pay services on a hundred channels—and all in living color.

3

The danger to network broadcasting during the forty years of its supremacy was therefore always a clear and present one. Any politician who felt that his toes had been stepped on by a news show, any FCC commissioner jealous of his high-mindedness, any president inclined to wage war against the "media establishment" might pull some regulatory stunt that would crack the industry wide open and let a hundred channels bloom. The networks made a lot of money in their day, but they looked over their shoulders all the way to the

bank, because they never knew when the elaborate system of ac-
commodations on which their fortunes had been built might collapse. Network television was constitutionally neurasthenic: the
slightest potential change in its environment induced a precaution-
ary frenzy.

The networks' commitment to news and other public-affairs
programs, for instance, has historically been a function of their
apprehension about government meddling: the higher the level of
official concern in Washington about exploitative programming or
monopolistic practices, the greater the number of shows devoted to
enlightening the public. Paley understood from the start the importance of maintaining a public-affairs profile: in 1931, all CBS press
releases bore the slogan "Columbia—The News Network," even
though CBS did not have a single news employee. CBS's reputation
as a prestigious news organization predated any actual news gathering. Though it was desirable to be identified with a commitment to
the news, the networks did not think it desirable to be identified
with the sorts of controversies a genuine commitment to the news
could create. By the accident that Edward R. Murrow, a CBS employee, was in Europe (though not as a reporter) when the Nazis
entered Austria, CBS radio was able to carry dramatic firsthand
coverage of the event. Murrow's radio broadcasts during the Blitz
(as noncontroversial a news event as one could hope for) made him
a great celebrity, his fame helped promote the network, and CBS
thus inadvertently began to acquire a prestigious news organization.

Paley made it a point not to socialize with his employees—even
with Stanton—but Murrow was an exception, and after Murrow's
return to New York at the end of the war the two men became
friends. When, in 1954, Murrow undertook to broadcast two shows
about Senator Joseph McCarthy on the news program *See It Now*,
though, Paley was careful to establish for his company what later executives would call "deniability." CBS refused, for instance, to buy
newspaper advertisements for either of the McCarthy broadcasts;
Murrow and his producer, Fred Friendly, had to pay for ads out of
their own pockets (something Smith unaccountably fails to mention). And after the first show had been broadcast, it was Babe Pa-

ley, not her husband, who placed the congratulatory call to Murrow. In the end, the response to the McCarthy broadcasts was favorable for CBS, but not universally so, and as Paley began to see the dangers that an unfettered investigative newsman invited, he began quietly to shut Murrow and Friendly down. By 1958, *See It Now* was off the air. That same year, Murrow publicly criticized the networks for their "escapism," and he and Paley did not have a civil conversation again until just before Murrow's death, in 1965. As it turned out, in 1959 the quiz-show scandal, which had attracted the attention of the FCC, gave CBS a fresh reason for demonstrating its commitment to public affairs, and the network promptly unveiled a new investigative series, *CBS Reports*.

The networks were anxious not just about politicians. They were anxious about everybody. Advertisers might take offense: "There should be no statement or situation in conflict with One-A-Day multiple vitamins," decreed the advertising agency for Miles Laboratories. (Miles Laboratories was sponsoring *The Flintstones*.) Powerful interest groups might take offense: for years, the American Medical Association advised the networks on medical dramas to ensure that doctors were portrayed in a favorable light; and the scripts, the casting, and the sponsorship of *The F. B. I.*, which was on the air from 1965 to 1974, were overseen by (sensibly, for who would want to make those people unhappy?) the FBI. Then there were the self-appointed watchdog groups, like the National Television Review Board, based in Chicago, which in the mid-1950s condemned *Howdy Doody* because it considered the show "loud," "confused," and "senseless" and the clown's role "too feminine."[3]

The networks always had a headache, and each time they moved to cure the pain some other part of their vast constituency gave them a new one. Efforts to design programs appealing to eighteen-to-thirty-four-year-old women, beloved of advertisers, led, for example, to the relatively sexy and violent television of the mid-1970s, which produced complaints from people who were (evidently) not eighteen-to-thirty-four-year-old women, which aroused the interest of the FCC. Panicked by the threat of regulation (or, much more alarming, deregulation), the networks proposed a "Family Hour," agreeing to broadcast between seven and nine o'clock in the evening only programs appropriate for "family viewing." That appeased the FCC, but annoyed independent producers of "mature" shows, such as *All in the Family*, which were being bumped to a later time. They sued the networks, and in 1976 a federal judge declared the Family Hour unconstitutional. It was enough to make anyone feel persecuted. When the networks pursued profits, they were told that the airwaves belonged to the public, and that their programming was not protected by the First Amendment; when they tried to regulate themselves in the name of the public interest, they were convicted of abridging the freedom of speech.

Where everyone must be pleased, even an autocrat can use some help, which is why, for instance, the creation of PBS was a welcome event for the networks: it excused them from the unremunerative duty of educating the public. The story of television programming in the network era is the story of what in another context might have seemed a utopian effort: the creation of something that millions of people would watch but that not a single person would be offended by. No wonder that almost half of all new shows were off the air within a year; few things that are bland enough to pass the test of everyone's sensibility have much flavor left. It was like trying to reinvent milk.

You do not have to think well of the results to appreciate the ordeal that the quasi-monopolistic nature of the broadcasting business condemned the networks to. Here were enterprises that were operated on purely commercial principles, but that could never seem cheap or sensational, that always had to give the appearance of being enlightened without ever taking a position on an issue on which people differed, that needed to attract the largest possible audience without being suspected of pandering. In those circumstances, it was obviously a great advantage to have at the head of the company a man as noted for his taste as William Paley. "I am not a highbrow," Paley once said. "I do not look down on popular taste. Oftentimes popular taste is my taste."[4] It hardly mattered whether this was true. What mattered was that government regulators and commercial sponsors were persuaded that the programs on CBS were compatible with the image Paley projected. A man who collected Picasso and Matisse, and whose wife was regularly named one of the most fashionable women in the world, might be trusted not to offer the public shabby cultural goods. It was not egomania (or not merely egomania) that inspired Paley, even after he had ceased to make decisions about other matters, to play a conspicuous role in his company's yearly programming meetings. It was smart business. In her biography of Paley, Smith presents him as a world-shaper, but the details of his story make it plain that he was only a man ideally suited to an industry whose prosperity depended on slavish adherence to a standard of utterly respectable mindlessness. There are suggestions throughout *In All His Glory* that if we could somehow get to the bottom of Paley's personal feelings we would understand something important about our culture; but the most important thing about Paley's feelings—as the sad episode with Murrow shows—was how easily he could set them aside in order to obey the commercial and political imperatives of his business.

A note of disapproval runs through Smith's biography of Paley, as it does through many books on the television industry. "The networks never allowed television to be all it might have been,"[5] as a leading historian, J. Fred MacDonald, puts it. Though the problem quite clearly was too much regulation—tying up the industry in a way that prevented alternatives to the networks from developing— these writers would apparently have preferred more regulation still. Had the government been willing, in the early days of radio, to impose "tighter regulations on commercial operators," Smith suggests, "broadcasting might have been a tool for greater enlightenment,"[6] and MacDonald echoes this sentiment. It is an easy chorus to join, for there is no doubt that television, considering its power to influence, has not been a particularly uplifting medium. But television's power to influence is just what makes one feel certain that active government interest in exploiting the medium's "educational" possibilities would have had regrettable consequences. In a way, the banality of network television was the best thing about it—just as the best thing about contemporary television is probably the sheer sensory confusion. Some powers are better left unchanneled.

The empire of the networks finally collapsed, at the end of the 1980s, in part because the pressure from rival technologies could no longer be resisted, but also because the networks lost the protection of the one federal regulation that seemed most restrictive: the rule that they could own only seven television stations apiece. In 1985, in the deregulatory spirit of the Reagan era, the FCC permitted each network to own up to twelve stations—which, since the ownership of a television station is effectively a license to print money, increased the networks' profitability and immediately made them candidates for takeovers. Paley's 1983 retirement had been a reluctant one, and some of the most engaging passages in Smith's book are devoted to a lengthy but lucid account of his conniving to regain at least the trappings of power. After Lawrence A. Tisch, the head of the Loews Corporation, acquired a controlling interest in CBS in 1985, he and Paley orchestrated the removal of the man Paley had named as his successor, Thomas H. Wyman. In 1987, when Tisch assumed the presidency of CBS, Paley returned to the chairmanship, and he remained active in company affairs until his death, in 1990, at the age of eighty-nine.

The power at CBS passed, though, to Tisch, who proceeded, after the manner of most takeover victors, to sell off some of the spoils, getting rid of two of the company's divisions, CBS Records and CBS Publishing, for cash. The cash was then used by CBS to buy back a portion of its own stock—some of which belonged to Tisch, who was thus able to recover much of his original investment, and some of which had belonged to Paley, whose estate reportedly needed the money to pay its taxes. All that remained of CBS was, essentially, the broadcasting network, which now had to make its way in a world no longer disposed to respect the prerogatives of broadcasting networks, or to glorify their emperors.

A Friend Writes:
The Old *New Yorker*

I

No one who wrote about William Shawn's *New Yorker*—the magazine that Shawn edited from 1952, when he was named to succeed its original editor, Harold Ross, until 1987, when he was replaced by Robert Gottlieb, the magazine now always referred to as "the old *New Yorker*"—ever failed to give offense. Sometimes, of course, offense was intended. When you have a reputation for being easily scandalized, people will be glad to find ways of helping you live up to it. In 1965, Tom Wolfe wrote an article about the *New Yorker* for the *New York Herald Tribune*'s Sunday magazine. On the eve of its publication, Shawn, having failed after repeated phone calls to dissuade the paper's editor from running the piece, sent a pleading letter to the *Herald Tribune*'s publisher, John Hay Whitney: "I know exactly what Wolfe's article is—a vicious, murderous attack on me and the magazine I work for. . . . In one stroke of the pen it puts the *Herald Tribune* right down in the gutter with the *Graphic*, the *Enquirer*, and *Confiden-*

tial. For your sake and for mine, and, in the long run, even for the sake of Wolfe and his editor, Clay Felker (God help me for caring about them), I urge you to stop the distribution of that article."[1] Who could resist that kind of encouragement? The *Herald Tribune* ran the piece. It may not have done much for Jock Whitney—the paper folded not long after—but the *Herald Tribune*'s Sunday magazine became *New York* magazine, Clay Felker became its editor, what became of Tom Wolfe everyone knows, and in 1966, the year after the offending article appeared, the *New Yorker* sold 6,143 pages of advertising, the highest number in its history. A little scandal is good for business.

Wolfe had every hope of doing harm; but even people who think they are doing the magazine a favor have been given reason to wish they hadn't bothered. No book did more to promote the image of the old *New Yorker* as a club every writer longed to join than James Thurber's *The Years with Ross* (1959). After it appeared, Thurber complained to Edmund Wilson that not a single person at the *New Yorker* offered a word of praise. Kenneth Tynan scolded Thurber for giving an insufficiently respectful picture of Harold Ross, the magazine's founding editor—who had died in 1951, seven years before Tynan joined the staff. Thurber's oldest and closest friend at the magazine, E. B. White, stopped speaking to him.

Brendan Gill's *Here at "The New Yorker"* (1975) tried the device of casting its author as a playful Eustace Tilley, examining his colleagues as though they were so many delightfully idiosyncratic butterflies. It was not, perhaps, a tactic calculated to please the butterflies; but Gill was only trying to do to *New Yorker* writers what *New Yorker* writers had done hundreds of times to the subjects of "Talk of the Town" pieces and "Profiles." Few writers appreciated finding themselves on the other side of the monocle. It took E. J. Kahn, represented in the book by a single harmless and ancient anecdote, ten years before he could bring himself to speak to Gill again. Gill's paragraphs on Katharine White, the magazine's longtime fiction editor, described her as a handsome and self-confident woman who deserved the credit for transforming the *New Yorker* into a serious literary magazine, and whose gracious but formidable editorial presence was considerably strengthened by her marriage to the indispensable E. B. White—which is pretty much the description found in every other account of Katharine White. When the book came out, she considered suing Gill for libel. Talked out of that by her lawyer and her family, she contented herself with compiling a long list of all the inaccuracies in *Here at "The New Yorker"*; but the book, she confided to a friend, had come "near to killing me."[2]

It is fair to say that most of these reactions flowed not from personal pride, but from pride in the magazine. Writers and editors don't like seeing their idiosyncrasies in print any more than anyone else does, and it obviously does no good to point out to them that putting other people's idiosyncrasies into print is how most writers and editors make their livings. The wasp does not excuse the exterminator because they're both in the same business. But besides the perfectly natural distaste for reading about themselves and their friends as characters in someone else's amusing story, people who worked at the *New Yorker* had a much stronger distaste for anything that suggested an incomplete respect for the dignity and integrity of the magazine.

This is a peculiarity in journalism. For most journalists not at the top of the masthead, loyalty to the craft ranks higher than loyalty to the publication. Even people who work at the *New York Times*, a publication whose opinion of itself is very exalted indeed, don't (with obvious exceptions) mind seeing it ridiculed a little; no one, in fact, can ridicule the *Times* with keener scorn than a *Times*person off hours. But at the old *New Yorker*, loyalty to the craft was identical with loyalty to the magazine. The *New Yorker* was identified with journalism in its most unadulterated state: the arts of writing and editing were practiced with every regard for the perfection of style, clarity, and accuracy, and with none for the two great ulterior motives of American journalism—selling copies and selling ads.

The firm and enforced separation between the editorial and business sides of the *New Yorker* forms the centerpiece of every description of the magazine, and of every account of its success. "Don't shoot! Editorial!" the writer John McNulty used to shout as he emerged from the elevator on the editorial floor of the magazine's offices on West Forty-third Street. For writers and editors were discouraged from fraternizing with people who worked on the business side—first by Ross, who feuded for years with the magazine's principal financial backer, Raoul Fleischmann, and then by Shawn. And business employees were not welcomed on the editorial floors. No doubt (as McNulty's joke suggests) there was something a little silly about the decorums that some *New Yorker* editors and writers felt they had to observe in order to protect the product from contamination. But the principle behind the decorums is not silly; and to write for a commercial publication that has a long record of commitment to editorial integrity—and to get paid quite decently for doing so— is indeed to belong to a club any writer might envy.

This explains the panic that many *New Yorker* writers and editors felt when the magazine was purchased by S. I. Newhouse in 1985, and that some of them expressed rather hysterically when Newhouse replaced Shawn with Gottlieb two years later. For two generations the Fleischmann family had run the *New Yorker* almost wholly benignly. (They were not, strictly speaking, the magazine's sole owners, for the *New Yorker* was a publicly traded company.) The reason for the benignity—as Gigi Mahon's business history of the magazine, *The Last Days of the "New Yorker"* (1988), makes clear—had less to do with an enlightened respect for art and literature than with a lackadaisical attitude toward business affairs that drove some of the other major stockholders on the magazine's board of directors to distraction. Newhouse's attitude toward business affairs is not lackadaisical, and the Condé Nast magazines, which are the chief magazine properties in his publishing empire, are unashamedly great, fat books of advertising: *Vogue, HG, Vanity Fair, GQ, Mademoiselle, Allure, Traveler,* and the rest. When ad revenues threaten to fall off at those magazines, editorial content is shaken up—and so, frequently, are mastheads. It must have sent a long, apprehensive shiver through *New Yorker* writers when they saw a picture of Ralph Lauren on the cover of *Vanity Fair,* a magazine once touted as Condé Nast's answer to the *New Yorker.*

The *New Yorker* was not immediately joined to the Condé Nast

group, though; it was run as a "stand-alone" entity. It was rumored
to be losing money after Newhouse acquired it (Newhouse's Advance Publications is a private company, and its finances are not
made public), though some reports suggested (inaccurately, as it
turned out) that the magazine had started to turn a profit again. Nor
was there any sign that, under Gottlieb, editorial content was being
shaped with a view to improving commerce. Some people criticized
the magazine for that, but there were just as many people who
would have criticized the magazine if it looked as though content
were being shaped with an eye to commerce. There were some new
bylines; there was some unaggressive editorial tinkering; there were
a few minor design changes. (It cannot have been pleasant to be an
editor who had only to make a tiny adjustment in the layout of the
table of contents to wake up the next morning and find a story about
it in the *New York Times*.) But things at the *New Yorker* seemed,
from the outside at any rate, to be running pretty much as they always had.

With one intangible difference: the mystique had evaporated.
This could only have been liberating to the people who worked
there; but if you looked back over the magazine's history, you had
to wonder about two things. The first was whether the magazine
would ever again be the magnificent cash cow it once was; and the
second was whether the place in American culture that the *New
Yorker* once occupied still existed.

2

These two questions are actually the same question. For the *New
Yorker*, too, was once a great, fat book of advertising, and the notion
that the magazine's editorial matter had nothing to do with the spec-
tacular forest of ads that grew up around it over the years is, of
course, pure myth. The *New Yorker* was invented by Ross, who had
a concept so precocious that it took the rest of the general-interest
magazine industry forty years to catch up to it. The concept was targeting. Why should, say, Bonwit Teller or Tiffany's spend money to
advertise in magazines edited to reach the greatest possible number

of readers, the majority of whom would never visit New York City, and, even if they did, could not afford the stuff that Bonwit's and Tiffany's were selling? Ross proposed a vehicle custom-designed for those advertisers: a general-interest magazine aimed specifically at people who did shop in New York City, and who could pay what Tiffany's was charging. When Ross wrote the famous line in the prospectus for his new magazine—"*The New Yorker* will be the magazine which is not edited for the old lady in Dubuque"—he wasn't talking to his readers (for surely the ladies of Dubuque appreciate clarity and accuracy and have a horror of prurience—values as central to Ross's editorial policy as they would later be to Shawn's). He was talking to his advertisers. Ross pestered potential backers for years with this harebrained notion of a magazine designed to squeeze a bigger profit out of a smaller circulation. In 1924, Raoul Fleischmann, a poker companion bored by his job running the family bakery, took the bait—whether because he grasped the genius of Ross's scheme or because he simply found the idea of owning a magazine charming is hard to know. The first issue appeared in February 1925.

The *New Yorker* started as a hectic book of gossip, cartoons, and facetiae. It wooed "upscale" readers with courtship techniques that magazines of the 1980s later made familiar. It pelted them with celebrities—with vignettes about actors, actresses, club owners, the idle rich, even the editors of more successful magazines. And it boasted repeatedly of its refusal to take anything seriously, a form of self-promotion in journalism that generally means nothing more scandalous than being irreverent about other people's self-promotions. John Held, Jr., an old friend of Ross's, did not actually draw a *New Yorker* cover, though he contributed some art for the inside; but there were many Held-like covers in the early years: loud, flat stylizations of city nightlife. (Some were by Rea Irvin, the artist who created both the monocled dandy who appears on the cover of the anniversary issue, and the *New Yorker*'s signature typeface.) The idea, apparently, was that urbane chat about New York high life was the way to reach the well-to-do, that it flattered those readers' sense of themselves as chic insiders. It didn't work. By summertime, circulation, which had started at fifteen thousand, had dropped below four thousand. Ads were down to three or four pages an issue. Fleischmann threw in the towel, but was persuaded to change his mind and throw in more money instead.

Then the weather turned. In the summer and fall of 1925, Katharine White (then Katharine Angell), Janet Flanner, the artists Peter Arno and Helen Hokinson, and the fashion writer Lois Long all came on. Issues began selling out. By Christmas, advertising contracts had been signed with B. Altman and Saks. In 1926, E. B. White, a disenchanted adman, was hired. In 1927, White brought on James Thurber, a disenchanted newspaper man, and Fleischmann rejected the first in what would turn out to be a long series of offers to buy the magazine—this one for $3 million. By 1928 profits exceeded a quarter million dollars on revenues of $1.8 million. An issue of the *New Yorker* from the late 1920s looks very much like the magazine forty years later: a glossy, tidily designed book, combining mild, literate wit with reporting and reviewing, all surrounded by column after column and page after page of luxury advertising.

Along the way, though, the urbanity was abandoned. In place of the insider chatter there rose up an entirely different kind of talk. It was bemused, but not smug; intelligent, but never smart; the talk of someone who knows where the party is and how to join it, but who is more disposed to stand, martini in hand, a step or two outside the circle of revelry, someone for whom the experience of ordinary life is the source of fully enough terror and ecstasy. In short, the *New Yorker* style was created.

3

People at the old *New Yorker* always tended to dismiss the suggestion that there was such a thing as a *New Yorker* style. The requirement for a story, they said, was that it be well written; the requirement for a drawing was that it be funny. No test for house sensibility was applied. This was undoubtedly true, but it doesn't mean that there was no *New Yorker* style. For the *New Yorker* was always a thoroughly—a famously thoroughly—edited magazine, and for sixty-two years under Ross and Shawn, its editorial principles were consistent. Whatever was knowing, allusive, or elliptical was amplified and clarified in the direction of perfect accessibility; whatever was suggestive, sensational, or offensive was carefully pruned of those excrescences. This seems—as it was meant to seem—like an entirely negative editorial policy. Nothing, after all, got added to the product. There was nothing that *must* be said; the ambition was merely to cure writing of the impurities that prevented it from saying whatever it was it wanted to be saying. No decent editor would reject this as a basic principle of good editing. What was distinctive about the *New Yorker* was that this basic principle became, by virtue of the single-mindedness of the magazine's commitment to it, the overriding principle as well. It took on content. How the *New Yorker* was edited came to be what the *New Yorker* was all about.

Every reader of the old magazine is familiar with the many ways in which this editorial policy made itself known. There was, to begin with, the *New Yorker*'s punctilio about correct punctuation and usage. The compulsion derived from Ross himself, who, while serving on the editorial staff of *Stars and Stripes* during the First World War, was once placed under house arrest for arguing too vehemently with a superior officer over the proper placement of a comma. The interesting thing about correct usage is that it manages to be democratic and elitist at the same time. Famous writers can't get away with eccentricities just because they are famous. The rules apply to everybody. On the other hand, knowing what's correct is one of the signs of a superior education. The newsbreaks—the examples of other people's solecisms that used to fill out the columns at the end of stories—highlighted the purity of the *New Yorker*'s text; and they were the magazine's tribute to the grammatical standards of its readers. A person might be excused for being unable to fix a toaster or to drive an automobile, they quietly suggested, but never for writing a sentence with a dangling participle. ("We'd use a pen.")

Then there was the *New Yorker*'s long-standing resistance to vulgarity. In the first theater review he submitted to the magazine, Tynan used the term *"pissoir,"* a word Shawn could not bring himself to put into print. After a long and amiable discussion, it was agreed that *"pissoir"* would be changed to read "a circular curbside construction." For most of the magazine's history this habit of mind was probably less inhibiting than it has been made out to be. There was plenty of frankness in the magazine's art and in its writing, and if prudish circumspection was exercised at the editor's desk, it rarely showed up on the page. But it is also true that the kind of work the *New Yorker* could attract was limited by the magazine's distaste for subject matter and vocabulary that eventually became utterly commonplace in virtually every other literary forum. Katharine White once wrote to Norman Mailer asking if he would care to contribute a story to the magazine. He would not, Mailer replied, because he did not have the freedom to say "shit" in the *New Yorker*. White wrote back to suggest that perhaps Mr. Mailer did not understand the true meaning of freedom. Mailer answered that he did indeed understand the meaning of freedom: freedom meant being able to say "shit" in the *New Yorker*.[3]

Well, "The Time of Her Time" is a story probably no one at the *New Yorker* was sorry to have missed the chance to publish. It's hardly a *New Yorker* story. On the other hand, one of the great deficiencies in the magazine's reporting was its coverage of the events of the 1960s, and Mailer's early political journalism, which did a lot to make *Harper's* and *Esquire* exciting magazines in those days, was just the kind of perfectly serious writing that lay outside the *New Yorker's* bounds. And some fiction the magazine probably *was* sorry to have missed. "Goodbye, Columbus" is reported to have been turned down because the story involves an item Shawn considered unprintable, a diaphragm. ("A circular cervical construction" was evidently not proposed as a substitute.)

For many people, the quintessence of *New Yorker* style was the style of "Talk of the Town"—the style of "We enjoy a parade as much as the next fellow, so when an invitation to the first annual Lite Beer Drinkers of America parade crossed our desk the other day," etc. The much-parodied first-person-plural voice was a consequence of the circumstance that for many years all "Talk" items were written by one person, relying on the notes of individual reporters. This was Thurber's job in the early days, and later it was Gill's. With the arrival of reporters like Mark Singer and Ian Frazier in the early 1970s, "Talk" became more of a competition of stylistic virtuosity; but the vestigial "we" tended to hang on.

"Talk" reflects Ross's hatred of knowingness, which is indeed the bane of much of the higher journalism in America. The tales of Ross's ignorance have been told often enough—that he once queried "William Blake" in a manuscript; that he asked a fact checker whether Moby Dick was the captain or the whale. The stories get repeated in part because a kind of virtue is understood to attach to such ignorance: it is, after all, superior to pretension. This is the virtue expressed in the ordinary-man style of "Talk of the Town." Thurber once submitted a "Talk" item to Ross for editing and got it back in this form (Ross's emendations are italicized):

> For those who exclaim over armor, *a thing pretty rare with us*, the three new suits the museum has just come by will prove enthralling. One of them, a richly ornamented Spanish war harness, has more pieces of réchange, *or you might say accessories*, than any other battle suit in the world. . . . Among other prizes of the New Accession Room is the lid of an amphora, *but we never did find out what an amphora is.*[4]

This is a style that has things all ways at once: the trendy or pretentious event (such as it is) is reported; any filaments of the experience that might be suspected of trendiness or pretension are mocked; and the mockery is ostensibly at the writer's expense, so no one need feel offended. The writer has found his way to the party, but he chooses to stay on the fringe. He'd *like* to be on the inside, maybe, but, oh dear, just finding a taxi was quite enough excitement for one afternoon. The attitude can be read as modesty, or as the politest possible put-down.

Thurber and White were masters of this persona, and S. J. Perelman produced a brilliantly rococo version of it. It showed a different face in the magazine's serious fiction, where the technological and epistemological befuddlement of the "Talk" and humor pieces was exchanged for the moral befuddlement that comes with life in the upper-middle-class bubble. *New Yorker* short-story writers succeeded in generating an extraordinary pathos from this befuddlement; and although it has long since been imitated to the point of cliché, the pathos was not a false one. The *New Yorker* story expressed with great precision the inner life of a certain kind of mid-century American: well off but insecure, well educated but without culture, enlightened enough to know how morally dark the world is in which he moves, but without a clue about how to live beyond it.

In its classic form, the story came in a lighter and a darker version. In the lighter—White's "The Second Tree from the Corner," John Cheever's "The Country Husband," John Updike's "The Happiest I've Been"—the ache is part of ordinary experience; it is first built up by the accumulation of trivial failures and humiliations, then soothed by the machinery of a momentary epiphany whose materials are taken from the world as it is. In the darker version—in Jean Stafford's "Children Are Bored on Sunday," Harold Brodkey's "Sentimental Education," J. D. Salinger's "A Perfect Day for Bananafish"—the ache does not belong to the world; it comes from some demon outside, so that the world is unequipped to console it, and the life breaks apart. The essential psychological condition in both versions, the condition that is the source both of the pathos and, when it happens, of the consolation, is powerlessness.

Something of the same spirit of self-effacement informs the most successful and inimitable of the magazine's genres, the *New Yorker* cartoon. Many longtime *New Yorker* subscribers liked to confess, in a typically *New Yorker* denial of cultural pretension, that they never *read* the thing, they only looked at the cartoons. (They rarely confessed to the obvious corollary to this, which is that they also looked at the ads. Subscribers may not have read anything in the *New Yorker*, but they turned every page. That's the behavior the cartoons were designed to stimulate.) The distinctive feature of the *New Yorker* cartoon, as Michael Wood pointed out many years ago, is that the comic situation is not visual but verbal.[5] In the beginning, in fact, *New Yorker* artists supplied only the drawings; the captions were considered too important to trust to them, and were provided by the writers. Helen Hokinson, for instance, the creator of a staple *New Yorker* caricature of the 1930s and '40s, the Ladies' Club president with the imperious bust, never wrote a single caption. The dialogue in the famous Carl Rose cartoon of a mother and child at the dinner table—"It's broccoli, dear." "I say it's spinach, and I say the hell with it"—was written by E. B. White.

Of course, there were *New Yorker* artists whose drawings didn't require captions (Saul Steinberg and William Steig, for example) or for whom the caption was often secondary to the image (Charles Addams and Gahan Wilson). But in the typical *New Yorker* cartoon, the drawing was the excuse for the caption, so that the same topoi tended to turn up again and again: two men at a bar, a man and a woman on a desert island, a pollster conducting an interview, a husband and wife in their living room, a man at his desk, people at a cocktail party, two animals talking. (Gill reported that once, in an effort to reduce the backlog of talking animal drawings, the magazine printed an issue that ran *only* talking animal drawings; he said that nobody noticed.)

The humor in these cartoons was always in the language. What was funny was not what was said—it was rarely a double entendre (as in, say, a *Playboy* cartoon) or topical satire (as in an editorial cartoon in a newspaper). What was funny was the language used to say it. If the scene was a cocktail party, the language was fatuous; if it was a man in a bathtub talking to his cats, it was grandiose; if it was a middle-aged couple in their living room, it was melodramatic. Children spoke with adult cynicism; barflies uttered solemn pedantries; animals talked in psychobabble. These captions were comic imitations of the speech of *New Yorker* readers, displaced onto harmless caricatures. It was a highly cultivated form of wit, one that flattered and teased at the same time. And as the history of the magazine proves, it was eternally reusable.

4

After the 1920s, the *New Yorker* began running cartoons on most of its covers. During the thirties the drawings tended to be composed of stock elements of upper-class life: doormen, butlers, chauffeurs, mink-stoled Park Avenue matrons, top-hatted clubmen—occasionally thrown into discomfiting contact with the lower orders. When the war began, the magazine executed one of its canny repositionings. Domestic circulation fell off, so a scaled-down edition of the magazine without advertising—called a "pony" edition—was made available to troops overseas. Serious reporters like Kahn, Robert Shaplen, and A. J. Liebling were dispatched to the front; cartoons of life in the armed forces began appearing on the covers and inside; and there were two powerful and uncharacteristic *New Yorker* covers, both by Christina Malman, that referred directly to the war: a 1940 charcoal of soldiers herding a crowd of civilians whose faces are turned away, and a 1945 drawing celebrating the human dimension of the Allied victory. By the end of the war, the pony edition was outselling the parent magazine; and when the soldiers returned and the great middle-class boom of the postwar era started up, the *New Yorker* had already won its slice of the new audience.

But the magazine was careful to continue to insist on just a slice. In the 1930s, Fleischmann had taken the trouble to keep the magazine's phone number unlisted in order to discourage new subscribers, and this policy of limiting readership was continued. By the mid-1950s the *New Yorker* ranked seventy-second in circulation among American magazines, but it ranked third in ad pages. Between 1957 and 1964, it sold more ad pages than any other magazine in the country; by 1963, it was realizing a 10 percent profit on a $21 million gross. In 1965, it sold 6,092 ad pages, beating its closest competitor, *Business Week*, by almost thirteen hundred pages.

And the magazine was turning down three-quarters of a million dollars in business a year. Ads for goods that were considered too down-market for *New Yorker* readers, such as ads for Sears, Roebuck, or that were deemed distasteful by Shawn, such as ads for lingerie, were routinely rejected. In 1966, the year after Tom Wolfe's "murderous" article, the *New Yorker* reached its sales peak with 6,143 ad pages. And then, very suddenly, the roller coaster began to run the other way. In 1967, the magazine lost five hundred ad pages; it lost another four hundred in 1968, five hundred more in 1969, seven hundred in 1970. Circulation began to slip. People who worked in the magazine's ad department started returning calls.

You can read what was happening on the covers. The human figure began to disappear from the *New Yorker* cover around the time
of the Cuban missile crisis; by the mid-1960s a steady annual pro-
portion of landscape covers has been established. By the seventies,
the cartoon cover with a human subject was a rarity. There were
Cape Cod cottage exteriors, cityscapes framed by apartment windows, flowers and teapots, Steigs and Steinbergs and Korens. But
apart from the occasional appearance of one of Charles Saxon's
overweight suburban dignitaries, the human caricature had mostly
vanished. The *New Yorker* had obviously lost its sense of its audience as a recognizable social type. It knew what its readers' *taste*
was, or ought to be. But it didn't have a very secure sense any longer
of what its readers looked like. By 1970, the *New Yorker* audience,
once a homogeneous, discrete social entity, had started to splinter.
It was holding together only through a common sensibility, a shared
bundle of tastes; and those tastes had begun to seem more and
more ephemeral, less and less worth preserving, every year.

In his introduction to a collection of *New Yorker* covers, published in 1989, John Updike suggested that one way you could en-
tertain yourself with the book was to pick a year that was eventful
for you and see what was on the covers. If you were born after 1945,
this is likely to be a fruitless exercise. These are some covers from
the summer of 1968: June 29, students studying quietly in a library;
July 6, dog sleeping on porch, American flag hanging from the railing; July 13, distant figures on a beach; August 10, middle-aged man
in a rowboat confronted by giant inflatable beach toy; August 17,
generic politician addressing half a dozen microphones; August 24,
sunflowers; August 31, middle-aged vacationer in jacket and bow-tie
preparing for a cocktail party at a beach house. In short, nothing to
suggest that the inner and outer life of the summer of 1968 was not
exactly like the inner and outer life of the summer of 1958.

If you look inside these issues at the "Notes and Comment" section—which serves, as, in effect, the *New Yorker*'s lead editorial—
you find, along with observations on the effects of the drought on
home gardening and a piece on jogging ("Joggers surround us these
days . . ."), two items of symptomatic importance. One is a reflection on current events:

> We grow increasingly disturbed these days, not just by the news
> but by its inexplicable lack of continuity. . . . In wartime, we for-
> merly kept a map of the world with colored pins, and were globally
> anxious, for there was never any question of the whole not being
> the sum of all the parts. . . . We have been thinking of getting out
> our map again, except that now it must be hopelessly out of date.
> Perhaps what we need is some sort of situation map of the world on
> our front pages.[6]

It is the return of the Thurberite nebbish, fretful that making sense
of the world is much too big a task, but not quite sure whether people who pretend to make sense of it are not being a little pompous.
Excuse us for being so unsophisticated, but maybe it's all really
much simpler than everybody seems to think; maybe we could put a
sort of situation map on the front page . . . It is a politics of whimsy,
and it is therefore a politics nobody in 1968 was likely to be paying
much attention to.

The second item of interest is a comment on an announcement
by the *Saturday Evening Post* of its plan to reduce circulation from
nearly seven million readers to three million: "The *Post* will focus on
the prime markets, forget the rest," the announcement said. The
"Notes and Comment" writer has great, derisory fun with this concept of limiting circulation to the desirable zip codes ("We found all
this hypnotic, and immediately began to wonder about our personal
zip code," and so forth), and finishes up with a parodic acceptance
of this crass new way of running a magazine: "There will be (as there
always are) some people who will carp at these developments, and
whine about the Media's Responsibility to the Demographically
Undesirable. . . ."[7] The point isn't simply that the editorial side of
the *New Yorker* had completely lost touch with the commercial
reality of its own enterprise. It's that the rest of the magazine world
had finally caught on to the *New Yorker*'s commercial secret, and
the editors of the *New Yorker* seem to have had no idea what was
happening.

But the magazine found a response. In January 1969, Shawn
made a move to solve the problem with the magazine's politics by
assigning political "Notes and Comment" pieces to Jonathan Schell,

who went on to produce over one hundred between 1969 and 1975. The magazine began providing serious, critical coverage of the Vietnam War, and it published the serial version of Charles Reich's *The Greening of America*—the counterculture for Ivy Leaguers. It had been compelled, against every instinct, to choose sides. The *New Yorker*'s choices were limited by its own tradition. It had never sponsored much more than a genteel (though global) antipolitics. White's "Notes and Comment" pieces of the early forties were primarily devoted to promoting the idea of world government. And the magazine's great reportorial coups "Hiroshima" and "Silent Spring," as politically influential as they proved to be, were the sort of pieces that appeal most to people whose distrust of—or indifference to—everyday politics is already fairly complete. The persona that pretended to regard getting a taxi as a trial of sensibility naturally tended to view greater issues in an apocalyptic light. "They never dreamed that the world's inelegance could become so dangerous,"[8] is the way Robert Warshow characterized the magazine's politics in 1947.

With Schell and Reich, the out-of-ordinary-politics tone became an above-ordinary-politics tone. The tone worked well for many readers when the issues of the day—Vietnam and Watergate—could be addressed by moral fervency alone. When the issues became politically more complex later in the decade, the fervency, in pieces by Schell and others, began to seem like stridency—and the writing even acquired, most uncharacteristically, a partisan political rhetoric. But the real problem was that simply to choose any side was, from the point of view of the demographic position the magazine commanded, to give up ground. "There was a change in the character of the readers" after 1969, J. Kenneth Bosee, the magazine's treasurer, told Gigi Mahon. "The numbers didn't change, but where there were top executives at Fortune 500 companies, now they were replaced by a bunch of kids. The thrust was to a lower audience. The demographics never went up again."[9]

Still, the roller-coaster ride bottomed out. The contents, after all, had remained strong. In that same summer of 1968, the magazine ran (looking at July and August alone): Jane Kramer's memorable two-part profile of Allen Ginsberg; long pieces on the Kennedy assassination conspiracy theorist Jim Garrison, by Edward Jay Epstein, and *The Graduate*, by Jacob Brackman; a joint profile of Chet Huntley and David Brinkley, by William Whitworth; a "European Diary," by Lewis Mumford; stories by Saul Bellow ("Mosby's Memoirs"), Donald Barthelme, Woody Allen, Larry Woiwode, Isaac Babel. These are not only things you would have been happy to read in 1968; these are things you would be happy to read in any magazine today.

In the 1970s, thanks to some uncharacteristically aggressive leadership on the business side, circulation did pick up slightly, the magazine sold more ad pages each year, and, most significantly, overall revenues increased substantially. But all the time other general-interest magazines were trying and succeeding where the *Saturday Evening Post* had failed—in targeting the same slice of the demographic pie the *New Yorker* had largely had to itself for fifty years. The mass-circulation magazine was being replaced by the magazine edited with an upper-quintile household income firmly in mind. *Life* and *Look* were giving way to *HG*. As the prestige of the *New Yorker* began to suffer from competition and from the critical sniping competition generated, Shawn seems to have fallen back on the belief that since it was the disinterested pursuit of editorial perfection that had made the *New Yorker* a success in the first place, an even more fiercely disinterested pursuit of perfection was the only remedy for whatever ailed it now. So that at times during Shawn's last years as editor, the magazine seemed like a parody of itself—running things like E. J. Kahn's enormous multipart series on corn, soybeans, potatoes, and rice; publishing reviews of unnoticed books months or years after they had come out; letting topical reports from Washington and reviews of Hollywood movies of no special moment run to many thousands of words; serializing memoirs of the childhoods of *New Yorker* writers.

In the eighties the great upper-middle-class economic boom inspired dozens of magazines to reposition themselves at the top of the market in order to attract luxury advertising, effectively finishing off the trend that had begun in the late 1960s. When the *New Yorker* failed to respond to these pressures from the rest of the industry, some major stockholders on the magazine's board of directors grew uneasy. When one of them decided to unload a sizable block of shares, Newhouse had his opportunity.

5

In 1985, soon after the *New Yorker* was sold, Shawn wrote a "Notes and Comment" piece designed to defend the magazine's editorial position against possible encroachments by the new ownership, and to reassure the magazine's readers. "We, the editorial people," he explained, "knew by instinct that to be able to make the *New Yorker* the magazine we wanted it to be we had to separate ourselves from the business side of the venture. . . . In this atmosphere of freedom, we have never published anything in order to sell magazines, to cause a sensation, to be controversial, to be popular or fashionable, to be 'successful.' "[10] The analysis is entirely correct, and it explains the true commercial genius of the *New Yorker*.

Nearly all American culture is commercial. It is either market-driven, as in the case of popular music, paperback fiction, and movies; or it is advertising-driven, as in the case of radio, television, newspapers, and magazines. And this culture is, of course, only an aspect of the American way of life generally, in which virtually every good—food, housing, furniture, clothing, cars, shaving cream—is understood to be designed to extract the greatest possible profit from the market conditions available, and to be susceptible to alteration the instant those conditions change. Because it is the chief tool for making conditions change, thereby creating new areas of demand and new sources of profit, advertising has become for most people the symbol of the thoroughgoing commercialism of American life.

Everyone participates in this system, and partakes of its benefits (individual economic opportunity and national economic expansion) and puts up with its drawbacks (cheap goods, an often banal and sometimes exploitative popular culture, financial uncertainty). The group that has benefited the most from this way of life, and that has done the most to shape it and to keep the system producing more of it, is the group of upper-middle-class professionals—lawyers, bankers, stockbrokers, designers, advertising executives, editors, publishers, business executives, television producers, and the college professors who educated them. These people were made possible—were made necessary, in fact—by the spectacularly successful commercialization of American life in the twentieth century; for they supply its creative and analytic intelligence. They are the society's most highly prized and highly rewarded members. But until recently, this group always demonstrated one peculiarity. Its tastes, its values, its lifestyle were all anticommercial. The Wall Street banker lived like a member of the English gentry in a mock-Tudor mansion in Mount Kisco. The Madison Avenue adman had a place in Vermont with outdoor plumbing and no electricity. The television producer bought his filet at an old-fashioned butcher, where it was wrapped in old-fashioned butcher paper. The publisher of a magazine for teenage girls watched public television—or had a passion for Mozart, or Trollope, or vintage wines. He vacationed in the cathedral towns of France. He didn't like motorboats, or billboards, or big American cars. And so forth. His face was turned away from the culture that gave him his living. The upper-middle-class professional had these tastes and values because they were part of his socialization. In midcentury America, this man was, prototypically, the graduate of an Ivy League college, married to the graduate of a select women's college or a major public university. His and his wife's education stressed the values of the liberal arts, which were understood to be opposed to everything transient and commercial. The consumables in their world were not mass-market: the features they shopped with an eye to were traditionalism, craftsmanship, longevity.

Of course, this couple represented a market—by virtue of their income and education, a highly desirable market. But they were not people susceptible to anything that smacked of opportunism or commercialism. Nor could they be reached by gossip about the successful and celebrated. Their taste—their great virtue, really—was for the self-effacing, the unpretentious, the literate and witty. They were secure enough to enjoy poking fun at themselves and their world; that was part of the nobility of their sense of humor. And it was a satisfaction, given their view of commerce and coercion, to imagine themselves to be ineffectual, silly, powerless. But they were genuinely insecure enough to require assurance that they would not be "out-browed"—that they would find their cultural experiences accessible and unthreatening, without being flavorless or incurious or prudish.

The old *New Yorker* looked terrific, as everyone knows, on a coffee table. Its covers were invariably pleasing, and some of them were modestly artful. But the most distinctive design feature of the *New Yorker* cover was that it said nothing about what was inside. Unlike the cover of every other commercial magazine in America, the cover of the *New Yorker* was not a piece of advertising. In fact, *nothing* in the old *New Yorker* was advertised. It ran no table of contents. Its reported pieces carried generic titles: "Reporter at Large," and, in much smaller print: "Soybeans." There might be, by way of illustration, a small, hand-lettered map. There was no accompanying blurb ("You will never feel the same way about this amazing foodstuff again!"). There were no pull-quotes or subheads. The writer's name appeared only at the end, in type that was the same point size as the type in which the article was printed. The cynical explanation for this is that the editorial matter in the *New Yorker* was subdued (for instance, no color) so that the ads would be more vivid. That may be how it worked for the advertisers; but Shawn was right. On the editorial side, the idea really was to give the *New Yorker*'s readers what they wanted: a straight dose of fiction, poetry, reportage, and criticism, without patronizing help or hype. If soybeans didn't interest you, you were free to turn the page (well, pages).

If you grew up in a household in which the *New Yorker* was a constant presence, you probably retain, whatever reservations your superior sophistication now requires you to make, a residual fondness for the magazine's cultural traditions. If you grew up in one of those households and had an interest in the arts, you are likely still to feel a debt to one or another of the magazine's regular critics:

Harold Rosenberg on art, Arlene Croce on dance, Pauline Kael on movies. And if you had an interest in becoming a writer yourself, the magazine almost surely formed part of your sense of what good writing was like. But the anticommercialism, the carefully maintained distance from the crass, capitalist world, will not mean to you what it meant to your parents. For among today's upper-middle-class professionals, the separation between culture and commerce has collapsed. Nor is the sense of membership in a common taste group as strong as it was. The social class of professionals is much less homogeneous than it used to be, and the education those people receive is less of a pious and clubby affair. And they do not find the pose of ineffectuality attractive.

Of course, upper-middle-class tastes still run to the traditional, the custom-built, the exclusive. But there is no special conscience about the relation between these tastes and the values of the marketplace. There is often, in fact, a kind of promiscuous delight in the commercialism of upscale pleasures, and an uninhibited interest in whatever mid- and mass-market experiences seem attractive. The younger professional today has become so adept at reading the language of advertisement and promotion that it has become a stimulation to be welcomed rather than a blight to be evaded. There are surely as many things that are hateful about this new upper-middle-class cast of mind as there were about the old one; but there are surely many things to be admired about it, too. It is an audience that could use a little help understanding which things are which, which is one of the needs magazines exist to serve.

Norman Mailer in His Time

In 1998, when he was seventy-five, Norman Mailer published *The Time of Our Time*, an anthology of his own writing, selected by him and arranged as a commentary on American life since the Second World War. Almost all of Mailer's books are represented in the volume, starting with *The Naked and the Dead* (1948), plus several magazine pieces that had not been reprinted before. Two of the excerpted books—*Ancient Evenings* (1983), which is set in the time of Ramses II, and *The Gospel According to the Son* (1997), a retelling of the Jesus story—do not have much to tell us about postwar American life; but they do have something to tell us about Norman Mailer, and they help to make the volume a surprisingly coherent recapitulation of Mailer's career.

What does Mailer think of postwar America? The answer (this is not the surprising part) is: something good and something bad. The something good is what Mailer calls "democracy," ordinarily a term of broad application, but by which he means specifically the conditions under which moral freedom and intellectual honesty are possible. He is not under the illusion that these qualities are sustainable to the same degree anyplace else in the world. That's the bright side of life in America. The dark side is what he calls "technology," ordinarily a term of specific application, but which he uses broadly to mean all efforts to clean up human messiness, to find a nice, rational, hygienic shortcut to satisfaction. His shorthand term for the results of such efforts is "plastic." Plastic, in his view, threatens freedom. It is a metaphor for creeping totalitarianism.

So far we are comfortably inside the realm of liberal middle-class culture. Everyone within that culture salutes the principles of moral freedom and intellectual honesty, and loathes the idea (without necessarily forgoing the convenience) of plastic. And this is Mailer's problem. In a nutshell: it is possible to have a nice, rational, hygienic contempt for plastic. A person can despise all the bogeymen of "technology" as Mailer identifies them in his essays and books— the military-industrial complex, the Hollywood studios, NASA, television, synthetics, high-rise buildings in which the windows don't open—and still suffer (by Mailer's measure) from moral cowardice and self-deception. Liberals are acculturated to feel superior to technology, even as they prosper, directly or indirectly, by its successes. In Mailer's view, though, technology isn't just depressing or tasteless or something to write editorials about. Technology is the devil. You don't beat the devil by writing editorials. You can't have a rational response to the threat of technology. Rationality is part of the disease.

Mailer spent the decade following the publication of *The Naked and the Dead* working this difficulty out. Though the elements of his solution were not original, their synthesis surely was. He began by biologizing the conflict between technology and freedom. The United States, he thought, was in danger of becoming just as totalitarian as the Soviet Union—a point he had already made in the closing section of *The Naked and the Dead*, where he portrayed, in the figure of a character named Major Dalleson, the postwar triumph of the bureaucratic mentality. Mailer thought that American totalitarianism would emerge under the guise of what he called, in *The Naked and the Dead*, "conservative liberalism,"[1] meaning that regimentation would be accomplished by subjecting dissidents to therapy rather than by sending them to Siberia or having them shot. Thus in two famous early stories, "The Man Who Studied Yoga" (1952) and "The Time of Her Time" (1959), the representative of technology is Freudianism, which paralyzes through introspection. (The man who studied yoga is able, after years of meditation, to unscrew his own navel. He does so, and his ass falls off.) The real danger, Mailer thought, was not economic; Marx had missed the point. The real danger was psychological. Our nervous systems were being invaded. The answer was not to argue but to act.

This much Mailer appears to have picked up from his Trotskyist friend Jean Malaquais, whom he met in Paris soon after finishing *The Naked and the Dead*; from Sartre, whose essay "Existentialism Is a Humanism" popularized the philosophy in the late 1940s; from Henry Miller and D. H. Lawrence, whose influence on Mailer's writing soon eclipsed the influence, evident in *The Naked and the Dead*, of James T. Farrell and John Dos Passos; from the Baltimore psychoanalyst Robert Lindner, who wrote a number of clinical studies of sociopathic behavior, including *Rebel without a Cause*; and from Wilhelm Reich, who politicized psychoanalysis by erecting (as it were) the liberated sexual instinct as the antagonist of the modern state. Mailer brought Sartre and Reich together by making sex the site of existential struggle. Where he differed from Sartre and Reich (and from all his other teachers except Lawrence) was in making sex the site of metaphysical struggle, as well. The quality of the orgasm became a matter not only of political but of cosmic significance. A bad orgasm—a thwarting or perversion of instinct—could lead (a Reichian idea) to cancer, which Mailer regarded as the biological equivalent of plastic. A good orgasm (an exhausting proposition, incidentally, if we are to rely on the example offered in "The Time of Her Time") was not only a victory over the machinery of psychological oppression; it was a victory on behalf of God in his war with the devil. In short, Mailer developed a Manichean version of Sartre's left-wing existentialism and Reich's left-wing Freudianism. Every choice became a choice between God and the devil, with the margin separating the two always razor-thin. Hence the existential frisson: to miss salvation by a hair was to risk damnation. Life was imagined as the psychic equivalent of rock-climbing (which, along with balancing on balcony railings while drunk, became a popular sport in Mailer's fiction). "The best move," as Mailer has liked to say, "lies close to the worst."

The *summa* of these meditations was "The White Negro" (1956). The essay is notorious for a passage in which the case of two eighteen-year-olds murdering a candy-store owner is proposed, without much qualification, as an example of "daring the unknown." ("One enters into a new relation with the police,"[2] as the essay explains.) Irving Howe, who published "The White Negro" in *Dissent* (it was reprinted in *Advertisements for Myself* [1959]), later expressed regret for having chosen to run it, as a "scoop" for his little magazine, rather than reject it for its endorsement of violence. (The best move lies close to the worst.) Mailer may have offered the piece to Howe with a view precisely to forcing such a dilemma on him; he regarded the American left as a culturally backward bunch that needed a shot of the morally outrageous. But "The White Negro" was not merely a provocation. It was a claim to turf. "I wrote it," Mailer said almost thirty years later, "with tremendous fear and agitation and great difficulty. . . . If I wanted to be a great writer—and by then being terribly fortified both by success *and* failure, I absolutely wanted to be a great writer—then I'd found a place where perhaps I could do it. I felt I had perceptions about these matters that I'd never read in anyone else's literature."[3]

The argument of "The White Negro" is built up from the proposition that American Negroes (by which Mailer means, of course, American Negro men), by virtue of their alienation from mainstream American society, are natural existentialists (they have "existential synapses"), and thus have better orgasms. They appreciate as well the cathartic effects of violence ("individual acts of violence are always to be preferred to the collective violence of the State,"[4] the essay suggests). The white American who would imitate them—the white Negro—is the Hipster. His goal is to be "with it."

> To be with it is to have grace, is to be closer to the secrets of that inner unconscious life which will nourish you if you can hear it, for

you are then nearer to that God which every hipster believes is located in the senses of his body, that trapped, mutilated, and nonetheless megalomaniacal God who is It, who is energy, life, sex, force, the Yoga's *prana*, the Reichian's orgone, Lawrence's "blood," Hemingway's "good," the Shavian life-force; "It"; God; not the God of the churches but the unachievable whisper of mystery within the sex, the paradise of limitless energy and perception just beyond the next wave of the next orgasm.

To which a cool cat might reply, "Crazy, man!"[5]

Mailer soon dropped the language of Hip (which was just the jargon of beatniks and jazz musicians). Over the years his enthusiasm for real violence was largely replaced by an enthusiasm for play violence—bullfighting, football, and, especially, boxing. As celebrity was visited upon him, his political animus relaxed. But "The White Negro" has remained the well from which his thought is drawn. What *The Time of Our Time* reveals (and this *is* the surprising part) is the extent to which Mailer has spent forty-five years occupying the ground he staked out in 1956. He is a man—in 2002, he is possibly the last man—of the 1950s.

Mailer is commonly regarded as a man of the 1960s, for it was in the sixties that he enjoyed his most productive and popular run as a writer: he published two novels, *An American Dream* (1965) and *Why Are We in Vietnam?* (1967); two volumes of essays, *The Presidential Papers* (1963) and *Cannibals and Christians* (1966); two works of reportage, *The Armies of the Night* (1968) and *Miami and the Siege of Chicago* (1968); and a collection of poems, called *Deaths for the Ladies (and Other Disasters)* (1962). He also turned his novel *The Deer Park* into a play, wrote and directed three movies, and ran for mayor of New York City. (He did not finish last.) He had good reason for considering it his favorite decade. But he was not really affected by anything that happened in the sixties. He had entered the decade with his own style of political radicalism and his own brand of sexual liberation already worked out; he did not have much to learn from the counterculture or the New Left. The war in Vietnam did not take him by surprise: it was exactly the sort of technocratic insanity he had been predicting since 1948. And the general attitude of "anything goes" was, he must have imagined, just the attitude he had prescribed in "The White Negro."

But it was not. In the end the social movements of the sixties were the undoing of every tenet of Mailer's radicalism, for they were not, despite appearances at the time, radical movements. They were liberal movements. Their purpose was to make life fairer by clearing away exactly the sort of mumbo-jumbo about race and sex that Mailer built most of his worldview around. The civil rights movement discredited the primitivist myth of black sexuality; the sexual revolution tried to get the language of sin out of talk about sex ("free love" was pretty much the antithesis of any notion of sex Mailer ever had in mind); gay liberation established homosexuality as something other than a heterosexual deformity; and women's liberation debunked the metaphysics of the orgasm. Mailer had gone to great lengths to mystify biology. The sixties demystified it. "Anything goes" did not mean that all is permitted on the understanding that the wrong move will cost you a piece of your soul. It just meant that all is permitted.

For most of the sixties Mailer was one of the things that was permitted, since anyone who seemed sufficiently far out held an appeal. And Mailer was a performer, a kind of celebrity the sixties loved. At the end of the decade, though, he ran into a wall. This was feminism. Mailer took feminism to be a tool of technology, an attempt to find a shortcut to sexual pleasure. Its aim, as he understood it, was to give women sexual independence from men, which meant making reproduction a laboratory exercise and orgasm a mechanical one. He could not see that there are just different kinds of sexual pleasure and different methods of reproduction, because for him unless these matters carry cosmic consequences, the universe is absurd. If a vibrator is as good as a penis, life has no meaning. Mailer's crusade against feminism was hopeless from the start, for he was fighting against one of the simplest and most powerful of human hopes, which is that happiness can be made a little easier to grasp. He offered some sort of truce with the movement (it was not accepted) in *The Prisoner of Sex* (1971) (which also includes defenses, against the strictures of Kate Millet, of Miller and Lawrence, that are, whatever one makes of the book as a whole, brilliant pieces of criticism). But he never really got it. He was done in by the clitoral orgasm.

Mailer's best writing in the sixties, therefore, was conceived in the skeptical spirit of a critic, not in the sympathetic spirit of a convert. The first half of *The Armies of the Night*, which tells the story of his participation in the 1967 march on the Pentagon, is almost certainly the strongest piece of journalistic writing Mailer ever did, and what gives it its sour brilliance is the author's barely suppressed animus against all the good liberals whose arms are linked with his. As a screed against the war, *The Armies of the Night* is not especially distinguishable from many other writings of the time. But as a mordant portrait of the culture of the antiwar movement, there is nothing to beat it.

After *The Prisoner of Sex* Mailer's projects became more diffuse—a biography of Marilyn Monroe, a book on the Apollo moon landing, another on the Ali-Foreman fight in Zaire, a "true-life novel" about Gary Gilmore, the novel set in ancient Egypt, another one set in Provincetown, a huge unfinished novel about the CIA, and books about Pablo Picasso, Lee Harvey Oswald, and Jesus. Mailer continued to cover presidential campaigns for various magazines, although he has not collected this work since *St. George and the Godfather* (1972). There are things to admire in this writing, but the intellectual approach is a little too familiar: the author divides his subject into redemptive and infernal elements, and then muses, at length, upon the possibilities. The general mystery addressed is whether events have a meaning. It is a perfectly respectable mystery to address: to uncover meaning is a reason for writing. What begins to wear the reader down is the Manichean insistence that all meanings are psychic meanings, and that there are only two ultimates. "The Beatles," Mailer once remarked (and not in the spirit of self-parody), "—demons or saints?"[6] There is never a middle possibility.

Thus, on the Apollo moon landing, in *Of a Fire on the Moon*:

> To make sense of Apollo 11 on the moon, to rise above the verbiage
> . . . that covered the event, was to embark on a project which could

not satisfy his own eye unless it could reduce a conceptual city of technologese to one simplicity—was the venture worthwhile or unappeased in its evil?[7]

On the subject of AIDS, in a magazine piece on the 1992 Republican National Convention:

> Was excrement a side-product of nature, offensive to some, as the Democrats would doubtless have argued, or was Satan in everyone's shit? Which, in turn, was a way of saying that the devil was present more often in homosexual than in heterosexual encounters—exactly the question that blazed in the divide. We are dying, said the victims of AIDS, and you have no mercy. Are you cold to our pain because we are the devil's spawn?—beware, then, for we will haunt you. That was the question. Was the gay nation guilty or innocent, victims of devils, damned by Jehovah or to be comforted by Christ?[8]

On Lee Harvey Oswald, in *Oswald's Tale*:

> It is virtually not assimilable to our reason that a small lonely man felled a giant in the midst of his limousines, his legions, his throng, and his security. If such a non-entity destroyed the leader of the most powerful nation on earth, then a world of disproportion engulfs us, and we live in a universe that is absurd. . . . Absurdity corrodes our species. The mounting ordure of a post-modern media fling (where everything is equal to everything else) is all the ground we need for such an assertion.[9]

One can come to feel that the reason the subjects in most of Mailer's later books tend to be about times other than the present is that the author has lost touch with the culture. He no longer stands in oppositional or even in skeptical relation to it because he no longer quite understands it. He wishes to fight the battles of forty years ago, but no one seems to know what he's talking about. Haven't all those battles been won? people wonder. Do we really need to hear about orgasms again? We can hear all about them on

MTV. There are, in this regard, two especially revealing late writings. The first is a review Mailer wrote in 1991 for *Vanity Fair* of a novel by Bret Easton Ellis called *American Psycho*. *American Psycho* is famous for having been dropped by its initial publisher, Simon and Schuster, just two months before publication and at a cost to the company of $300,000, after the chief executive read it and was offended by its deadpan descriptions of the torture and murder of women. The novel was picked up immediately by Vintage Books, but it had already become a scandal, and it was universally panned. (Vintage abstained from advertising the book. It was a best-seller anyway.)

Mailer's review is very fine to a point—he is an exceptional critic—but he cannot get past the point. He is sympathetic to the use of grossly offensive imagery to shock audiences into some awareness of the technological horror of their spiritual condition. He has always relied heavily on obscenity in his own fiction with that end in mind. But he can find, in Ellis's sadistic narrative, no there there. "If one is embarked on a novel that hopes to shake American society to the core," he complains, "one has to have something new to say about the outer limits of the deranged—one cannot simply keep piling on more and more acts of machicolated butchery. . . . Blind gambling is a hollow activity and this novel spins into the center of that empty space."[10] It is a little like watching Ernst Gombrich trying to elucidate the iconography in a work by Jeff Koons. The idea that a work of literature should have "something new to say," or even that it should have an interesting way of saying it, is just one of the aesthetic values that Ellis is trying to show his contempt for, along with every other value of ordinary civilized life. Mailer thinks that Ellis hasn't imagined horror; he has only copied it from schlock movies. "We are being given horror-shop plastic,"[11] he suspects. We are. That's the idea. Lenny Bruce was the last obscene man in America. Even Mailer cannot be obscene any longer. Everyone has heard it all.

The other interesting selection is an interview with Madonna Mailer conducted for *Esquire* in 1994. Madonna seems so clearly Mailer's kind of girl, and he works like a madman to get her up to his conception of her. But to no avail. He cannot shock her, and he cannot persuade her to regard herself from anything like a Maileresque point of view. There are many choice moments of crossed frequencies. Madonna is, of course, a leading spokesperson for safe sex.

> Mailer: Well, condoms are one element in a vast, unconscious conspiracy to make everyone part of the social machine. Then we lose whatever little private spirit we've kept.

> Madonna: On the flip side, couldn't you say: If it makes everybody stop and question who they're sleeping with, then isn't that a good thing, too? . . . Maybe it's a way of getting people to think how much they care about this person they're sleeping with? You know what I mean?

Oh, he does, he does. Flatter her sense of self-importance as he may, Mailer cannot shake her free of the cant of liberal sexology.

> Mailer: Well, you're a revolutionary. What will this revolution be in the name of?

> Madonna: In the name of human beings relating to other human beings. And treating each other with compassion.[12]

Crazy, man.

2

The Time of Our Time rests its case for Mailer's importance on Mailer's views. This seems the wrong square on which to place the chips. Those views made few converts in their time, and they deserve none now. As motives for fiction, they have not proved enduringly stimulating. Mailer's novels seem today to enact a panic about masculinity that has a very midcentury flavor to it. The sort of gender roles central to Mailer's imagination have disappeared from the repertoire of contemporary identity. His importance lies in another corner of the board altogether.

One of the most interesting literary developments in the last forty years has been the challenge to the way we think about nonfiction. The notion of the realist novel as an impersonal mirror of reality (to the extent that anyone ever seriously entertained it) was exploded by the modernists, who placed artifice clearly in the foreground of their work. A novel by Joyce or Woolf or Nabokov is, above all else, *written*. Transparency is not the claim. But impersonality and transparency remain, to a great extent, the claims of contemporary journalism. Anyone who has had the smallest thing to do with journalists knows that newspaper pieces are not called stories for too little (to borrow a Mailerism). But to make a point of this is to invite a defensive reaction. We cannot seem to acknowledge that writing, of whatever kind, is a technology like any other, a human invention for human uses. We cling to the belief that there must be one kind of writing that is a clear window on "the facts."

Great cultural anxiety is therefore always triggered when "real" material is treated in a style that does not seem conventionally appropriate to nonfiction. This is the flip side of the anxiety triggered when works of fiction like *American Psycho* represent, without explicitly condemning, antisocial behavior. In both cases, the fear is that people are unable to separate the textual from the real—the fear, basically, that people do not know how to read. But the activity of reading a book is not the cognitive equivalent of being hit over the head with a brick. It is, like the activity of *writing* a book, a process of selection, a continual assertion and withdrawal of assent to the representations being made by the language. In the end, what matters isn't the literal accuracy of every word; there is no such thing as literalness where words are concerned. What matters is whether the writer has, in the reader's judgment, got it right. There are many ways to get there.

Since 1960, American literary culture has become fascinated by these issues. The names usually mentioned in connection with the mainstream interest in them are Tom Wolfe and Truman Capote, who are credited with inventing the New Journalism, which was defined by Wolfe as journalism that uses the techniques of fiction, and the nonfiction novel, which was the term Capote cleverly chose to categorize *In Cold Blood* (1965). Wolfe and Capote certainly popularized the idea that expectations about fiction and nonfiction could be challenged in entertaining ways. But they did not, except for the purposes of self-presentation, have much that was interesting to say about what they were doing, and their work, from a literary point of view, is of relatively minor interest.

Mailer was there before them, and he went much deeper into the possibilities released by the undermining of traditional distinctions between journalism and fiction. The techniques of fiction are what made his piece on the 1960 Democratic National Convention, which nominated John F. Kennedy, "Superman Comes to the Supermarket," such a famous performance when it appeared in *Esquire* in 1960, three years before Wolfe is supposed to have invented the New Journalism. Mailer viewed politicians with a novelist's eye; he read the inner man from the outer:

> [Kennedy's] style in the press conferences was interesting. Not terribly popular with the reporters . . . he carried himself nonetheless with a cool grace which seemed indifferent to applause, his manner somehow similar to the poise of a fine boxer, quick with his hands, neat in his timing, and two feet away from the corner when the bell ended the round. . . . Yet there was an elusive detachment to everything he did. One did not have the feeling of a man present in the room with all his weight and all his mind. Johnson gave you all of himself, he was a political animal, he breathed like an animal, sweated like one, you knew his mind was entirely absorbed with the compendium of political fact and maneuver; Kennedy seemed at times like a young professor whose manner was adequate for the classroom, but whose mind was off in some intricacy of the Ph.D. thesis he was writing. Perhaps one can give a sense of the discrepancy by saying that he was like an actor who had been cast as the candidate, a good actor, but not a great one—you were aware all the time that the role was one thing and the man another, they did not coincide, the actor seemed a touch too aloof (as, let us say, Gregory Peck is usually too aloof) to become the part. Yet one had little sense of whether to value this elusiveness or to beware of it. One could be witnessing the fortitude of a superior sensitivity or the detachment of a man who was not quite real to himself.[13]

There is nothing in Wolfe to match the sheer intuitiveness of this writing; Wolfe got his effects by other means. Still, Mailer was only elevating the form. He had not broken it open. That happened when he wrote about the 1967 march on the Pentagon for *Harper's*, the story that became *The Armies of the Night*. There he did what no other New Journalist except, later, Hunter Thompson did (and Hunter Thompson went to school to Norman Mailer), which was to insert himself, as a character called Mailer, into the reportage. He did it again, under the name Aquarius, in *Of a Fire on the Moon*, again as Norman in *The Fight*, and by one name or another in virtually every piece of journalism he has done since. Most readers have chalked the device up to ego; but it was not ego, or it was not only ego. It was a way of placing directly before the reader's attention the circumstance that the text was written by a man armed with such-and-such prejudices, operating under such-and-such moral and physical limitations, altering events by his presence in such-and-such a way, and (as in *The Fight*, for example) induced to undertake the work by the promise of such-and-such a fee. The conditions of production are visible right there in the story, since they are in the story whether they are visible or not.

In Cold Blood was a great triumph for Capote, and no doubt Mailer pondered a little on Capote's example, and whether he wanted to be perceived as emulating it, before embarking on his most successful book, *The Executioner's Song* (1979). *The Executioner's Song* is based on a story, the 1976 execution of Gary Gilmore, in Utah, that brought together many of Mailer's obsessions—the psychology of the psychopath, the technology of punishment, existential risk and rebirth. He scarcely needed to add a thing, and it was his genius (though it was not characteristic of his genius) to realize it. "What I had was gold," as he once said about the story, "if I had sense enough not to gild it."[14]

He was referring, of course, to the sort of cosmological interpolations his readers had grown, with some resignation, to expect. But it is a mistake to think that he turned himself into a tape recorder. His first artistic decision was to solve a problem that had plagued Capote's book, which was the problem of direct quotation. Capote had conducted interviews for his book, but he was reduced in most cases to re-creating dialogue out of his own head. The results, particularly in the case of the secondary characters, are often stagy, an Easterner's idea of what Kansans talk like. And having flattened down the dialogue to suit the characters (it did not help that Capote was writing the book for the *New Yorker*, which imposed implicit restrictions on the kind of language he could use, even for his murderers), Capote flattened his own prose down to match it. The writing is genteel, careful, perpetually on the edge of cliché, as though a fresh expression might suggest some sort of authorial attitude, and throw off the journalistic "balance." The consequence, as usually happens when a writer with as large an ambition as Capote self-consciously suppresses his or her personality, is a story utterly dominated by Capote. Except for the killers, whom he interviewed and who frequently speak in something approximating their own voices, the characters in *In Cold Blood* are just cogs in the machine of Capote's prose.

Mailer's idea was to render the language of his real-life characters in the novelistic style known as free-indirect discourse—that is, to paraphrase them in language drawn from their own way of talking. He essentially created a voice between speech and narration.

> Brenda knew her power in conversations like this. She might be that much nearer to thirty-five than thirty, but she hadn't gone into marriage four times without knowing she was pretty attractive on the hoof, and the parole officer, Mont Court, was blond and tall with a husky build. Just an average good-looking American guy, very much on the Mr. Clean side, but all the same, Brenda thought, pretty likable. He was sympathetic to the idea of a second chance, and would flex it out with you if there was a good reason. If not, he would come down pretty hard. That was how she read him. He seemed just the kind of man for Gary.[15]

This style enabled Mailer to avoid the reductionism that was the consequence of Capote's decision to maintain the impression of journalistic detachment, and it allowed him to create open characters—that is, characters who are not entirely subjected to the mediating distortions of the authorial voice—without losing control of his narrative.

Having withdrawn his own voice from the text, on the other hand, Mailer could not place his involvement in its creation in the foreground, as he had done in *The Armies of the Night*. This problem he solved by elevating the character of Lawrence Schiller to a key role in the second half of the book. Schiller, the man who went out to Utah to buy up the rights to Gilmore's story and who eventually signed Mailer up to write it, is more than the representative of the journalist. He is a continual reminder that Gilmore's death (and the deaths of the two men Gilmore killed) is being turned to commercial use. You think, What a carrion bird is this Larry Schiller. Then you realize that you are holding in your hands the very commodity he has created. You are a shareholder in Gilmore, Inc. *The Executioner's Song* brings the old question about fiction that modernism had apparently drained of interest—Can the text justly mirror reality?—back to life. It raises the ethical stakes of reading.

In keeping himself out of *In Cold Blood*, Capote was working for an illusion of transparency. He wanted to be a mirror to events. He had his own interpretation of the killers, but it was a psychological interpretation, and he quoted an article from a psychology journal to express it. He did not see a literary significance in his material. What Mailer saw in *his* material—as Schiller had already shaped it, according to which rights he could secure and which he couldn't; but we are privy to all the machinations—was a love story. What makes *The Executioner's Song* novelistic is not the character of Gilmore but the character of Gilmore's girlfriend, Nicole Barrett. She, not Gary, is the hero of the story, and the recognition that she is dramatically the equal of Gilmore is crucial to an appreciation of the book.

Half of the Gilmore story has to do with his struggle to force the Utah authorities to execute him, but the other half has to do with his struggle to persuade Nicole to die with him by committing suicide, and this second struggle is the novelist's home ground. Nicole is a promiscuous and scatterbrained young woman, with two kids,

living on welfare, and Gilmore is a cold and clever con. His whole
personality is driven by the desire to control; this, more than anything else, is what motivates his crusade to have his death sentence
carried out on his terms. He wishes (to offer the textual analogy) to
be the author of all destinies, and he needs to suck Nicole into the
grave with him. But she breaks free. Gilmore is about death, and
Nicole is, in the end, for life. There is no one quite like her in contemporary American literature, and she is possibly Mailer's greatest
creation. One wonders if he knows it.

Life in the Stone Age

I

If you advised a college student today to tune in, turn on, and drop out, she would probably call campus security. Few things sound less glamorous now than "the counterculture," a term many people are likely to associate with Charles Manson. Writing about that period feels a little like rummaging around in history's dustbin. Just thirty-five years ago, though, everyone was writing about the counterculture, for everyone thought that the American middle class would never be the same. The American middle class never is the same for very long, of course; it's much too insecure to resist a new self-conception when one is offered. But the change that the counterculture made in American life has become nearly impossible to calculate—thanks partly to the exaggerations of people who hate the sixties, and partly to the exaggerations of people who hate the people who hate the sixties. The subject could use the attention of some people who really don't care.

The difficulties begin with the word "counterculture" itself. Though it has been from the beginning the name for the particular style of sentimental radicalism that flourished briefly in the late

1960s, it's a little misleading. For during those years the countercul-ture *was* the culture—or the primary object of the culture's atten-tion, which in America is pretty much the same thing—and that is really the basis of its interest. It had all the attributes of a typical mass-culture episode: it was a lifestyle that could be practiced on weekends; it came into fashion when the media discovered it and went out of fashion when the media lost interest; and it was, from the moment it penetrated the middle class, thoroughly commercial-ized. Its failure to grasp this last fact about itself is the essence of its sentimentalism.

The essence of its radicalism is a little more complicated. The general idea was the rejection of the norms of adult middle-class life; but the rejection was made in a profoundly middle-class spirit. Middle-class Americans are a driven, pampered, puritanical, self-indulgent group of people. Before the sixties, these contradictions were rationalized by the principle of deferred gratification: you exer-cised self-discipline in order to gain entrance to a profession, you showed deference to those above you on the career ladder, and ma-terial rewards followed and could be enjoyed more or less promiscu-ously. To many people, the counterculture alternative looked like simple hedonism: sex, drugs, and rock 'n' roll (with some instant so-cial justice on the side). But the counterculture wasn't hedonistic; it was puritanical. It was, for that matter, virtually Hebraic: the par-ents were worshiping false gods, and the students who tore up (or dropped out of) the university in an apparent frenzy of self-destruction—for wasn't the university their gateway to the good life?—were, in effect, smashing the golden calf.

There was a fair amount of flagrant sensual gratification, all of it crucial to the pop culture appeal of the whole business; but it is a mistake to characterize the pleasure-taking as amoral. It is only "fun" to stand in the rain for three days with a hundred thousand chemically demented people, listening to interminable and in-escapable loud music and wondering if you'll ever see your car again, if you also believe in some inchoate way that you are partici-pating in the creation of the New World. The name of the new god was authenticity, and it was unmistakably the jealous type. It demanded an existence of programmatic hostility to the ordinary modes of middle-class life, and even to the ordinary modes of consciousness—to whatever was mediated, accomodationist, materialistic, and, even trivially, false. Like most of the temporary gods of the secular society, the principle of authenticity was merely paid lip service to by most of the people who flocked to its altar; and when the sixties were over, those people went happily off to other shrines. But there were some people who took the principle to heart, who flagellated their consciences in its service, and who, even after the sixties had passed, continued to obsess about being "co-opted."

There are two places in American society where this strain of puritanism persists. One is the academy, with its fetish of the unconditioned. The other is the high end of pop music criticism—the kind of criticism that complains, for instance, about the commercialism of MTV. Since pop music is by definition commercial, it may be hard to see how pop music commercialism can ever be a problem. But for many people who take pop music seriously, it is *the* problem, and its history essentially begins with *Rolling Stone*.

2

Rolling Stone was born in the semi-idyllic, semi-hysterical atmosphere of northern California in the late sixties. It began in San Francisco in 1967, and was edited there for ten years before it was moved to New York. The man who founded it, and who remains its publisher today, was Jann Wenner. In many accounts of *Rolling Stone*—and notably in the excellent history of the magazine by Robert Draper—Wenner figures as both the hero and the villain of the tale, the man who seized the moment and then betrayed it. This verges on making Wenner a little more complicated than he actually is. An opportunistic, sentimental, shrewd celebrity hound, Wenner was the first person in journalism to see what people in the music business already knew, and what people in the advertising business would soon realize: that rock music had become a fixture of American middle-class life. It had created a market.

Wenner knew this because he himself was the prototypical fan.

He was born in 1946, in the first wave of the baby boom—his father would make a fortune selling baby formula for the children to whom the son later sold magazines—and he started *Rolling Stone* (he is supposed to have said) in order to meet John Lennon. He met Lennon; and he met and made pals with many more of his generation's entertainment idols, who, once they had become friends, and with or without editorial justification, turned up regularly on the covers of his magazine. Wenner was not looking for celebrity himself; he was only, like most Americans, a shameless worshiper of the stars. "I always felt that Jann had a real fan's mentality," one of his friends and associates, William Randolph Hearst III, explained. "He wanted to hang out with Mick Jagger because Mick was cool, not because he wanted to tell people that *he* was cool as a result of knowing Mick."[1]

The person who is interested in Mick mainly because he thinks that Mick is cool is the perfect person to run a magazine devoted to serious fandom. But he is a potential liability at a magazine devoted to serious criticism. Wenner was not a devotee of the authentic, not even a hypocritical one. He was a hustler; he believed in show biz, and he saw, for instance, nothing unethical about altering a review to please a record company he hoped to have as an advertiser. "We're gonna be better than *Billboard*!" is the sort of thing he would say to encourage his staff when morale was low.[2] Morale was not thereby improved. For the people who produced Wenner's magazine took the sixties much more seriously than Wenner did. It wasn't merely that, like many editors, Wenner demonstrated a rude indifference to the rhythms of magazine production, commissioning new covers at the last minute and that sort of thing. It was that he didn't seem to grasp the world-historical significance of the movement that his magazine was spearheading. "Here we were," Jon Carroll, a former staffer, said, "believing we were involved in the greatest cultural revolution since the sack of Rome. And he was running around with starlets. We thought that Jann was the most trivial sort of fool."[3]

Draper's view, in his book on the magazine, is an only slightly less inflated version of Carroll's view. "Quite correctly," he writes of

the early years, "the employees of *Rolling Stone* magazine saw themselves as leaders and tastemakers—the best minds of their generation."[4] *Rolling Stone* covered the whole of the youth culture, though
it generally steered clear, at Wenner's insistence, of radical politics.
("Get back," Wenner pleaded with his editors in 1970, after the
shootings at Kent State inspired them to try to "detrivialize" the
magazine, "get back to where we once belonged.")[5] But the back-
bone of the magazine always was its music criticism, and its special
achievement was that it provided an arena for the development of
the lyrical, pedantic, and hyperbolic writing about popular music
that is part of the sixties' literary legacy. *Rolling Stone* wasn't the only
place where this style of criticism flourished, but it was the biggest.
Rolling Stone institutionalized the genre.

This is what Draper responds to in the magazine, and where his
sympathies as a historian lie. His principal sources are from the editorial side of the magazine, because that is his principal interest. He
writes at some length about the editorial staff's travails, but he gives
a perfunctory account, as though he found it too distasteful to inves-
tigate, of, for example, the business staff's "Marketing through Music" campaign—a newsletter for "Marketing, Advertising, and Music
Executives," circulated in the mid-eighties, that encouraged corporate sponsorship of rock concerts and the use of rock stars and rock
songs in advertising. The business deals are mentioned in his book,
but they are generally treated from the outside, and always as inimi-
cal to the true spirit of the magazine. From the point of view of social
history, though, "Marketing through Music" is the interesting part of
the story. For rock music, like every other mass-market commodity,
is about making money. Everyone who writes about popular music
knows that before Sam Phillips, the proprietor of Sun Records,
recorded Elvis Presley in 1954, he used to go around saying, "If I
could find a white man who had the Negro sound, I could make a
million dollars."[6] But Elvis himself is somehow imagined to have
had little to do with this sort of gross commercial calculation, and
when Albert Goldman's biography of Elvis appeared in 1981 and described Presley as a musically incurious and manipulative pop star,
the rock critical establishment descended on Goldman in wrath.

All rock stars want to make money, for the same reasons everyone else in a liberal society wants to make money: more toys and more autonomy. Bill Wyman, when he went off to become the Rolling Stones' bass player, told his mother that he'd only have to wear his hair long for a few years, and he'd get a nice house and a car out of it at the end.[7] Even the Doors, quintessential late-sixties performers who thought they were making an Important Musical Statement, began when Jim Morrison ran into Ray Manzarek, who became the group's keyboard player, and recited some poetry he'd written. "I said that's it," Manzarek later explained. "It seemed as though, if we got a group together, we could make a million dollars."[8] Ray, meet Sam.

Pop stars aren't simply selling a sound; they're selling an image, and one reason the stars of the sixties made such an effective appeal to middle-class taste is that their images went, so to speak, all the way through. Their stage personalities were understood to be continuous with their offstage personalities—an impression enhanced by the fact that, in a departure from Tin Pan Alley tradition, most sixties performers wrote their own material. But the images, too, were carefully managed. The Beatles, for example, were the children of working-class families: they were what the average suburban teenager would consider tough characters. Their breakthrough into mainstream popular music came when their manager, Brian Epstein, transformed them into four cheeky but lovable lads, an image that delighted the suburban middle class. The Rolling Stones, apart from Wyman, were much more middle-class. Mick Jagger attended (on scholarship) the London School of Economics; his girlfriend Marianne Faithfull, herself a pop performer, was the daughter of a professor of Renaissance literature. Brian Jones's father was an aeronautical engineer, and Jones, who founded the band, had what was virtually an intellectual's interest in music. He wrote articles for *Jazz News*, for instance, something one cannot imagine a Beatle doing. But when it became the Stones' turn to enter the mainstream, the lovable image was already being used in a way that looked unbeatable. So (as Wyman quite matter-of-factly describes it in his memoir, *Stone Alone*) *their* manager, Andrew Oldham, cast them as rude boys, which delighted middle-class teenagers in a different and even more thrilling way.

These images enjoyed long-term success in part because they suited the performers' natural talents and temperaments. But it is pointless to think of scrutinizing them by the lights of authenticity. One reason popular culture gives pleasure is that it relieves people of this whole anxiety of trying to determine whether what they're enjoying is real or fake. Mediation is the sine qua non of the experience. Authenticity is a high-culture problem. Unless, of course, you're trying to run a cultural revolution. In which case you will need to think that there is some essential relation between the unadulterated spirit of rock 'n' roll and personal and social liberation. "The magic's in the music," the Lovin' Spoonful used to sing. "Believe in the magic, it will set you free." The Lovin' Spoonful was an unpretentious teenybopper band if there ever was one; but those lyrics turn up frequently in Draper's book. For they (or some intellectually enriched version of them) constitute the credo of the higher rock criticism.

The central difficulty faced by the serious pop exegete is to explain how it is that a band with a manager and a promoter and sales of millions of records that plays "Satisfaction" is less calculating than a band with a manager and a promoter and sales of millions of records that plays "Itchycoo Park" (assuming, perhaps too hastily, that a case cannot be made for "Itchycoo Park"). Theorizing about the difference can produce nonsense of an unusual transparency. "Rock is a mass-produced music that carries a critique of its own means of production," the British pop-music sociologist Simon Frith has explained; "it is a mass-consumed music that constructs its own 'authentic' audience."[9] To which all one can say is that when you have to put the word *authenticity* in quotation marks, you're in trouble.

The problem is more simply solved by reference to a pop music genealogy that was invented in the late 1960s and that has been embraced by nearly everyone in the business ever since—by the musicians, by the industry, and by the press. This is the notion that genuine rock 'n' roll is the direct descendant of the blues, a music whose authenticity it would be a sacrilege to question. The historical scheme according to which the blues begat rhythm and blues, which begat rockabilly, which begat Elvis, who (big evolutionary leap here) gave us the Beatles, was canonized by *Rolling Stone*. It is the basis for *The Rolling Stone Illustrated History of Rock 'n' Roll* (1976), edited by Jim Miller, which is one of the best collections of classic rock criticism; and it's the basis for *Rock of Ages: The Rolling Stone History of Rock 'n' Roll* (1986), by Ed Ward, Geoffrey Stokes, and Ken Tucker, which reads a little bit like the kind of thing you would get if you put three men in a room with some typewriters and a stack of paper and told them that they couldn't come out until they had written *The Rolling Stone History of Rock 'n' Roll*.

All genealogies are suspect, since they have an inherent bias against contingency, and genealogies to which critics and their subjects subscribe with equal enthusiasm are doubly suspect. The idea that rock 'n' roll is simply a style of popular music, and that there was popular music before rock 'n' roll (and not produced by black men) that might have some relation to, say, "Yesterday" or "Wild Horses" or "Sad-Eyed Lady of the Lowlands"—songs that do not exactly call Chuck Berry to mind, let alone Muddy Waters—is largely unknown to rock criticism. The reason that the link between Elvis Presley and the Beatles feels strained is that we are really talking about the difference between party music for teenagers and pop anthems for the middle class—between music to jump up and down to and music with a bit of a brow. Even the music to jump up and down to is a long way from the blues: adolescents from Great Neck did not go into hysterics in the presence of Blind Lemon Jefferson. An entertainment phenomenon like Mick Jagger, with his mysteriously acquired Cockney-boy-from-Memphis accent, surely has as much relation to a white teen idol like the young Frank Sinatra as he does to a black bluesman like Robert Johnson. Except that Robert Johnson is the real thing. Of course some of the music of Jagger and Richards and Lennon and McCartney appropriated the sound of American black rhythm and blues: that's precisely the least authentic thing about it.

This is not to say that rock 'n' roll (or the music of the young Frank Sinatra, for that matter) doesn't come from real feeling and doesn't touch real feeling. And it's not to say that there aren't legitimate distinctions to be made among degrees of fakery in popular music. When one is discussing Percy Faith's 1975 disco version of "Hava Nagilah," it is appropriate to use the term "inauthentic." But the wider the appeal a popular song has, the more zealously it resists the terms of art. The most affecting song of the 1960s was (let's say) the version of "With a Little Help from My Friends" that Joe Cocker sang at Woodstock on August 17, 1969—an imitation British music-hall number performed in upstate New York by a white man from Sheffield trying to sound like Ray Charles. On that day, probably nothing could have sounded more genuine.

3

Spiro Agnew thought that the helpful friends were drugs, which is a reminder that the counterculture was indeed defining itself against something. The customary reply to a charge like Agnew's was that he was mistaking a gentle celebration of togetherness for a threat against the established order—that he was, in sixties language, being uptight. Agnew's attacks were ignorant and cynical enough; but the responses, though from people understandably a little uptight themselves, were disingenuous. Few teenagers in 1967 thought that the line "I get high with a little help from my friends" was an allusion to the exhilaration of good conversation. "I get high" is a pretty harmless drug reference. But it is a drug reference.

The classic case of this sort of thing is "Lucy in the Sky with Diamonds," also on the *Sgt. Pepper's* album. When the press got the idea that the title encrypted the initials LSD, John Lennon, who had written the song, expressed outrage. "Lucy in the Sky with Diamonds," he allowed, was the name his little boy had given a drawing he had made at school and brought home to show his father; and this bit of lore has been attached to the history of *Sgt. Pepper's* to indicate how hysterically hostile the old culture was to the new. No doubt the story about the drawing is true. On the other hand, if "Lucy in the Sky with Diamonds" is not a song about an acid trip, it is hard to know what sort of song it is.

Drugs were integral to sixties rock 'n' roll culture in three ways.

The most publicized way, and the least interesting, has to do with the conspicuous consumption of drugs by rock 'n' roll performers, a subject that has been written about ad nauseam. Lennon eating LSD as though it were candy, Keith Richards undergoing complete blood transfusions in an effort to cure himself of heroin addiction ("How do you like my new blood?" he would ask his friends after a treatment)—these are stories of mainly tabloid interest, though they are important to rock 'n' roll mythology, since addiction and early death are part of jazz and blues mythology, as well. The drug consumption was real enough (though one doesn't see it mentioned that since the body builds a resistance to hallucinogens, it is not surprising that Lennon ate acid like candy: he couldn't have been getting much of a kick from it after a while). Some people famously died of drug abuse; many others destroyed their careers and their lives. But overindulgence is a hazard of all celebrity; it's part of the modern culture of fame. That rock 'n' roll musicians overindulged with drugs is not, historically, an especially notable phenomenon.

Then there are the references to drugs in the songs themselves. Sometimes the references were fairly obscure: "Light My Fire," for instance, the title of the Doors' biggest hit, was a phrase taken from an Aldous Huxley piece in praise of mescaline (as was the name of the group itself, taken from the title of Huxley's book *The Doors of Perception* [1954]). Sometimes the references were overt (Jefferson Airplane's "White Rabbit," or the Velvet Underground's "Heroin"). Most often, though, it was simply understood that the song was describing or imitating a drug experience: "Lucy in the Sky with Diamonds," "Strawberry Fields," "Mr. Tambourine Man," "A Whiter Shade of Pale." The message (such as it was) of these songs usually involved the standard business about "consciousness expansion" already being purveyed by gurus like Allen Ginsberg and Alan Watts: once you have (with whatever assistance) stepped beyond the veil, you will prefer making love to making war, and so forth. Sometimes there was the suggestion that drugs open your eyes to the horror of things as they are—an adventure for the spiritually fortified only. ("Reality is for people who can't face drugs," as Tom Waits used to say.) The famous line in the Beatles' "A Day in the Life" was meant to catch both senses: "I'd love to turn you on." It was all facile enough; but the idea was not simply "Let's party."

What was most distinctive about late-sixties popular music, though, was not that some of the performers used drugs, or that some of the songs were about drugs. It was that late-sixties rock was music designed for people to listen to while they were on drugs. The music was a prepackaged sensory stimulant. This was a new development. Jazz musicians might sometimes be junkies, but jazz was not music performed for junkies. A lot of late-sixties rock music, though, plainly advertised itself as a kind of complementary good for recreational drugs. This explains many things about the character of popular music in the period—in particular, the unusual length of the songs. There is really only one excuse for buying a record with a twelve-minute drum solo.

How the history of popular music reflects the social history of drug preference is a research topic that calls for some fairly daunting field work. It was clear enough in the late sixties, though, that the most popular music was music that projected a druggy aura of one fairly specific kind or another. Folk rock, for example, became either seriously mellow (Donovan or the Youngbloods) or raucous and giggly (Country Joe and the Fish), sounds suggesting that marijuana might provide a useful enhancement of the listening experience. Music featuring pyrotechnical instrumentalists (Cream or Ten Years After) had an overdriven, methedrine sort of sound. In the 1970s, a lot of successful popular music was designed to go well with cocaine, a taste shift many of the sixties groups couldn't adjust to quickly enough. (The Rolling Stones were an exception.)

But the featured drugs of the late sixties were the psychedelics: psilocybin, mescaline, and, especially, LSD. They were associated with the Beatles scene through Lennon, who even before *Sgt. Pepper's* had apparently developed a kind of religious attachment to acid. And LSD was the drug most closely identified with the San Francisco scene, especially with the Grateful Dead, a group that had been on hand in 1965 when Ken Kesey and the Merry Pranksters took their "acid test" bus trips, and whose equipment had been paid for by Timothy Leary himself. It would seem that once a person was on a hallucinogen, the particular kind of music he or she was listening to would be largely irrelevant; but there were bands, like the Dead, whose drug aura was identifiably psychedelic.

You didn't have to be on drugs to enjoy late-sixties rock 'n' roll, as many people have survived to attest; and this is an important fact. For from a mainstream point of view, the music's drug aura was simply one aspect of the psychedelic fashion that between 1967 and 1969 swept through popular art (black-light posters), photography (fish-eye lenses), cinema (jump cuts and light shows), clothing (tie-dye), coloring (Day-Glo), and speech ("you turn me on"). Psychedelia expressed the counterculture sensibility in its most pop form. It said: spiritual risk-taker, uninhibited, enemy of the System. It advertised liberation and hipness in the jargon and imagery of the drug experience. And the jargon wasn't restricted to people under thirty, or to dropouts. In the late sixties, the drug experience became a universal metaphor for the good life. Commercials for honey encouraged you to "get high with honey." The Ford Motor Company invited you to test-drive a Ford and "blow your mind." For people who did not use drugs, the music was a plausible imitation drug experience because almost every commodity in the culture was pretending to some kind of imitation drug experience.

Psychedelia, and the sensibility attached to it, was a media-driven phenomenon. In April 1966, *Time* ran a story on the Carnaby Street, mods and rockers, Beatles and Rolling Stones scene in London. In fact, that scene was on its last legs when the article appeared; but many Americans were induced to vacation in London, which revived the local economy, and the summer of 1966 became the summer of "Swinging London." Swinging London was perfect mass-media material—sexy, upbeat, and fantastically photogenic. So when twenty thousand people staged a "Human Be-In" in Golden Gate Park in January 1967, the media were on hand. Here was a domestic version of the British phenomenon: hippies, Diggers, Hell's Angels, music, "free love," and LSD—the stuff of a hundred feature stories and photo essays. The media discovery of the hippies led to the media discovery of the Haight-Ashbury, and the summer of 1967 became the San Francisco "Summer of Love," that year's edition of Swinging London. *Sgt. Pepper's* was released in June, and the reign of psychedelia was established. The whole episode lasted a little less than three years—about the tenure of the average successful television series.

Once the media discovered it, the counterculture ceased being a youth culture and became a commercial culture for which youth was a principal market—at which point its puritanism (inhibitions are a middle-class superstition) became for many people an excuse for libertinism (inhibitions are a drag). LSD, for instance, was peddled by Leary through magazines like *Playboy*, where, in a 1966 interview, he explained that "in a carefully prepared, loving LSD session, a woman will inevitably have several hundred orgasms." This was exactly the sort of news *Playboy* existed to print, and the interviewer followed up by asking whether this meant that Leary found himself irresistible to women. Leary allowed that it did, but proved reluctant to give all the credit to a drug, merely noting that "any charismatic person who is conscious of his own mythic potency awakens this basic hunger in women and pays reverence to it at the level that is harmonious and appropriate at the time."[10]

Playboy is not a magazine for dropouts, and the idea that counterculture drugs were really aphrodisiacs was an idea that appealed not to teenagers (who do not require hormonal assistance) but to middle-aged men. ("Good sex would have to be awfully good before it was better than on pot," Norman Mailer mused, presumably for the benefit of his fellow forty-five-year-olds, in *The Armies of the Night*, in 1968.)[11] It was not teenagers who put Tom Wolfe's account of Kesey's LSD quackery, *The Electric Kool-Aid Acid Test* (1968), on the hardcover best-seller list. Hippies did not buy tickets to see *Hair* on Broadway, where it opened in 1968 and played over seventeen hundred performances, or read Charles Reich's homage to bell-bottom pants in the *New Yorker*. People living on communes did not make *Laugh-In*, Hollywood's version of the swinging psychedelic style, the highest-rated show on television in the 1968–69 season. And, of course, students did not design, manufacture, distribute, and enjoy the profits from rock 'n' roll records. Those who attack the counterculture for disrupting what they take to have been the traditional American way of life ought to look to the people who ex-

ploited and disseminated it—good capitalists all—before they look
to the young people who were encouraged to consume it.

4

After the Altamont concert disaster, in December 1969, when a fan
was killed a few feet from where the Rolling Stones were performing, psychedelia lost its middle-class appeal. More unpleasant news
followed in 1970—the Kent State and Jackson State shootings, the
Manson Family trials, the deaths by overdose of famous rock stars.
And even more quickly than it had sprung up, the media fascination with the counterculture evaporated. But the counterculture,
stripped of its idealism and its sexiness, lingered on. If you drove
down the main street of any small city in America in the 1970s,
you saw clusters of teenagers standing around, wearing long hair
and bell-bottom jeans, listening to Led Zeppelin, furtively getting
stoned. This was the massive middle of the baby-boom generation,
the remnant of the counterculture—a remnant that was much bigger than the original, but in which the media had lost interest.
These people were not activists or dropouts. They had very few public voices. One of them was Hunter Thompson's.[12]

Thompson came to *Rolling Stone* in 1970, an important moment
in the magazine's history. Wenner had fired Greil Marcus, a music
critic with an American studies degree who was then his reviews editor, for running a negative review of an inferior Dylan album called
Self-Portrait (it was one of Wenner's rules that the big stars must
always be hyped); and most of the politically minded members of
the staff quit after the "Get Back" episode following Kent State.
There were financial problems as well. By the end of 1970, *Rolling
Stone* was a quarter million dollars in debt. Hugh Hefner, who is to
testosterone what Wenner is to rock 'n' roll, offered to buy the magazine, but Wenner found other angels. Among them were the record
companies. Columbia Records and Elektra were delighted to advance their friends at *Rolling Stone* a year's worth of advertising;
Rolling Stone and the record companies, after all, were in the same
business.

The next problem was to sell magazines. (*Rolling Stone* relies heavily on newsstand sales, since its readers are not the sort of people who can be counted on to fill out subscription renewal forms with any degree of regularity.) Here Wenner had two strokes of good fortune. The first was a long interview he obtained with John Lennon, the first time most people had ever heard a Beatle not caring to sound lovable. It sold many magazines. The second was the arrival of Thompson.

Thompson was a well-traveled, free-spirited hack whose résumé included a stint as sports editor of the *Jersey Shore Herald*, a job as general reporter for the *Middletown Daily News*, freelance work out of Puerto Rico for a bowling magazine, a period as South American correspondent for the *National Observer* (during which he suffered some permanent hair loss from stress and drugs), an assignment covering the 1968 presidential campaign for *Pageant*, two unpublished Great American Novels, a little male modeling, and a narrowly unsuccessful campaign for sheriff of Aspen, Colorado. He had actually been discovered for the alternative press by Warren Hinckle, the editor of *Ramparts*, which is when his writing acquired the label "gonzo journalism." But Thompson was interested in *Rolling Stone* because he thought it would help his nascent political career by giving him access to people who had no interest in politics (a good indication of the magazine's political reputation in 1970). A year after signing on, he produced the articles that became *Fear and Loathing in Las Vegas* (1972), a tour de force of pop faction about five days on drugs in Las Vegas. It sold many copies of *Rolling Stone*, and it gave Thompson fortune, celebrity, and a permanent running headline.

Many people who were not young read *Fear and Loathing in Las Vegas* and thought it a witty piece of writing. Wolfe included two selections from Thompson's work in his 1973 anthology, *The New Journalism* (everyone else but Wolfe got only one entry); and this has given Thompson the standing of a man identified with an academically recognized "movement." But Thompson is essentially a writer for teenage boys. *Fear and Loathing in Las Vegas* is *The Catcher in the Rye* on speed: the lost weekend of a disaffected loser who tells his story in a mordant style that is addictively appealing to adolescents with a deep and unspecified grudge against life. Once you understand the target, the thematics make sense. Sexual prowess is part of the Thompson mystique, for example, but the world of his writing is almost entirely male, and sex itself is rarely more than a vague, adult horror; for sex beyond mere bravado is a subject that makes most teenage boys nervous. A vast supply of drugs of every genre and description accompanies the Thompson protagonist and maintains him in a permanent state of dementia; but the drugs have all the verisimilitude of a fourteen-year-old's secret spy kit: these grownups don't realize that the person they are talking to is *completely out of his mind* on dangerous chemicals. The fear and loathing in Thompson's writing is simply Holden Caulfield's fear of growing up—a fear that, in Thompson's case as in Salinger's, is particularly convincing to younger readers because it seems to run from the books straight back to the writer himself.

After the Las Vegas book, *Rolling Stone* assigned Thompson to cover the 1972 presidential campaign. His reports were collected in (inevitably) *Fear and Loathing on the Campaign Trail* (1973). The series began with some astute analysis of primary strategy and the like, salted with irreverent descriptions of the candidates and many personal anecdotes. Thompson's unusual relation to the facts—one piece, which caused a brief stir, reported that Edmund Muskie was addicted to an obscure African drug called Ibogaine—made him the object of some media attention of his own. But eventually the reporting broke down, and Thompson was reduced at the end of his book to quoting at length from the dispatches of his *Rolling Stone* colleague Timothy Crouse (whose own book about the campaign, *The Boys on the Bus* [1973], became an acclaimed exposé of political journalism). Since 1972, Thompson has devoted his career to the maintenance of his legend, and his reporting has mostly been reporting about the Thompson style of reporting, which consists largely of unsuccessful attempts to cover his subjects, and of drug misadventures. He doesn't need to report, of course, because reporting is not what his audience cares about. They care about the escapades of their hero, which are recounted obsessively in his writings, and some of which were the basis for an unwatchable movie called *Where the Buffalo Roam*, released in 1980 and starring Bill Murray.

Thompson left *Rolling Stone* around 1975 and eventually became a columnist for the *San Francisco Examiner*. He began repackaging his pieces in chronicle form in 1979, and collections of his articles' and his correspondence have been coming out regularly ever since. Thompson, in short, is practically the only person in America still living circa 1972. His persona enacts a counterculture sensibility with the utopianism completely leached out. There are no romantic notions about peace and love in his writing, only adolescent paranoia and violence. There is no romanticization of the street, either. Everything disappoints him—an occasionally engaging attitude that is also, of course, romanticism of the very purest sort. Thompson is the eternally bitter elegist of a moment that never really was—it is significant that his favorite book is *The Great Gatsby*—and that is why he is an ideal writer for a generation that has always felt that it arrived onstage about five minutes after the audience walked out.

5

If all popular culture episodes were only commercial and manipulative, they would not matter to us. The late-sixties counterculture was not, by any means, the shabbiest episode in the postwar era, even if it now seems the most antique. It was imaginative and infectious, and it touched a nerve. A lot of those old idols deserved to be overthrown. And maybe it is a generational thing, but the music still seems tonic. But the faith in popular music, consciousness expansion, and the nonconformist lifestyle that made up the countercultural ethos is likely to strike us today as clearly misplaced. You wonder why it didn't dawn on all those disaffected *Rolling Stone* writers and editors that Wenner was successful precisely because he wasn't the anomaly they took him to be. He was closer to what the moment was all about than they were. But faith in anything can be a valuable sentiment; and what young people in the sixties thought their faith made it possible to do was to tell the truth. Telling the truth turned out to be much harder than they thought it would be, and the culture they imagined was sustaining them turned out not to be "authentically" theirs, and not really sustainable, after all. But those people had not yet become cynics.

The silliest charge brought against the sixties is the charge of moral relativism. Ordinary life must be built on the solid foundations of moral values, the critics who make this charge argue, and the sixties persuaded people that the foundations weren't solid, and that any morality would do that got you through the night. The accusation isn't just wrong about the sixties; it's an injustice to the dignity of ordinary life, which is an irredeemably pragmatic and ungrounded affair. You couldn't make it through even the day if you held every transaction up to scrutiny by the lights of some received moral code. But that is exactly what radicals and counterculture types in the sixties did. They weren't moral relativists. They were moral absolutists. They scrutinized everything, and they believed they could live by the distinctions they made.

There are always people who think this way—people who see that the world is a little fuzzy and proceed to make a religion out of clarity. In the sixties their way of thinking was briefly but memorably a part of the popular culture. Gered Mankowitz, a photographer who accompanied the Rolling Stones on their American tours in the 1960s, once told a story about two groupies who dedicated themselves to the conquest of Mick Jagger. After several years of futile pursuit, they managed to get themselves invited to a house where the Stones were staying, and Mick was persuaded to take both of them to bed. Afterward, though, the girls were disappointed. "He was only so-so," one of them complained. "He tried to come on like Mick Jagger, but he's no Mick Jagger."[13] The real can always be separated from the contrived: wherever that illusion persists, the spirit of the sixties still survives.

The Popist:
Pauline Kael

auline Kael began reviewing movies for the *New Yorker* in
1967. She was not a "discovery." She was forty-eight years
old, and she had already written for nearly every well-
known magazine in America but the *New Yorker*, including
the *New Republic, Partisan Review*, the *Atlantic, Mademoiselle, Holiday, Vogue, Life*, and *McCall's*. Before coming to New York, in the
mid-sixties, she had made weekly radio broadcasts about movies on
KPFA in San Francisco; she had been contributing regularly to jour-
nals like *Film Quarterly* and *Sight and Sound* since 1953; and a collection of her pieces, *I Lost It at the Movies*, had come out in 1965
and sold 150,000 paperback copies. Mr. Shawn was not taking a
gamble on a rookie.

In 1967, the *New Yorker* was the most successful magazine in
America. It owed its prosperity to a formula that can no longer be
duplicated: it was a general-interest commercial magazine for
people who disliked commercialism and who rarely subscribed to
general-interest magazines—a magazine, essentially, for people who

didn't read magazines. For in the fifties and sixties, a literate and un-
stuffy anticommercialism was still a cherished ingredient of upper-
middle-class taste, and by catering to it, the *New Yorker* was able to
deliver to advertisers several hundred thousand well-educated and
affluent people who could be reached through almost no other
medium.

It did so with an editorial product rigorously manufactured to
avoid any semblance of the sensational, the prurient, or the merely
topical—any semblance, that is, of the things educated people
could be assumed to associate with commercial media. It also
avoided, less famously but with equal diligence, anything that
hinted at cultural pretension. And this policy, too, was based on a
genuine insight into the psychology of its audience. For *New Yorker*
readers, though proud of their education and their taste, were intellectually insecure. They did not need to be told who Proust and
Freud and Stravinsky were, but they were glad, at the same time,
not to be expected to know anything terribly specific about them.
They were intelligent people who were nevertheless extremely wary
of being out-browed. The *New Yorker* was enormously attentive to
this insecurity. It pruned from its pieces anything that might come
across as allusive or knowing, and it promoted, in its writing and
cartoons, a sensibility which took urbanity to be perfectly compatible with a certain kind of naïveté. The *New Yorker* made it possible
to feel that being an antisophisticate was the mark of true sophistication, and that any culture worth having could be had without special aesthetic equipment or intellectual gymnastics.

Pauline Kael made it possible for people to feel this way about
the movies, and although that sounds like a modest accomplishment, it was not. It required disarming both phobias in the sensibility the *New Yorker* had so successfully identified: the fear of too low
and the fear of too high. It meant overcoming the intelligent person's resistance to the pulpiness, the corniness, and the general
moral and aesthetic schmaltz of Hollywood movies, but without re-
fining those things away by some type of critical alchemy. The *New
Yorker*'s readers did not want an invitation to slum. But they didn't
want to be told that appreciating movies was something that called
for a command of the "grammar of film," either. They needed to be-

lieve that it was possible to enjoy the movies without becoming either of the two things *New Yorker* readers would sooner have died than be taken for: idiots or snobs.

This was precisely the approach to movies Kael had devoted her pre–*New Yorker* career to perfecting. She heaped scorn on the moguls, and she heaped scorn on the cinéastes. She joined the magazine at the moment the movies seemed to many people suddenly to have caught up with the rest of American culture: her first piece was a seven-thousand-word defense of *Bonnie and Clyde*. She kept the attention of the magazine's readers during a time when movies seemed to mean a great deal to them. And she continued to keep it well after the movies ceased being important in most of those readers' lives. By the time she retired, in 1991, the *New Yorker's* traditional readership had lost its cohesion as a distinctive taste group, and the type of movies Kael had made her name by championing had nearly vanished, too. After her retirement, she stopped reviewing; she died in 2001. But she had produced a generation of epigoni, and the manner of appreciation she invented has become the standard manner of popular-culture criticism in America.

2

Kael was born in Petaluma, California, in 1919. Her parents were Jewish immigrants from Poland; they ran a chicken farm. Like many people who fall in love with the movies, Kael succumbed when she was a teenager. She became enamored of two completely different kinds of movies, and the simplest way to describe her career is to say that she awoke in middle age to find them miraculously reborn together on a single screen. Her first infatuation was with the Hollywood genre movies of the 1930s: newspaper pictures like *The Front Page* (1931), comedies like *Million Dollar Legs* (1932) and *Duck Soup* (1933), and, especially, the screwballs, which began appearing in 1934—"the year," as she put it in her long and swoony essay on Cary Grant, "when *The Thin Man* and *Twentieth Century* and *It Happened One Night* changed American movies."[1] It was also the year Kael turned fifteen.

Kael thought that these were great movies, but it was not "as movies" that she admired them. She did not esteem them for their realization of the possibilities of cinematic form. She esteemed them for their indifference to the idea of "the possibilities of cinematic form," and in particular for the death blow they delivered to the high-minded sentimentality—what she described as the "calendar-art guck"—of the silent tradition. The silents, she thought, had encouraged a kind of "dream aesthetic," which associated film with the movements of the subconscious and led to the production of a lot of misty allegories about "purity" and "morality." When characters started speaking, the mists went away, and so did the purity and morality. "The talkies," as she once put it, "were a great step down."[2]

Two things, in her view, made those thirties movies go: the writing and the acting. Her 1971 essay on *Citizen Kane* is usually remembered as an attack on Orson Welles and the cult of the director, a kind of sequel to her polemic against auteur theory, "Circles and Squares" (1963). But the point of the essay is that the reason it is wrong to talk about *Citizen Kane* as a bolt from cinema heaven is not that Welles was not really a genius; Kael thought he really was a genius. It is because *Citizen Kane* (released in 1941) was the crowning achievement of thirties movie-making, the capstone of the tradition *The Front Page* had started. It was, she thought, simply "the biggest newspaper picture of them all."[3] What made it great was the script—by Herman J. Mankiewicz, who had been involved, as a writer or producer, in many of the movies Kael loved, including *Million Dollar Legs* and *Duck Soup*—and the acting. Charles Foster Kane was the one role in his career in which Welles was perfectly cast; for Welles was a sort of Kane himself, a theatrical *monstre sacré*, a boy wonder and a mountebank. Welles may have stolen half the writing credit from Mankiewicz, but Mankiewicz showed Welles naked to the world.

Then the parade ended. The commercial failure of *Citizen Kane*—the critics acclaimed it, but the industry, intimidated by the other real-life Kane, William Randolph Hearst, failed to stand behind it—drove Welles into the movie wilderness. And it marked,

Kael believed, the demise of the supremely smart but supremely accessible Hollywood entertainments of the 1930s. Except in odd corners of the business, such as the comedies of Preston Sturges, irreverence disappeared from the screen. The movies fell into the hands of self-righteous, fellow-traveling hacks: earnestness was prized above wit, and politically correct mediocrity was promoted over talent. "Morality" was back in the saddle. It remained there for twenty-five years.

Kael had a second infatuation, though, and it was with a kind of movie that had nothing generic about it, a kind of movie in which the director *was* the star. This was the European realist tradition, above all the early movies of Jean Renoir—*Boudu Saved from Drowning* (1931), *Grand Illusion* (1937), and *The Rules of the Game* (1939)—but also the work of the Italian neorealists, like Roberto Rossellini's *Open City* (1945) and Vittorio De Sica's *Shoeshine* (1946) and *Miracle in Milan* (1951), and of Max Ophuls, particularly *The Earrings of Madame De . . .* (1953), a movie Kael called "perfection."[4] The technical term for the quality many of these movies (though not Ophuls's) share is "open form." The camera directs its gaze with equal empathy at every facet of the world viewed. Ordinary things are not scanted or rushed over, since the gods, if there are any, are probably in the details; but grand things are not put into quotation marks, or set up to be knocked down, either, since great emotions are as much a part of life as anything else. The door is opened onto the world "as it is," without scrims or stage directions; and the world is left, at the end, in the same condition, unarranged, and unboxed by moral resolution.

When Kael arrived at the *New Yorker*, these were her touchstones—Cary Grant and Carole Lombard, Rossellini and Renoir. It was a canon exceptional less for what it included than for what it left out. Kael's taste for genre pictures, for instance, was not indiscriminate. She had a distant respect for the early Westerns of John Ford, like *Stagecoach* (1939), because they handled popular iconography in a classical spirit; but she hated *High Noon* (1952), *Shane* (1953), and *The Man Who Shot Liberty Valence* (1962) for their moralism and their mythic fakery, and she rarely passed up an occasion to say so. She had no special enthusiasm, either, for film noir, a genre barely mentioned in her enormous final collection from all her writings, *For Keeps* (1995), or for other low-rent forms, such as horror and science fiction.

Her line about Frank Capra is famous: "No one else can balance the ups and downs of wistful sentiment the way Capra can," she said of *Mr. Smith Goes to Washington* (1939), "and if anyone else should learn to, kill him."[5] She dismissed most of Hollywood's postwar efforts at serious moral drama, movies like *The Best Years of Our Lives* (1946) and Chaplin's *Limelight* (1952), as embarrassing imitations of European art films. She regarded *The Red Shoes* (1948) as kitsch on stilts. She considered Fellini pretentious and overrated, and Bergman a "northern Fellini."[6] And for the high-end imports reverentially mulled over by cinéastes in the early sixties— *Hiroshima, mon amour* (1959), *Last Year at Marienbad* (1961), *Red Desert* (1964)—she had pure contempt. She called them "come-dressed-as-the-sick-soul-of-Europe parties,"[7] and she considered them prime specimens of the philistinism of antiphilistinism, intellectual clichés to which repetition and obscurity had given the illusion of profundity.

There were two imports, however, which she did admire: Jean-Luc Godard's *Breathless* (1959; released in the United States in 1960) and François Truffaut's *Shoot the Piano Player* (1960). She was drawn to them because they were, in effect, the sum of the two types of movies that had won her heart in the thirties. They were genre pictures whose forms had been imaginatively opened up: pop plus poetry. So that when *Bonnie and Clyde*, directed by an American disciple of Godard and Truffaut, Arthur Penn, appeared in 1967, it was as though a dream Kael had been having for twenty-five years had come to life. *Bonnie and Clyde* announced, for her, a Hollywood new wave. It was a movement that lasted a decade, and produced a series of stylish entertainments people could care about without feeling trivial or pedantic. The first two *Godfather* movies (1972 and 1974) define the type: straight gangster pictures, but with the visual and moral depth of field of a Renoir.

In the seventies Kael consequently became, despite her dispar-

agement of auteur theory, a devotee of directors. Her favorites—
Coppola, Martin Scorsese, Robert Altman, Bernardo Bertolucci,
Sam Peckinpah, Brian De Palma, Jonathan Demme, Paul Mazursky, Steven Spielberg—were artists of the popular. They loved,
without condescension, exactly what the audience loved and went
to the movies to see: pursuit and capture, sex and violence, love and
death. They loved the story. Spielberg won Kael over in his first feature, *The Sugarland Express* (1974), by his orchestration of one of
the most mundane staples of seventies movie-making, a car chase,
which she described in her review as though it had been a masked
ball shot by Ophuls: "He patterns them; he makes them dance and
crash and bounce back. He handles enormous configurations of ve-
hicles; sometimes they move so sweetly you think he must be woo-
ing them. These sequences are as unforced and effortless-looking as
if the cars themselves—mesmerized—had just waltzed into their idiot formations,"[8] and so on. Even the most authorial of her auteurs,
Bertolucci, showed his understanding of big-screen aesthetics in
his casting: Trintignant, Sanda, Brando, De Niro, Lancaster, Depar-
dieu. People go for the faces.

The reverse side of Kael's taste for cleverness was her distaste for
cynicism. She disliked most of Stanley Kubrick's movies because
she thought they were unfeeling and aloof; she disliked most of
John Cassavetes' because she felt that they showed contempt for
the audience's desire to be entertained. She disliked *The Graduate*
because it seemed to her patently manipulative while pretending to
be original and sincere; and she disliked the Dirty Harry movies because they exploited the visceral appeal of blood. She despised any
filmmaker who assumed that because a thing is popular it must also
be cheap, or that an audience drawn to sex or violence deserves to
have its nose rubbed in it. This standard is the nub of the problem
in her critical judgment.

For the more compelling the movie, the trickier the distinction
between cleverness and cynicism becomes. It's not just that there is
an element of cold-blooded calculation in all successful entertainment; Kael was the last person to have disputed that. It's that the
cold-bloodedness in some of the movies she championed can some-

times seem a little more genuine than the entertainment. Barbara Harris's pathetic anthem in the final scene of *Nashville*, the protracted slow motion of the pig's blood sequence in De Palma's *Carrie*, Brando sticking his chewing gum under the railing at the end of *Last Tango in Paris*: these are scenes that seem to have been created not so much to rip away the last veil of our innocence as to gratify the director's desire to have the last laugh on humanity. Kael didn't defend moments like these in the movies she admired. She just read them differently. She knew perfectly well that De Palma enjoyed being manipulative, but she found his movies playful and witty, rather than smarmy and cynical, just as she found *Nashville* generous and funny, rather than patronizing and dyspeptic. She sensed pathos in places where less partisan or less enraptured viewers sensed satire and even disgust. Kael wasn't interested in satire and disgust. She was a romantic.

3

Between 1967 and 1978, the American film industry turned out *Bonnie and Clyde*, written by David Newman and Robert Benton and produced by Warren Beatty; *Shampoo*, produced by Beatty and written by Robert Towne; Roman Polanski's *Chinatown*, written by Towne; Coppola's first two *Godfather* movies and *The Conversation*; George Lucas's *American Graffiti*, produced by Coppola; Altman's *M*A*S*H*, *McCabe & Mrs. Miller*, and *Nashville*; Peckinpah's *The Wild Bunch* and *Straw Dogs*; Scorsese's *Mean Streets*, which he wrote, and *Taxi Driver*, written by Paul Schrader; Spielberg's *Close Encounters of the Third Kind*, which he wrote; Woody Allen's *Annie Hall*, which he wrote with Marshall Brickman; Mazursky's *An Unmarried Woman*, written by him; *Midnight Cowboy*; *The Graduate*; *Five Easy Pieces*; *The Outlaw Josie Wales*; *Easy Rider*; *The Last Picture Show*; and *The Deer Hunter*. Kael did not admire all these movies; she panned a few. But she responded intensely to most of them (she divided her *New Yorker* column during those years with Penelope Gilliatt), and she shared the sense many of her readers had that these were movies that somehow cut to the bone of the

American experience. She was old enough to appreciate the seren-
dipity of the phenomenon, and she assumed the role of its grand in-
terpreter. She was the Hollywood Dr. Johnson.

Then, in 1978, she actually went there. She was invited by
Beatty, who wanted her help with a movie he was producing. That
project fell through, and she became a story consultant at Para-
mount instead. After six months she was back at the magazine. She
denied it in interviews, but the view of Hollywood from the inside
seems to have turned her stomach; and in 1980, she published a jeremiad called "Why Are Movies So Bad? Or, The Numbers," which
blamed everything on the money.[9]

Well, it usually *is* the money. That happens to be the flag that
commercial culture salutes. But whether it was because material
conditions really had changed, as her essay claimed, or because
Hollywood's imaginative juices had somehow dried up, or simply
because the major screen breakthroughs had all been accomplished, by the end of the 1970s the connection between enjoying a
movie and feeling a shock of recognition, a connection that had
come to seem almost automatic in the decade before, was severed.
It might have been adolescent to have walked out of *Shampoo* or
Five Easy Pieces or *Mean Streets* feeling that you must change your
life, but not even adolescents walked out of *Beverly Hills Cop* or *The
Empire Strikes Back* or *Batman* feeling that way. They were happy to
feel they had gotten the price of the ticket.

Kael responded to this decline in the cultural authority of the
movies in a peculiar way. She began to overpraise. Hyperbolic abandon had always been the virtual signature of her style. The stakes
could never be too high. She equated *Nashville* and the second
Godfather with Melville and Whitman; she equated the opening
night of *Last Tango in Paris* with the opening night of *Le Sacre du
Printemps*. "There are parts of *Jaws*," she wrote in 1976, "that suggest
what Eisenstein might have done if he hadn't intellectualized himself out of reach."[10] And when she didn't like a movie, she wasn't
just irritated or bored; she was the victim of an intellectual mugging.
She condemned *The French Connection* as "total commercial opportunism passing itself off as an Existential view."[11] (Well, yes, but
how was the picture?) She condemned the earnest *Lenny* as "the ul-

timate in modern show-biz sentimentality."[12] Words like "corrupt," "dishonest," "decadent," and, for a while, "fascist" were part of her regular critical vocabulary. *Dirty Harry* she pronounced "a deeply immoral movie."[13]

"Shallowly immoral" would probably have done it. But you cannot compare the movies you love with *Moby Dick* and then let the ones you hate off with a shrug. You have to keep writing as though souls are being saved and lost down at the cineplex every night. In the years when many of her readers found it exciting to treat movies as tests of character, Kael's rhetoric was just excessive enough. You argued about the movie with your friends, and then you picked up the *New Yorker* and argued about it with Kael. But when the same people eventually found themselves content to describe the movies they enjoyed as "a lot of fun" and the movies they didn't enjoy as "pretty stupid," Kael's rhetoric began to seem a little curious.

So did her judgment. It became possible to read one of her rapturous reviews—of, for instance, Philip Kaufman's *Invasion of the Body Snatchers* (1978) ("It may be the best movie of its kind ever made")[14] or Robert Zemeckis's *Used Cars* (1980), which inspired comparisons with *Bringing Up Baby*, *Shampoo*, *Close Encounters of the Third Kind*, and Melville's *The Confidence Man*—and then find the actual movie, when you went to see it, almost unrecognizable. What had made her pulse race so fast? The less portentous the buzz around a movie she wanted to like, the more hyperkinetic her exertions seemed to become. Unpopular or unexceptional efforts by old favorites began to receive shameless raves—as in: "I think De Palma has sprung to the place Altman achieved with films such as *McCabe & Mrs. Miller* and *Nashville* and that Coppola reached with the two *Godfather* movies—that is, to a place where genre is transcended and what we're moved by is the artist's vision."[15] She was reviewing *Blow Out* (1981). And when the whole movie couldn't honorably be rhapsodized, a single scene or even a single line would be given a prominently placed homage, a sort of verbal trailer. This is the lead paragraph of Kael's review of *Tequila Sunrise* (1988), a slightly underpowered romance/thriller that happens to have been written and directed by Robert Towne:

Michelle Pfeiffer tells Mel Gibson how sorry she is that she hurt his feelings. He replies, "C'mon, it didn't hurt that bad," pauses, and adds, "Just lookin' at you hurts more." If a moviegoer didn't already know that *Tequila Sunrise* was the work of a master romantic tantalizer, Gibson's line should cinch it. That's the kind of ritualized confession of love that gave a picture like *To Have and Have Not* its place in moviegoers' affections. What makes the line go ping is that Mel Gibson's blue eyes are wide with yearning as he says it, and Michelle Pfeiffer is so crystalline in her beauty that he seems to be speaking the simple truth. . . . It's a line that Gary Cooper might have spoken to Marlene Dietrich. . . .[16]

Stop! I give up! I'll see the movie!

What had evaporated was the consensus that it all mattered. The result was a dissociation between the experience and the commentary. Kael's disquisitions on the psychology of the American movie audience, which characterized her early criticism, gave way to page after page of word-painting. She would paraphrase almost the whole story line, and every clever bit in the movie seemed to end up in the review. After you had read her review of *Zelig*, the movie itself felt like something you had already seen, and not quite as ingenious as you remembered it. She was a pioneer, in effect, of the condition movies suffer from today, when by the time a big-budget production hits the screen, it has been so overexposed in magazines and on television that there is almost no point in bothering to go see it. Which is fine, of course, with magazine publishers and television producers. The coverage competes with the product.

Kael's manner of overpraising and overdamning has itself been so overpraised and overdamned that rereading her reviews is a little like rereading Hemingway after listening to too many parodies: why can't she stop trying to sound so much like Pauline Kael? The trademark Kaelisms now trip you up on every page: the second-person address; the slangy heighteners, "zizzy," "zingy," "goosey," "plummy," and so on, and put-downs, like "frowzy," "whorey," "logey" (her word for Claude Lanzmann's *Shoah*); the high-low oxymorons, like "pop classic" (for the remake of *King Kong*) or "trash archetype" (for *Car-*

rie); and her most exasperating locution, the conditional universal superlative, which she used promiscuously and frequently bathetically: "The scene is perhaps the wittiest and most deeply romantic confirmation of a marriage ever filmed"[17] (*The Right Stuff*); "He may be the most natural and least self-conscious film actor who ever lived"[18] (Jeff Bridges).

Her writing is all in the same key, and strictly *molto con brio*. There is no modulation of tone or (which would be even more welcome) of thought. She just keeps slugging away. She is almost always extraordinarily sharp, but she is almost never funny. And (as she conceded in the introduction to *For Keeps*) she is clearly working her way through her feelings about the movie as she writes, and this produces garrulousness and compositional dishevelment. Writing in the *New Yorker* gave her a huge space advantage over other reviewers; she did not always profit by it. Her reviews are highly readable, but they are not especially rereadable. James Agee, in his brief service as movie critic of the *Nation*, reviewed many nondescript and now long-forgotten pictures; but as soon as you finish reading one of his pieces, you want to read it again, just to see how he did it. Kael does not provoke the same impulse.

Still, fine writing is not the name of the game. W. H. Auden once praised Agee's column by saying that he never went to the movies, but that he looked forward to reading what Mr. Agee had to say about them every week. Many people have said the same thing about Stanley Kauffmann, the longtime reviewer for the *New Republic* who is, in critical terms, pretty much the UnKael. Kael was not a reviewer for people who didn't go to movies. She was the ideal person to read when you had just seen a movie and couldn't make up your mind what you thought about it. At her best, she argued it through on the page for you. You know what you think about *Bonnie and Clyde* by now, though, and so her insights have lost their freshness. On the other hand, she is a large part of the reason you think what you do.

And her influence is everywhere. Kael was, by all accounts, a journalistic queen bee. If she did not orchestrate opinion (something she was accused of many times), she certainly took pleasure in orchestrating the orchestrators. She maintained, even before her *New Yorker* days, a circle of admirers whose careers she cultivated and whose degree of orthodoxy she monitored closely; and she became an object of personal infatuation for many younger writers who never met her. She has a number of protégés and ex-protégés among active movie reviewers: Terrence Rafferty, who succeeded her at the *New Yorker*; David Denby, who succeeded Rafferty; Michael Sragow; Roger Ebert; John Powers; Peter Rainer. But her impact extended far beyond movie reviewing. The television critics James Wolcott (who now writes about more than television) and Tom Shales, the art critics Jed Perl and Sanford Schwartz, the music critic Greil Marcus, and the sportswriter Allen Barra are all her fans, and there is a long list of other writers, in many genres, whose work would be almost unimaginable without her example. There are also two celebrity epigoni: Camille Paglia, whose style is a virtual pastiche of Kael's but who (such is the anxiety of influence) has almost never mentioned her name in print; and the Hollywood wunderkind Quentin Tarantino, who mentions her name at almost every opportunity. And properly so; for Tarantino's *Pulp Fiction* is a dish for which Kael spent forty years writing the recipe.

Kael's followers are sometimes referred to, a little dismissively, as "the Paulettes." The standard complaints about them are that they imitate Kael's enthusiasm for the cheap-thrill element of popular culture, and that they are prisoners of her journalistic mannerisms. This is unfair to their talents, but there is no question that Kael's style proved highly infectious; and there is no question, either, that her appetite for sensationalism, for blood and sex, helped to shape educated movie taste. Cataloguing stylistic tics, though, is not the most accurate way to measure Kael's influence. For her importance has, in the end, very little to do with her style of writing or even her taste in movies. It is much greater than that.

4

The problem Kael undertook to address when she began writing for the *New Yorker* was the problem of making popular entertainment respectable to people whose education told them that popular entertainment is not art. This is usually thought of as the high-low problem—the problem that arises when a critic equipped with a highbrow technique bends his or her attention to an object that is too low, when the professor writes about *Superman* comics. In fact, this rarely is a problem: if anything profits from (say) a semiotic analysis, it's the comics. The professor may go on to compare *Superman* comics favorably with Tolstoy, but that is simply a failure of judgment. It has nothing to do with the difference in brows. You can make a fool of yourself over anything.

The real high-low problem doesn't arise when the object is too low. It arises when the object isn't low enough. *Meet the Beatles* doesn't pose a high-low problem; *Sgt. Pepper's Lonely Hearts Club Band* does. Tom Clancy and "Who Wants to Be a Millionaire" don't; John Le Carré and *Masterpiece Theater* do. A product like *Sgt. Pepper's* isn't low enough to be discussed as a mere cultural artifact; but it's not high enough to be discussed as though it were *Four Quartets*, either. It's exactly what it pretends to be: it's entertainment, but for educated people. And this is what makes it so hard for educated people to talk about without sounding pretentious—as though they had to justify their pleasure by some gesture toward the "deeper" significance of the product.

One of Hollywood's best-kept industrial secrets is that the movies are entertainment for educated people, too. This was a finding that surprised the studios when, in the 1940s, they first undertook to analyze their audience: frequency of movie attendance increases with income and education. Even today, when people complain that they don't make movies for grownups anymore, the percentage of people who say they are "frequent moviegoers" is more than half again as great among people who have gone to college (31 percent) as it is among people who have only finished high school (19 percent). The belief that education makes people snobbish about moviegoing is the opposite of the case: 20 percent of people who have been to college say they "never" go to movies, but the figure is 39 percent among adults who have only finished high school and 57 percent among adults with even less education than that. Kael didn't persuade *New Yorker* readers to go to the movies; they were already going. That wasn't the problem. The problem was teaching them how to think critically about it.

One way to think critically about it, the way consistent with modern thinking about the arts generally, is to identify the formal properties of the medium and to judge movies by how fully and intelligently they use them. So that the assertion "*Stagecoach* is a great movie" might be defended against the person who wants to know if that means it is as great as *King Lear* by replying that *Stagecoach* is great "in cinematic terms." This is to defend your judgment with an abstraction; for when you say things like "in cinematic terms," you are on your way toward developing a theory of film. Kael had devoted her entire pre–*New Yorker* career to demolishing this way of thinking. By 1967, her anti-aesthetic had been completely worked out. She hated theories. She didn't oppose only auteur theory; she opposed all theoretical preconceptions. "Isn't it clear that trying to find out what cinema 'really' is, is derived from a mad Platonic and metaphorical view of the universe," she wrote, in an unreprinted essay, in 1966, "—as if ideal, pure cinema were some pre-existent entity that we had to find? Cinema is not to be found; but movies are continuously being made."[19] And, more famously, in "Is There a Cure for Movie Criticism?" (1962), an attack on the film theorist Siegfried Kracauer: "Art is the greatest game, the supreme entertainment, because you discover the game as you play it. . . . We want to see, to feel, to understand, to respond in a new way. Why should pedants be allowed to spoil the game?"[20]

Kael was the most brilliantly ad hoc critic of her time, and she made it possible to care about movies without feeling pompous or giddy by showing that what comes first in everyone's experience of a movie isn't the form or the idea but the sensation, and that this is just as true for moviegoers who have been taught to intellectualize their responses to art as it is for everyone else. The idea that a movie critic needs to work from sensations was not new with her, of course. Agee's persona in the *Nation* had been that of the ordinary intelligent guy who just happens to love going to movies (and who also just happens to write like James Agee). Robert Warshow, who

wrote about movies for *Commentary* and *Partisan Review* in the
1940s and '50s, warned that the critic who trucks a load of sociology
and aesthetics into the movie theater will end up missing the show.
"A man watches a movie," as he once famously, and perhaps a shade
sententiously, put it, "and the critic must acknowledge that he is
that man."[21]

When Warshow wrote about *Scarface* and Agee wrote about *National Velvet*, they didn't have much trouble being that man. But
that is because the high-low problem doesn't kick in with *Scarface*
and *National Velvet*. It kicks in with a movie like *Monsieur Verdoux*,
Chaplin's black comedy about a serial killer, which very few people
have patience for anymore, but which Agee and Warshow both went
solemnly bananas over. Agee and Warshow thought that Chaplin
had Something Important To Say in *Monsieur Verdoux*, and they
therefore bent over backward in their appreciation of the movie in
order to give him credit for his good intentions.

Kael never gave anyone credit for good intentions. "Art," as she
put it back in 1956, "perhaps unfortunately, is not the sphere of good
intentions."[22] She wasn't interested in abstractions like "social significance" or "the body of work." She had to be turned on all over
again each time. Her favorite analogy for the movie experience got
seriously overworked, and was lampooned as a result, but it does
have the virtue of simplicity: a movie, for her, was either good sex or
bad sex. For the quality of sex doesn't necessarily have anything to
do with the glamour of the partner. The best-looking guy in the
room may be the lousiest lover—which is why nothing irritated Kael
more than a well-dressed movie that didn't perform. "If a lady says,
'That man don't pleasure me,' " she explained to the readers of *Holiday* in 1966, "that's it. There are some areas in which we can still decide for ourselves."[23] She thought that people who claimed to enjoy
2001: A Space Odyssey more than *The Thomas Crown Affair* were either lying or were guilty of sex-in-the-head. There were a lot of people like that around before 1967. "What *did* she lose at the movies?"
asked a puzzled Dwight Macdonald when he reviewed *I Lost It at
the Movies*, in 1965.[24] Case in point.

Kael's contention that "serious" movies should meet the same standard as pulp—that they should be entertaining—turned out to be an extremely useful and widely adopted critical principle. For it rests on an empirically sustainable proposition, which is that although people sometimes have a hard time deciding whether or not something is "art," they are rarely fooled into thinking they are being entertained when they are not. It was Kael's therapeutic advice to the overcultivated that if they just concentrated on responding to the stimulus, the aesthetics would take care of themselves. What good is form if the content leaves you cold?

The kind of approach Kael promoted is antiessentialist. It is a reaction against the idea, associated with modernist literature, painting, and architecture, that the various arts have their own essential qualities—that poetry is *essentially* a matter of the organization of language, that painting is *essentially* a matter of figure and ground, that architecture is *essentially* a matter of space and light. The undoing of these assumptions is often taken to have been the work of high critical theory, of semioticians, Derrideans, and postmodernists. And that undoing is associated with highbrow, avant-garde art and literature—it is thought of as a distinctly elitist cultural movement. In fact, the cultural work was done long before "postmodernist" became a theoretical concept in the academy, and it was done by people whose audience was entirely mainstream. If we need to give it a brow, this reaction against modernist formalism and essentialism was a middlebrow phenomenon. Its champion practitioners were Warhol (in painting), Mailer (in fiction), and Tom Wolfe (in journalism)—all perfectly accessible figures who played to a large, nonintellectual audience. Its "theoreticians" were people like Susan Sontag, who was a freelance writer, Robert Venturi and Denise Scott Brown, who were architects, and Kael, who never finished college. For the notion that serious art must be appreciated formally before anything else was actually not so much a feature of modernist art itself—it's not something most of the major modernists would have claimed about what they were doing—as it was the result of the way modern art and literature were taught to people like the people who read the *New Yorker* in the 1950s and early 1960s. Formalism was a middlebrow oppression. It didn't frighten poets; it frightened moviegoers. It made them think there was something they ought to know about called the "grammar of film."

This liberation of art from a priori principles was one of the great achievements of American culture in the 1960s. It has since been attacked for encouraging the dangerously relativist notions that "It's art if I say it's art" and "Anything goes." People said those things in the sixties, and I suppose people say them now, but those are not the necessary conclusions of the lesson Kael helped to teach. A dislike of formalism does not entail a dislike of form. And openness to mass culture does not entail identification with the mass audience; it doesn't require an attitude of *épater les intellectuels*, or a belief that if it's "of the people," it must be counterhegemonic. The critical attitude Kael represented only means approaching a work of art without bias about what "a work of art" is supposed to be. It is predicated on the notion that modern culture is fluid and promiscuous, and therefore that nothing is gained by foreclosing the experience of it—particularly if you are a critic. Pauline Kael understood these things, and she consciously built her practice as a reviewer around them. And that is why she is a supremely important figure even for writers who, although they grew up reading everything she wrote, strove, in their own work, never to sound like Pauline Kael.

Christopher Lasch's Quarrel with Liberalism

odern life, to some of its critics, looks like a giant wrecking yard of traditions, with no one around to pick up the mess. In the middle of the yard there is a small tin shed, and inside the shed the apologists of fragmentation sit. These are the liberals. They explain how it is that we are better off without guides to conduct that are any more substantive than the right of each of us to pick up whatever pieces catch his or her fancy, and why it is that life inside the yard counts as liberation.

People who are unhappy with modernity, on this description, have two alternatives: they can gather together bits of the failed traditions and construct from them a philosophy of conduct that might supplant liberalism's emptiness, or they can choose, intellectually at least, to live outside the yard altogether. The first way is the perilous way, since it runs the risk of producing simply another trophy of liberalism's sterile value of "inclusivity," another sign that the system is working for everyone, even for the people who pretend to hate it.

This is why it is not enough for the opponents of liberalism simply to construct alternative models; they must never cease to insist that liberalism is actively the enemy—that it is not the consequence of modernity, but its original mad inventor.

Christopher Lasch began his career as a historian and critic of American liberalism. His analysis of liberalism led him to an analysis of some of the alternatives to liberalism in American political thought and, eventually, to a long excursion into social history and cultural criticism. It was clear from this work that he was unhappy with the dominant political and intellectual traditions in American life, and distressed by the mess he thought those traditions had gotten us into. But it was not clear what he thought we might do to organize our lives more propitiously until the publication of *The True and Only Heaven* (1991), in which he returned to the criticism of liberalism with which he started, but this time offered a prescription.

What did Lasch mean by "liberalism"? Beyond the broad idea that liberalism is the philosophical foundation of the modern condition, the term has been used to describe such a variety of specific views that it has become a vexing one to define. Some people we call liberals—those associated with the War on Poverty in the 1960s, say, and with George McGovern's 1972 presidential campaign—believe that the government should provide, in some measure, for the basic welfare of its citizens. Others—Michael Dukakis and Bill Clinton, for instance—think that a vigorous and expanding free-market economy is more likely to produce prosperity. Some liberals want foreign policy to be dictated by a concern for human rights and democratic values, as Jimmy Carter did; others, like Richard Nixon—in this respect a traditionally liberal president—believe that our relations with other nations should be governed by an unsentimental assessment of our own interests.

These disagreements among liberals are not a recent development, a splitting up of what was once a unified core of beliefs. Liberal thought has been divided along similar lines since at least the early years of the century, when liberals argued about America's entry into the First World War, about the growing dominance of large corporations in the American economy, and about the true character of Soviet Communism. But in Lasch's view, all liberals, whether they dislike corporate capitalism or welcome it, whether they approve of American intervention in foreign conflicts or deplore it, share a common attitude: they are all optimists, believers in moral and material progress. Liberals believe that as civilization advances (by which, Lasch thought, liberals usually mean "as people become more liberal"), more wants and desires are satisfied, and fewer prejudices and superstitions inhibit us. Once life was made miserable by bad kings and bad teeth; now we have democracy and dentists, political freedom and physical comfort, and thus we can say that people have become happier, and that life is improving.

It was this faith in progress, Lasch argued in his first book, *The American Liberals and the Russian Revolution* (1962), that made it so difficult for many liberals in 1917 to understand the Communist revolution in Russia as the malign event it was. For to do so would have meant calling into question this central tenet of liberal faith: that history is a continuous progression from tyranny toward freedom, whose advance is marked by a series of democratic revolutions. Liberals are themselves the heirs of a revolutionary tradition, Lasch pointed out; how were they to accept the fact of a revolution that rejected the liberal ideal? And even if Soviet Communism proved to be antiliberal and antidemocratic (as, of course, it did), liberals insisted on regarding its emergence as only a temporary setback in the advance of progress. In the end, liberalism must triumph even in Russia, because the triumph of liberalism was destined to be universal. *The American Liberals and the Russian Revolution* is a detailed study of the political debate during the years of the First World War—from 1914 to 1919. But the argument was clearly addressed to the liberals of Lasch's own day. When Lasch wrote that "liberalism in America, no less than communism in Russia, has always been a messianic creed, which staked everything on the ultimate triumph of liberalism throughout the world,"[1] he was describing, he thought, not only the liberalism of 1919—of Woodrow Wilson and Walter Lippmann—but the liberalism of the Kennedy administration, as well.

This was an ingenious and antithetical point to make. For to

describe liberalism as a messianic creed in 1962 was to call the vampire killer a vampire—as the titles of two standard expositions of liberal political theory in the early cold war era suggest: Arthur M.
Schlesinger, Jr.'s *The Vital Center* (1949) and Daniel Bell's *The End
of Ideology* (1960). Contemporary liberalism, for those writers, was
precisely not an absolutist, world-transforming politics. It was a
problem-solving, consensus-reaching politics, one that "dedicates
itself," as Schlesinger suggested, "to problems as they come."[2] Such
pragmatism could only be impeded by prior ideological convictions,
which Bell analyzed specifically as displaced religious and messianic impulses. "Ideology, which once was a road to action, has
come to be a dead end," he claimed. "Few serious minds believe any
longer that one can set down 'blueprints' and through 'social engineering' bring about a new utopia of social harmony."[3] "People who
know they alone are right find it hard to compromise," was the way
Schlesinger put it; "and compromise is the strategy of democracy."[4]
A little utopianism might be fine as a spur to political engagement,
but the business of politics lay in fine-tuning the machinery that
maintains social and economic freedoms, and in resisting ideology
and messianism wherever they threaten those freedoms. Liberals
were not supposed to become obsessed with the ends (or "the end")
of history.

It is possible to be messianic in the effort to root out messianism, though. Even pragmatism can suffer from hubris; and Lasch's
detection of a self-aggrandizing impulse, a secret determination to
convert the world to its own "anti-ideological" ideology, in the ostensibly instrumentalist politics of midcentury liberalism was an insight whose accuracy was confirmed, for many people, by America's
subsequent entanglement, under a series of liberal administrations,
in Vietnam. Lasch's accusation was also, of course, one that any liberal disenchanted with the self-righteous certainty of some of his
fellow liberals might have made.[5] It need not have led anyone to
abandon liberalism. After all, a liberal might reasonably ask, so long
as we don't force people to become like us, why *shouldn't* we hope
that liberal institutions—democratic societies and free markets—
become universal?

For Lasch, however, the point had a different consequence. He began to see not only liberalism, but the whole march of "progress" itself as a creeping tyranny of centralized social and political control. Though liberalism was the ascendant political theory of this historical process, even many of the adversaries of liberalism, Lasch concluded, shared its optimism and its passion for transforming people's lives. In *The New Radicalism in America* (1965) and *The Agony of the American Left* (1969), he considered some of these adversaries: the "cultural radicals," such as Mabel Dodge Luhan and Randolph Bourne; the turn-of-the-century populists and socialists; and the leaders of the progressive movement, which, during the first two decades of the century, sought to restore a sense of "civic virtue" to American political and economic life. Among these, only populism and socialism—"two broad patterns of opposition to corporate capitalism, occasionally converging but ideologically distinct"[6]—seemed to Lasch to have offered a genuine alternative to the corporate economy and the liberal state. Their failure, early in the century, marked for him the death of all real dissent.

For the reformers and cultural radicals, he decided, were in the end only participating in the general effort to "enlighten"—and thus remold—the citizenry from the top down, through public education and artistic and literary culture; and this was an enterprise so congenial to the liberal mentality that liberals found it easy to adopt the radical style, and to patronize intellectual culture, in a way that rendered those traditions powerless. The Kennedy administration, with its indulgence of artists and intellectuals enthralled by the illusion that they were having an influence on the exercise of political power, represented, as Lasch saw it, the culmination of this process. As for the progressive movement, associated with the followers of Theodore Roosevelt and with liberal militants such as Herbert Croly, Walter Lippmann, and Walter Weyl, it was progressive "chiefly in attacking the archaic entrepreneurial capitalism the existence of which impeded the rationalization of American industry," and thus "actually served the needs of the industrial system."[7] In seeking to reform the system rather than to resist it—to discover ways for more people to partake of the material prosperity capitalism provided rather than ways to prevent big business from turning people into well-fed "wage slaves"—the progressives only smoothed capitalism's path. So that by midcentury, Lasch concluded, it had become "almost impossible for criticism of existing policies to become part of political discourse. The language of American politics increasingly resembles an Orwellian monologue."[8]

Having come to the bottom of the political barrel, Lasch turned first to social history and then to jeremiad. *Haven in a Heartless World* (1977) proposed that the history of modern society could be described as "the socialization of production, followed by the socialization of reproduction."[9] By the first phrase, Lasch meant the division of labor that accompanied the emergence of industrial capitalism, and that, by depriving people of control over their work, deprived them as well of the virtues unalienated labor instills. A day on an assembly line spent fixing the heads on pins, to use Adam Smith's famous example of specialization in *The Wealth of Nations*, is not likely to lead a person to an elevated conception of life, or to give him a sense of independence and self-confidence. (This was a warning about the moral effects of specialization that Smith himself recorded elsewhere in his writings.) By "the socialization of reproduction," Lasch meant the proliferation, beginning in the nineteenth century, of the so-called helping professions: the doctors, psychologists, teachers, child-guidance experts, juvenile court officers, and so forth, who, by their constant intervention in people's private lives, "eroded the capacity for self-help and social invention."[10]

This second development constitutes, in Lasch's view, liberalism's worst betrayal. For liberalism, he argued, had struck a deal: in return for transforming the worker from an independent producer of goods into a fixer of heads on pins, it was agreed that people would be free to pursue happiness and virtue in their private lives in whatever manner they chose. The workplace was thus severed from the home, and the family became the "haven in a heartless world." But no sooner was the deal made, Lasch argued, than liberalism reneged. Private life was immediately made prey to the quasi-official helping professions and the "forces of organized virtue," led by "feminists, temperance advocates, educational reformers, liberal ministers, penologists, doctors, and bureaucrats."[11] "From the moment the conception of the family as a refuge made its historical appearance, the same forces that gave rise to the new privacy began to erode it. . . . The hope that private transactions could make up for the collapse of communal traditions and civic order"[12] was killed by organized kindness.

Modern life, in Lasch's conception, is thus predicated on one basic transaction: the exchange of genuine independence for pseudo-liberation. Liberals and reformers will free us from the repressiveness of the patriarchal family, of the closed ethnic community—even of our own unhappiness. All we have to do is to surrender ourselves to the benevolent paternalism of the sociologists, psychiatrists, educators, and corporate and welfare bureaucrats. But those "helpers" have effectively destroyed the very institutions, such as the nuclear family, through which character and independence were traditionally instilled. The responsibility for raising children has been lifted from the shoulders of parents (thus discrediting their authority) and placed in the offices of medical and educational professionals and experts; a pattern of "normal" development is now enforced by the public schools, whose purpose has been reconceived as socialization—turning people into good citizens on the liberal model, rather than simply introducing them to knowledge. "Liberating" people has meant, in short, converting them into permanent dependents of the modern state and its "human science" apparatchiks.

Lasch's argument, at this point in his work, had begun to show some similarity to that of Michel Foucault, whose analysis of modern institutional benevolence as a tyrannical system of social controls Lasch wrote about approvingly.[13] Perhaps a stronger, or more immediate, influence was Philip Rieff's notion of "the triumph of the therapeutic"—the idea that the twentieth-century belief in personal liberation has created a new culture organized around a new type of human being, whom Rieff called "psychological man." It was Lasch's development of this argument of Rieff's that yielded the work for which he is famous.

2

The Culture of Narcissism (1979) was a book of its moment. It appeared at the close of a depressing decade and near the close of an unpopular presidency. Lasch was, in fact, one of the luminaries invited to Camp David to help Jimmy Carter organize his thoughts for the speech in which he proposed that Americans were suffering from malaise (a word that did not actually appear in the speech itself), and this well-publicized distinction no doubt helped put the book on the best-seller list. Its argument is a little more complicated than people whose knowledge of it came largely at second hand may have assumed. Lasch proposed that the modern developments he had examined in his earlier work—the demise of the family and the erosion of private life generally—had produced "a new form of personality organization."[14] If (as he thought) people were behaving and feeling differently, it was because a fundamental change had taken place not only in beliefs and values—in what people thought moral, or permissible, or desirable—but in the structure of the mind itself. Our "social arrangements live on," he proposed, "in the individual, buried in the mind below the level of consciousness."[15]

The principal evidence for this assertion—beyond sociological observations about a "sense of inner emptiness," the "decline of the play spirit," and so forth—were psychiatric reports on contemporary personality disorders, which were (Lasch claimed) increasingly assuming a "narcissistic" pattern. Lasch was not, as some of his more casual readers may have assumed, using "narcissism" in the everyday sense of "self-centered" or "hedonistic." He was using the term in a clinical sense that had been developed in a psychoanalytic tradition arising out of Freudian theory—in the work of Heinz Kohut, Otto Kernberg, and the object-relations psychologist Melanie Klein. In this literature, a "narcissist" is not someone with an overweening sense of self, but, on the contrary, someone with a very weak sense of self.

In order to make the psychoanalytic data he had assembled fit the case he was making about the emergence of a new personality type in society at large, Lasch made one further assumption: that "pathology represents a heightened version of normality"[16]—that is, that a clinically disordered personality, of the kind reported in psychoanalytic studies, is representative of the current "normal" personality type. This made for a rather elaborate theoretical contraption. The reader was being called upon to make the following assumptions, any one of which is clearly vulnerable to challenge: that changes in education, the role of the family, the nature of work, and so on are capable of producing fundamental changes, "below the level of consciousness," in people's psychological makeup; that the changes in American life over the last hundred years have been extensive and unidirectional enough to create an entire population dominated by this new personality type; that the pathological personality does indeed present a version of the normal personality; and that the particular examples of narcissistic behavior adduced by Lasch in 1979—among them the Manson Family killings, the kidnapping of Patty Hearst, the attack on theatrical illusion in contemporary drama, "the fascination with oral sex,"[17] and the streaker craze—are evidence of long-term personality disintegration, rather than isolated responses to a confusing but transitory historical moment. (There was also the problem that a writer who had elsewhere suggested that psychiatry was, in the hands of some of its practitioners, at least, one of the corrupting forces in modern life was relying rather heavily on a psychiatric conception of the "normal.") *The Culture of Narcissism* was thus a book it was easy to misunderstand. Lasch was not saying that things were better in the 1950s, as conservatives offended by countercultural permissiveness probably took him to be saying. He was not saying that things were better in the 1960s, as former activists disgusted by the "me-ism" of the seventies are likely to have imagined. He was diagnosing a condition that he believed had originated in the nineteenth century.

The Minimal Self (1984) was written to correct the misapprehensions of the earlier book's admirers. The "narcissistic" self, Lasch explained, was really a type of what he was now calling the "minimal" self—"a self uncertain of its own outlines, [yet] longing either to remake the world in its own image" (as in the case of technocratic reformers and other acolytes of "progress") "or to merge into its environment in a blissful union"[18] (as in the case of counterculturalists, feminists, and ecological utopians). Authentic selfhood lies between these extremes, he wrote—in an acceptance of limits without despair. But the conditions in which such a self might be forged were being destroyed.

What is distinctive about Lasch's criticism of modern life, besides its unusually broad scope, is its moral and personal intensity. For it is one thing—and not an uncommon thing among academic intellectuals—to analyze modern democratic society as a system of social controls masquerading as personal freedoms, without concluding anything more radical (or less banal) than that all societies must hold themselves together somehow, and that an officially "open" society will find means for doing so that are designed to appear as uncoercive as possible. But Lasch showed no interest in this kind of analytic detachment, which he regarded as just the sort of superior sociological "expertise" he associated with the bureaucratic and professionalist mentality he abhorred.[19] He was (or he gave, in his work, the impression of being) a man who believed he had caught "the modern project"[20]—his phrase for the group of social and political tendencies he analyzed—in an enormous lie, and who cannot rest until the lie has been exposed. There is an invasion-of-the-body-snatchers urgency to his writing; and this gave it, over the years, an increasingly aggrieved, and sometimes paranoid, tone. It also drew him to a style of relentless and contentious assertion which can be, to put it gently, extremely off-putting. It was an unusual style for a scholar to resort to, and I think he meant it, quite deliberately, to be offensive: an affront to the modern taste for cool and logically seamless forms of persuasion. If he did mean it that way, it works.

3

The True and Only Heaven was the first place in which Lasch tried to suggest, with some degree of comprehensiveness, a way out of the regrettable condition he thought the modern liberal view had left us in. It is much the longest of his books, and it suffers from many of the faults one has come to associate with his work: it lingers pedantically on minor matters and dashes through major ones; it makes much of points almost everyone would concede and ignores obvious objections to its more controversial assertions; and it is written from a position that had hardened into something like dogmatism. Lasch was, after all, a writer who had argued that "all medical technology has done is to increase patients' dependence on machines and the medical experts who operate [them]";[21] that "new ideas of sexual liberation—the celebration of oral sex, masturbation, and homosexuality—spring from the prevailing fear of heterosexual passion, even of sexual intercourse itself";[22] that the reliance on medical intervention during pregnancy "helped women in their campaign for voluntary motherhood by raising the cost of pregnancy to their husbands—not only the financial cost but the emotional cost of the doctor's intrusion into the bedroom, his usurpation of the husband's sexual prerogatives";[23] that the imposition of child labor laws "obscured the positive possibility of children working alongside their parents at jobs of recognized importance";[24] and that "the prison life of the past looks in our time like liberation itself."[25]

Like all of Lasch's books, *The True and Only Heaven* was clearly designed to be responsive to contemporary anxieties—in this case, to concern about the ecological dangers that are bound, it seems, to accompany the spread of market economies across the globe. Lasch argued that if we continue to believe, as the religion of progress encourages us to believe, that somehow everyone in the world can be given the standard of living of a middle-class American, the planet will be used up long before we ever arrive at that dubious utopia. He was not the first person to sound this warning, but he did, as usual, sound it in a provocative manner.

By the time of *The True and Only Heaven*, Lasch had come to regard the belief in progress not as simply an interesting paradox in twentieth-century liberal thought, but as the dominant ideology of modern history. It is in the name of progress, he thought, that traditional sources of happiness and virtue—work, faith, the family, even an independent sense of self—are being destroyed; and he began his book with an analysis of the false values of the modern liberal outlook, proposing, for each value or attitude to be rejected, an alternative. This discussion is filled with references to various thinkers and ideas, as is the case throughout *The True and Only Heaven*; but references to specific policies or social arrangements are scarce, so that the analysis has a theoretical or abstract cast. Lasch's purpose, evidently, was to establish a vocabulary.

Lasch argued, as he had in his first book, nearly thirty years earlier, that liberals are optimists: they believe in an unlimited ability to provide for an ever-expanding array of human wants. A worthier sentiment, he felt, is "hope"—an acceptance of limits without despair (as he had described it in *The Minimal Self*). Liberals espouse a kind of Enlightenment universalism; they regard their truths as self-evident to all reasonable people, and therefore as applicable to everyone. He recommended instead an emphasis on particularism—a recognition of the persistence of national and ethnic loyalties. Nostalgia, he argued, is progress's "ideological twin,"[26] since it is a way of thinking about the past that makes it seem irrecoverable, and makes change seem inevitable. He proposed "memory" as an alternative, a way of seeing the past and present as continuous. Instead of the modern conception of people as consumers, working only to provide themselves with the means to satisfy material wants, he suggested a conception of people as producers, working in order to acquire the virtues labor instills—among them independence, responsibility, and self-sufficiency. And in place of "self-interest," which defines the economic man of liberal individualism, he proposed "virtue," which defines the citizen ready to take an active part in community life.

This much of Lasch's argument, directed at the mentality that sees no limits to economic growth, and that understands the ends of social and economic policy to be simply the creation and satisfaction of more consumers, had a timely appeal. The collapse of the communist economies was greeted in some quarters, as Lasch in 1962 suggested it would be, as evidence of the inevitable global triumph of liberalism—the theoretically predicted "end of history," in the catchphrase made popular by Francis Fukuyama. And on these matters, as Lasch quite rightly pointed out, there is no longer an appreciable difference in mainstream American political thought between "liberals" and "conservatives." The "New Right," in this respect, proved a sham: Ronald Reagan was no less a worshiper of progress—no less an optimist, a nostalgist, a global crusader for the American way—than any classic liberal one might name.

Much of the attention Lasch's book received when it appeared was therefore preoccupied with its attack on the "progressive" worldview; and the general terms that define the substitute worldview the book proposed are plainly attractive. Who would want to defend "optimism" against "hope," "nostalgia" against "memory," "self-interest" against "virtue"? So long as the discussion remains at this level of abstraction, there is very little to argue. But Lasch had a broader purpose: he had undertaken to reconstruct a political and moral tradition in which his "alternative" values are rooted. This tradition he called "populism," and it is not possible to engage his argument in a serious way without confronting the challenges that this tradition makes (or that Lasch understood it to make) to modern liberal assumptions.

Lasch meant by "populism" something more than the late-nineteenth-century political movement the term ordinarily denotes. Indeed, the book contains very little discussion of William Jennings Bryan, for instance, or of the Southern populist leader Tom Watson.[27] The populist tradition Lasch described has been transmitted through an oddly assorted sequence of thinkers. These thinkers all share one attitude, of course: an antagonism to the modern liberal outlook as Lasch had defined it. This may express itself in an appreciation for the "civic virtues"—the virtues derived from personal independence, political participation, and genuinely productive labor; in an acceptance of "fate" (one of the book's key terms) and of the idea of limits; or in an admiration for a set of characteristics that Lasch identified with lower-middle-class, or "petty-bourgeois," culture: moral conservatism, egalitarianism, loyalty, and the struggle against the moral temptation of resentment (that is, the capacity for forgiveness).

Among the social and political critics Lasch regarded as populists are writers who defend small-scale producers (farmers, artisans, and so forth), who despise creditors, and who oppose the culture of uplift and universal philanthropy because of its disruptive intervention in personal and family life. These sentiments are, he thought, particularly strongly expressed in the writings of Tom Paine; the English radical William Cobbett; the nineteenth-century editor, Transcendentalist, and controversialist Orestes Brownson; and the author of the classic of populist political economy *Progress and Poverty* (1879), Henry George. Two labor-movement theorists from the turn of the century are important to Lasch's tradition as champions of small-scale producers: the French syndicalist Georges Sorel, whose *Reflections on Violence* (1908) was admired by critics of the Third Republic in France and of liberalism in England, and the British guild socialist G. D. H. Cole. By proposing to restore control over production to the worker, Lasch argued, syndicalism and guild socialism represented genuine alternatives to corporate capitalism. What socialists and the labor movement generally ended up settling for, he felt (and Cole is his example), was a top-down welfare system that turned the worker into a consumer, and left him, though more secure in his job, even more dependent.

This tradition of political and economic criticism is complemented, Lasch argued, by a parallel tradition of moral criticism—and this proposal is the chief novelty of *The True and Only Heaven*, and the key to its creation of an alternative to liberal fragmentation. The major figure is Emerson, whose recognition, in the late essay on "Fate" (1860), that "freedom lies in the acceptance of necessity" Lasch regarded as the philosophical centerpiece of populist thought. Emerson's fatalism is ignored, he thought, by the Emersonians—"those professional Pollyannas"—and he proposed to restore us to a proper understanding, principally by reading Emerson by the lights of the Puritan divine Jonathan Edwards. Two other writers, both readily associated with Emerson, are said to share the populist moral vision: Thomas Carlyle, in *Sartor Resartus* (1834) and the essays on heroes and hero worship published in 1841, and William James, in the discussion of the "twice-born" in *The Varieties of Religious Experience* (1902) and in the essay "The Moral Equivalent of War" (1910).

Lasch traced the course of populist ideals in a group of

twentieth-century American writers: Josiah Royce, Randolph
Bourne, Herbert Croly, Waldo Frank, John Dewey, the New Dealer
Thurman Arnold, and Reinhold Niebuhr. In some of these cases, he
was reconsidering writers whose ideas he had once criticized. Croly,
for instance, whose *The Promise of American Life* (1910) Lasch once
regarded as a typical example of the progressive's naïve understanding of the nature of corporate power,[28] was praised for recognizing,
in a later book, *Progressive Democracy* (1914), the importance of en-
dowing the worker with a sense of responsibility—and for perceiv-
ing that the specialization required by big business and mass
production would destroy the possibilities for meaningful work.
Niebuhr (one of the heroes of Schlesinger's *The Vital Center*) was
attacked by Lasch in *The New Radicalism in America* for taking an
uncritical and Manichean view of the struggle between American
liberal democracy and Soviet totalitarianism—for assuming too
readily the inherent virtue of the American way and the monolithic
evil of Soviet communism.[29] In *The True and Only Heaven*, though,
Niebuhr appears as a critic of liberalism. His defense of "particularism"—of the innate desire of groups to protect their difference and
autonomy against the liberal inclination to force compromises on
competing interests—now seemed to Lasch to make him a misun-
derstood antagonist of liberal ideology.

Niebuhr is also important to the populist tradition, as Lasch interpreted it, because of his insistence on the desirability of forgiveness, and the futility of resentment, in struggles for social justice;
and Lasch's consideration of this aspect of Niebuhr's thought leads
directly to the only political success story in the book: Martin
Luther King, Jr.'s leadership of the Southern civil rights movement. King succeeded, Lasch believed, by appealing to the populist
virtues of lower-middle-class communities in the South—both
black and white—and by preaching the doctrine of "a spiritual discipline against resentment." Blacks in King's movement did not
seek revenge for the injustices they had suffered, since they understood (or King, who had studied Niebuhr as a divinity student, understood) Niebuhr's teaching that to combat injustice and coercion
with more injustice and coercion is only to perpetuate a cycle of

conflict. But, Lasch argued, when King and his associates attempted to mobilize victims of poverty in the inner cities of the North, they could no longer appeal, as they had in the South, to communities of people who understood the value of forgiveness. Resentment against the powerful became instead the motivating emotion of the struggle, with disastrous results.

Lower-middle-class virtues persist, Lasch thought, but as an endangered moral species, preyed upon by the social-engineering schemes of the liberal professional classes. The controversy between suburban liberals and working-class city residents over the busing of school children to achieve racial integration and the argument over abortion rights are, he suggested, recent instances of liberal imperialism. In the Boston busing wars, and in the struggles for open housing in the suburbs of Chicago, lower-middle-class white communities were reviled, and even demonized, by liberals; yet their "only crime," Lasch said, "so far as anyone could see, was their sense of ethnic solidarity."[30] The populist solution, apparently, would have entailed an attempt to transform the inner city into a "real community," rather than to compel people to ignore their ethnic and racial differences—though Lasch was vague about how this transformation would take place.

In the case of abortion rights, one might imagine that pro-choice advocates, because of their insistence that the decision to have an abortion should be left to the individual woman rather than foreclosed by the state, would have had the stronger case for Lasch. But Lasch regarded the procedure of abortion itself as an instance of technological intrusion into the natural process of reproduction, and he accused the proponents of abortion rights of advocating social engineering—of trying to use medical advances to eliminate the "unwanted" in the name of social improvement. (This view of the pro-choice mentality derives mainly from a single sociological study, Kristin Luker's *Abortion and the Politics of Motherhood* [1984].) And yet in these cases there is at least some engagement between the classes. In general, Lasch thought, "neither left- nor right-wing intellectuals . . . seem to have much interest in the rest of American society."[31] A revived populist tradition, he concluded, would challenge the ideologues of progress, and help to answer "the great question of twentieth-century politics":[32] how we are to restore a spirit of civic virtue in our lives.

This does not mean that Lasch was proposing a resurrection of the populist political and economic program (though his lengthy and often quarrelsome elaboration of that program sometimes made it appear otherwise). As he conceded, much of populist economic theory—with its hatred of creditors and landlords, its monetary gimmicks and paper money schemes, its call for a return to small-scale production—was anachronistic even in the nineteenth century. Many populist political convictions are similarly outdated: the belief that armed conflict breeds virtue in the citizenry, for example, surely died in the Battle of the Somme. Lasch was not suggesting that all the facts of modern history could be repealed, or that some-day we might all become yeoman farmers, with our ancestral rifles hanging over the fireplace—though he would perhaps have liked us to think more respectfully of yeoman farmers.

The real argument of his book was a more philosophical one, having to do with the juxtaposition of populist economic theory, such as it is, with the tradition of moral criticism Lasch found in Edwards, Emerson, Carlyle, James, Niebuhr, and others. His point seemed to be that we need a political economy that matches the moral economy (as Lasch believed those writers understood it) of the universe. The universe, in this conception, is a place in which we earn our way, and do so in part by recognizing that there are lim-its to how far we can go and forces militating against us which we cannot control. Character is built by striving to perform the role fate has assigned us, and a society that recognized this truth would be one which understood that conditions a modern person finds op-pressive—obedience to family discipline, acceptance of the re-strictions of place and class, military conscription, demeaning or unremunerative work—are really the conditions that make a full and independent life possible. The reason populists give for agitat-ing against capitalists, creditors, and landlords is that those are classes of people who profit without producing. In doing so, they violate the principles of an economics based on a labor theory of value—the foundation of not only populist and Marxist but even liberal economic theory in the nineteenth century. More than that, though, they violate the universe's moral principle of just compensation. You must give something to get something back. Only if we are producers will we deserve to consume. And to be a "producer" in the larger, moral sense means to feel oneself responsible for all of what one does in one's life.

This is not an unattractive philosophical conception. But what happens when it touches ground in the thought and practice of a particular "populist" writer? Consider the case of Georges Sorel, whose militant version of socialist syndicalism appealed to Lasch because of its rejection of both liberal and Marxist utopianism. Among the less attractive features of Sorel's thought, Lasch noted in passing, is "probably" anti-Semitism.[33] But a man who compared France's struggle against the Jews to America's against the "Yellow Peril," who wrote that "the French should defend their state, their customs, and their ideas against the Jewish invaders" and that "the so-called excesses of the Bolsheviks were due to the Jewish elements that had penetrated the movement," and who referred, in two of the works Lasch cited, *Reflections on Violence* and *The Illusion of Progress*, to "big Jew bankers," is not just "probably" an anti-Semite.[34] Nor was Sorel's anti-Semitism simply a detachable element of his general outlook. It was the obvious, if not the inevitable, consequence of an economic theory that demonized financiers and creditors.

And this side of populist thought is of a paranoid piece throughout: the dislike of professional armies, as an instance of specialization that deprives citizens of the virtue-making activity of war; the dislike of those who lend the state the money to pay its armies, and who therefore supposedly find it in their interest to foment war between states; the defense of local religious and ethnic communities—these are all classic sources of anti-Semitism. They are also among the sources of fascism, particularly in France. "The intellectual father of fascism," one French admirer called Sorel in the 1920s;[35] and although Lasch noted Sorel's close association with the Action Française and his enthusiastically reciprocated admiration for Mussolini (later complemented by an equally fervent admiration for Lenin), he did not explain why this aspect of Sorel's thought, of which he plainly did not approve, should be regarded as irrelevant to the aspects he had praised. And the same is true of the racism, jingoism, and demagoguery associated with populist political move-ments generally: Lasch acknowledged these tendencies, but asked his readers to ignore them—occasionally by the discreditable tactic of throwing their suspicions back in their faces. He addressed the question of Sorel's connections to fascism, for instance, simply by remarking that "liberals' obsession with fascism . . . leads them to see 'fascist tendencies' or 'proto-fascism' in all opinions unsympa-thetic to liberalism."[36] This may or may not be true, but it is not an argument.

The True and Only Heaven was, one assumes, intended to pro-voke many such disputes about the selective readings and unortho-dox interpretations of various figures. But there are two larger criticisms that I think Lasch invited, and they have application not only to that book, but to his work generally. Of the many peculiari-ties about the moral tradition Lasch constructed in The True and Only Heaven, the most astonishing is the omission of Freud—a writer who had played an important part in Lasch's earlier thinking. For surely the Freudian notion of psychic economy involves exactly the principle of compensation, and exactly the tragic sense of life, that Lasch so passionately admired in thinkers of far smaller intel-lectual stature. But a writer like Freud could not figure in Lasch's account, and the reason is that Freud has already been accepted as one of the heroes of modern culture. And this is also why the writers who do have a prominent place in Lasch's tradition are either minor and eccentric figures, like Brownson and George, or major ones who are supposed to have been misread by everyone else, like Emerson and Niebuhr. For to have conceded that the "populist" moral conception is simply a limited and somewhat cranky version of a moral conception we find everywhere in modern culture would mean conceding that values modernity is supposed to have made obsolete are actually to be found at the very heart of modern life.

If, as Lasch suggested in his work on the family, there is a "deal" on which modern liberal society was founded, it is that we shall have the freedom to criticize the conditions in which we live. This bargain has given us an enormous body of literary and intellectual work, fiercely protected by liberal institutions, whose moral intention is to complicate all the issues that traditional liberal theory makes too simple. Lionel Trilling wrote a famous book to make this point; but *The Liberal Imagination* was not mentioned by Lasch. He seemed, and not only on the evidence of *The True and Only Heaven*, simply deaf to literature. "Misgivings were destined to be confined to a shadowy half-life on the fringes of debate,"[37] he wrote of the spread of specialization and the division of labor in the early years of the Industrial Revolution. It is as though Wordsworth, Dickens, and Thoreau had never written, or their books never been read.

At the core of Lasch's condemnation of liberalism is the familiar charge that liberalism is effectively without content—that "liberal man" is a wind-up contraption that chases its own short-term interests, and the liberal state a night watchman that only keeps the streets clean and the fights fair (or, at least, "efficient"). But liberalism does have a moral conception of the self, which is expressed in the political doctrine of rights. There is virtually no mention of rights in Lasch's attack on the elements of the modern liberal outlook, or in his analysis, in *The True and Only Heaven*, of particular political events, such as the disputes about busing and abortion. Elsewhere, he linked modern feminism's attachment to medical technology to the eighteenth-century idea of individual rights: the progressive mentality, he thought, regards access to reproductive technology as an enhancement of the woman's right to choose whether to bear children.[38] And it is clear that, like many other critics of liberalism, he wanted to replace talk of rights in our political vocabulary with talk of duties—talk of what we owe to our society and to each other, rather than what is owed to us. "Rights-bearers," he claimed, near the end of his life, in a symposium on the subject, "are regarded as autonomous individuals, and that is precisely the style of thinking we are trying to avoid."[39]

This seems to me to be an insufficient account of rights. It is insufficient historically because the recognition of individual rights figures crucially in the liberal idea of what counts as progress. And it is insufficient morally, as well, since our notion of exactly what a right entails—to speak freely, or to bear arms, or to travel or own property—and under what circumstances it must give way to other claims, is the subject of continual debate. The history of United States Supreme Court decisions alone is ample evidence of the intellectual and moral complexity of the idea of rights. It is true that from one perspective rights appear to uphold private interests against public goods—to protect my desire to publish obscene material, for example, against the community's desire to maintain standards of good taste. But from another perspective, a system of enumerated rights against the state, such as the Bill of Rights provides, is precisely an acknowledgment of the *general* claim of society as a whole against the individual. This was the view taken by some liberal contemporaries of Lasch's turn-of-the-century populists: that it is only because we recognize the legitimacy of society's claims generally that we undertake to respect the need for people to be exempted from those claims in specified types of behavior.

Because the subject is dismissed altogether from *The True and Only Heaven*, rights have no place in the book's account of the Southern civil rights movement, and this seems a telling omission. For what saves Lasch's populist tradition from being merely a bouquet of the values left strewn in the wake of progress is his contention that the populist spirit continues to have a life in real communities. Since the South has been the breeding ground for many populist politicians in this century, and since the South was itself a classic example of antiliberal "particularism"—"the preindustrial society par excellence," as Lasch once called it[40]—one would have expected him to give special attention to the character of Southern life. But prominent Southern populists go almost unmentioned in *The True and Only Heaven*. Huey Long's name, for example, appears only twice, in lists of the sort of people liberals unfairly associate with populism. George Wallace turns up more often; but although Lasch seemed to disapprove of the politics of resentment Wallace practiced during his days as a segregationist, his remarks on Wallace were otherwise not unkind, and he noted

Wallace's eventual acceptance of racial integration approvingly as testimony to the ability of one local ethnic constituency—lower-middle-class Southern whites—to respond to a moral appeal from another.

It is true that the Montgomery bus boycott of 1955–56, which is where the modern civil rights movement began, is one of the noblest political events in American history, and that it was made possible by the religious faith of a lower-class ethnic community—Southern blacks—essentially untouched by legalistic ways of thinking. But it is not true, as Lasch suggested it is, that the boycotters' victory, or the victories in other civil rights campaigns in the South, came about because lower-middle-class Southern whites understood the justice of the blacks' moral appeal. Southern whites did not take a notable part in the Montgomery protest except to oppose it and to humiliate and harass its participants. The protest succeeded because on the day a local judge issued the injunction that would have broken the boycott, the Supreme Court ruled that the black citizens of Montgomery had the right to sit where they chose on city buses. There was no "local solution" to the problem of racial segregation in the South because the principle at stake was not a local principle.

Lasch was always at his most acerbic in his criticism of middle-class liberals who impose the values of their culture on lower-middle-class communities and families, and he had much to say in his discussion of subjects like the busing controversy and the abortion debate about the attitude of moral superiority some liberals assume toward the less educated people who oppose them. There is indeed some ugliness in the middle-class attitudes he described; but to take note of the ugliness does not dispose of the matter.

Back in the 1960s, a group of filmmakers, Drew Associates, was invited by the Kennedy administration to film its enforcement of the court-ordered desegregation of the University of Alabama—the incident that culminated in George Wallace's famous "stand in the schoolhouse door." The film that was produced, *Crisis: Behind a Presidential Commitment*, covers events both at the White House and in Alabama. It is sometimes shown on public television, and it dramatizes the cultural friction Lasch writes about. Robert Kennedy, in the White House, and his deputy, Nicholas DeB. Katzenbach, in Alabama—Ivy League liberals, supremely assured of their virtue—are seen discussing their strategy for handling Wallace as though Wallace were an inconvenient road hazard, a man, in their calculus, of no moral account whatever. And Wallace is seen arriving at the university and accepting expressions of support from the people waiting to greet him with the easy familiarity of a man who knows them and is part of a genuine community.

Wallace was as successful a populist as the postwar era produced, and the Kennedy administration was undoubtedly the incarnation of the modern liberal mentality as Lasch conceives it. There is something slightly chilling about the confrontation, as there is when you watch any ancient and deeply rooted thing smoothly and expertly obliterated by the forces of "progress." But Kennedy and Katzenbach were right, and Wallace was wrong.

Lust in Action:
Jerry Falwell and Larry Flynt

I

The People vs. Larry Flynt opened on Christmas Day, 1996. It is the story of a free-spirited entrepreneur who dares to flout every canon of piety and taste. Though his irreverence is ratified by an enormous commercial success, he is persecuted incessantly by hypocritical bluenoses, convicted of absurd charges, imprisoned for contempt, and paralyzed by a would-be assassin's bullet. Confined to a wheelchair and in constant physical pain, he sinks into drugs, despair, and near-madness, but he never quits, and in the end his perseverance is rewarded by a unanimous Supreme Court victory in a suit brought against him by the most sanctimonious moralizer of the day. Through it all, he is sustained by the great soul-love of his wife, a woman who has overcome poverty and abuse through indomitable spunk, but she dies tragically on the eve of his triumph, and his moment of vindication is made bittersweet by the memory of the more precious thing he has lost. Still, thanks to this man's determination to stand on his rights when all around him, even his attorney, were ready to give him up, we live in a freer country today.

Well, this was certainly one way to tell the story of Larry Flynt, the publisher of *Hustler* magazine and the victor in the famous Supreme Court case of *Hustler v. Falwell*. "It's a Capra movie with porn!"[1] was the reaction the movie's screenwriters, Scott Alexander and Larry Karaszewski, said they got when they first pitched the idea to Columbia Pictures, and they were able to attract an exceptional team of filmmakers who evidently shared the sentiment, including the director Milos Forman, who had not made a movie since 1989, and the producers Oliver Stone, Janet Yang (who produced *The Joy Luck Club*), and Michael Hausman (who produced *Silkwood*). Larry Flynt is played by Woody Harrelson as a charming, "gotta be me" good ol' boy who just happens to love the ladies, and who, no matter how much he is made to suffer for it, is simply incapable of inhibition or deceit. His wife, Althea, is played by the rock star Courtney Love—the personal choice for the part, Forman let it be known, of Mr. and Mrs. Václav Havel. The young actor Ed Norton is Alan Isaacman, Flynt's straight-arrow attorney, and small parts are played by James Carville (against type) as Simon Leis, the Cincinnati prosecutor who got Flynt convicted, briefly, on pandering, obscenity, and organized crime charges, and Donna Hanover, then still the wife of Rudolph Giuliani, as Ruth Carter Stapleton, Jimmy Carter's evangelical sister, who got Flynt converted, also briefly, to Christianity. The real Larry Flynt himself appears in the role of William Morrissey, a Cincinnati judge who once sentenced Flynt to seven to twenty-five years in prison (he served six days). The screenplay adapts Flynt's story beautifully to the classic three-act bio-pic format (he's up, he's down, he's up), and the courtroom scenes are both plausible and entertaining, which is an extremely rare coincidence in motion picture history. The movie is of course laced with nudity, obscenity, and tastelessness, but it is all, as it were, in the best of taste. Apart from fleeting glimpses of a few well-known images, such as the notorious *Hustler* cover picturing a woman being fed into a meat grinder, nothing remotely repulsive or titillating is shown. The story may be smutty, but the film is so clean it practically squeaks.

The movie was screened in October 1996 at the close of the New York Film Festival, and the immediate response was enthusiastic. Frank Rich, in the *New York Times*, called it "the most timely and patriotic movie of the year,"[2] and his column was reprinted, complete and unabridged, in advertisements for the film. Soon after, though, there was a liberal backlash. The *Times* itself ran a long story, by Nina Bernstein, headed "A Hero of Free Speech? It's Not So Simple," in which prominent liberals such as Cass Sunstein and Burt Neuborne, a former legal director of the American Civil Liberties Union who had a small part in the movie as Jerry Falwell's attorney, criticized the film as one-sided on the free speech issues, and the *New Republic* ran an article by Hanna Rosin which criticized the film as one-sided on pretty much all the issues. "This Christmas," as she put it, "pond scum is intellectually chic."[3]

There were several distinct questions in this response. The first had to do with the verisimilitude of the movie itself. It was not impeccable. Alexander and Karaszewski, in their introduction to the published screenplay, admitted to a few emendations. Contrary to what is shown in the movie, they confessed, Alan Isaacman was not Flynt's attorney in all his cases. Nor were the editors of *Hustler* the same group of people from the start. In real life, Flynt used many lawyers and fired his editorial staff regularly. The screenwriters argued, reasonably, the need to avoid confusion in a picture meant to cover fifteen years of a man's life. But there are many episodes in the movie that depart from even the account Flynt himself provided in *An Unseemly Man*, an autobiography published to accompany the film.

In the opening scenes of the movie, for instance, we are shown ten-year-old Larry—"bursting with a Huckleberry Finn industriousness," as the screenplay puts it (I think they mean "a Tom Sawyer industriousness"; Huckleberry Finn was distinctly not the industrious type)—peddling moonshine in his native backwoods Kentucky. But Flynt never sold moonshine. When he was sixteen or seventeen, he tells us in *An Unseemly Man*, he made some money driving liquor from a neighboring wet county into the dry county where his family lived—also illegal, but less adorable. In the movie's account of Flynt's first meeting with Althea, she seduces him within three minutes right in his office ("So how come you haven't tried to ball *me*?" she says), and they have sex there until he pleads exhaustion. The autobiography, by comparison, is positively chivalrous. Flynt asks Althea out after work ("She was coy about it,"[4] he reports) and they spend much of the night just talking. In the movie Althea proposes marriage to Flynt after a bout of group sex in a hot tub; in the autobiography, they are driving somewhere together in a car.

In the movie, Flynt is initiated into the business of "adult" publishing by a local printer who explains that he can't just print photographs of naked women without some sort of text as a legal "beard." But this story does not appear in the book, nor is there any suggestion there that it was ever Flynt's intention, in launching *Hustler*, to publish only photographs of naked women, or that he was naive about anything except the amount of work involved in putting out a magazine. And when Althea dies, by drowning in a bathtub, the movie has Flynt alone with her in his bedroom, tragically unable, because of his paralysis, to help her or to get help. In the book we learn that there was a nurse in the room the whole time.

Then there are those facts of Flynt's life, magazine, and legal adventures that are simply elided. Hanna Rosin points out, for instance, that viewers are not told that Althea was actually the fourth of Flynt's five wives, or that Flynt has fathered five children, none of whom have lived with him, or that *Hustler* routinely runs cartoons lampooning black people and prints pictures of naked three-hundred-pound women, women with penises, women with diarrhea whose feces are shown running down their legs, and so on. The legal history is similarly selective. Viewers would not know, for example, that *Hustler v. Falwell*, decided in 1988, was not Flynt's first encounter with the Supreme Court. In 1984, the Court heard arguments in a suit against *Hustler* by Kathy Keeton, who was the wife of the publisher of *Penthouse*, Bob Guccione, and whom *Hustler* had portrayed in a cartoon suggesting that she had contracted venereal disease from Guccione. As the justices adjourned, Flynt, whose request to represent himself in oral arguments had been denied, shouted from the audience, "You're nothing but eight assholes and a token cunt!"[5] He was arrested, though the charges were eventually dropped. In a movie whose director has claimed that "the hero [is] the Supreme Court of the United States,"[6] this would seem a relevant episode.

If completeness and verisimilitude were the standards, of course, no movie or novel based on "real-life" events would ever pass the test. A movie isn't supposed to reproduce the facts; it's supposed to dramatize them, and the question for the viewer is substantially the same in the case of a movie claiming to be based on historical events as it is in the case of a movie that concerns a topical subject but is otherwise fictional. It is whether the essence of the movie experience somehow squares with, or "gets at," the essence of the lived experience. It's a mistake, I think, to assume that what we're meant to be "getting at" in *The People vs. Larry Flynt* is the real Larry Flynt. That was the way the filmmakers sometimes talked about what they tried to do, and the movie does have a biographical structure. But this is mostly because a movie about a person is much easier to get people interested in seeing than a movie about an issue. What matters isn't whether the real Larry Flynt is a smut peddler with a heart of gold or merely a smut peddler with a wheelchair of gold, something that is probably indeterminable anyway. What matters is how we are led to think about the phenomena with which Larry Flynt's life happened to intersect in the period covered by the movie, which runs from 1972, when Flynt was operating a string of striptease clubs in Ohio, to 1988, when the *Falwell* opinion was handed down—that is, pornography, the religious right, and First Amendment law.

2

The emphasis of the movie is almost entirely on the development of First Amendment law, and especially on the legal matter at issue in *Hustler v. Falwell*—which explains the enthusiasm of commentators like Frank Rich. On the subject of pornography, *The People vs. Larry Flynt* seems to have nothing more to say than that it's a harmless amusement which some people have a taste for and some people don't, and that the people who actively seek to suppress it are a good deal more dangerous than the people who produce it. On the subject of the religious right, the movie regards Jerry Falwell as a smug pomposity, but it is careful not to cast him in a particularly lurid light—a treatment it reserves instead for Charles Keating, who, before he became famous for his involvement in the savings-and-loan scandal, was once a vigorous antipornography crusader, and was Flynt's real-life nemesis in Cincinnati back in the 1970s.

This emphasis on the law rather than the pornography is arguably warranted by the fact that *Hustler v. Falwell* was not an obscenity case; it was a defamation case. The fact that Flynt was the publisher of a raunchy magazine had no bearing on the legal issues involved. The case arose from a parody of a Campari ad. Campari used to market its product with advertisements featuring celebrities who spoke, in a mock interview format, about their "first time"— meaning their first drink of Campari, but suggestive of their first sexual experience. In 1983, *Hustler* published a parody of this ad that featured Falwell, who was made to disclose that his "first time" had been with his mother, and that the memorable event had taken place in an outhouse. He was also made to admit that he often preached while drunk. The piece was listed as "fiction" in the table of contents, and underneath the ad, in small type, were the words "Ad parody—not to be taken seriously."

Falwell sued in United States District Court for the Western District of Virginia, his home state. His complaint listed three grounds for recovery: invasion of privacy (that is, the appropriation of his name and face for commercial purposes), libel, and the intentional infliction of emotional distress. After a raucous trial—featuring a surreal deposition of Flynt, who, heavily medicated and in prison on an unrelated contempt citation, began by giving his full name as Christopher Columbus Cornwallis I. P. Q. Harvey H. Apache Pugh, and proceeded to offer, over Isaacman's objections, a considerable quantity of uncensored and self-damaging testimony—the jury found for Flynt on the invasion of privacy claim (since the appropriation was not made for purposes of trade) and the defamation claim (since no one could be expected to believe the ad), but for Falwell on the third count, intentional infliction of emotional distress, and it awarded him $200,000 in damages. The verdict was upheld on appeal in 1986, and the case went before the Supreme Court in the following year, where, in a unanimous opinion written by Chief Justice Rehnquist, the emotional distress judgment was finally reversed.

It would be misleading to say that *Hustler v. Falwell* extended the scope of First Amendment speech protections. What the Supreme Court did, essentially, was to preserve the scope that already existed, which they did by rejecting an effort by the Appeals Court to allow a public figure, absent a finding of libel, to recover on a claim of emotional distress. The Appeals Court had conceded that Falwell's defamation claim was ruled out by the landmark case of *New York Times Co. v. Sullivan* (1964), which held that a public official cannot recover from a newspaper for libel unless he proves "actual malice" on the part of the paper, and by the subsequent decision in *Curtis Publishing Co. v. Butts* (1967), which extended the rule to cover "public figures" (not just "public officials") generally. The constitutional logic in these cases involves the concept of "breathing space": the Court felt that the press requires some leeway in matters of fact if public debate is to be uninhibited, as the First Amendment presumably intends it to be. Public figures are people who, although they do not hold public office, have made themselves participants in public debate, a definition that clearly applied to Falwell. (An effort to extend the protection to cover the unintentional defamation of private citizens in stories relating to matters of public *interest* was rejected by the Court in *Gertz v. Robert Welch, Inc.* [1974].) But the appellate court did conclude that a public figure's claim of emotional distress could survive a failure to prove "actual malice" under the *New York Times* standard. So long as *Hustler* acted recklessly and with an intention to inflict emotional distress (as Flynt essentially conceded that it had), Falwell was entitled to damages.

The Supreme Court regarded this as an attempt to make an end run around *New York Times*. The lower court decision meant that a public figure who cannot establish that he has been defamed can still argue that he has been distressed. In rejecting this theory,

Rehnquist drew an analogy between the Campari parody and a political cartoon. It is in the nature of satire and parody, he said, to wound, and "in the world of debate about public affairs, many things done with motives that are less than admirable are protected by the First Amendment."[7] If Falwell had been a private figure—or, presumably, if the communication of the insult had been private—there might have been a tort. But in the public realm, the Constitution washes the insult clean.

The classic analysis of *Hustler v. Falwell* is by Robert C. Post, in an article which appeared in the *Harvard Law Review* in 1990 and which he reprinted in his book *Constitutional Domains*.[8] The case, as Post demonstrates in penetrating detail, represents a collision between two types of legal claims—a claim of personal injury made by Falwell versus a constitutional claim of free speech asserted by Flynt—which represents in turn a collision between two radically different theories of civil society. Falwell sued on the basis of the so-called dignitary torts: defamation, invasion of privacy, and emotional distress. We allow individuals to recover for these injuries to their dignity not because we wish to chill or restrict public debate, but because we wish to *foster* that debate by sanctioning expressions which have no purpose except to wound or intimidate other speakers. In the case of the infliction of emotional distress, the standard for determining when speech becomes tortious is the standard of outrageousness, which is, necessarily, a community standard. Behavior is outrageous, as the second *Restatement of Torts* helpfully explains, when "the recitation of the facts to an average member of the community would . . . lead him to exclaim, 'Outrageous!' "[9] *Hustler*'s Campari ad parody is clearly justiciable under such a standard.

Flynt's defense against Falwell rests, as Post sees it, on a different theory. The First Amendment law on which Flynt relied posits a realm of "public discourse," populated by "public figures" like Falwell and Flynt and operating through media like *Hustler* (and the *New York Times*), in which community-based norms of civility, such as its notion of outrageousness, do not apply. In extending First Amendment protections, the Court has generally argued that in a diverse society, a society of many values and tastes, one man's outrage is another man's sincere opinion. The realm of "public discourse" is thus not only characterized by immunity from liability for giving offense; one might even say that it is *defined* by that immunity. The paradox is this: by extending the protections of the First Amendment we seek to ensure the fullest possible participation in the democratic determination of communal norms and values, but we simultaneously prevent ourselves from using those norms and values to regulate expression which we consider, as a community, detrimental.

Post has put his finger on what is unsettling, for many people, about the opinion in the *Falwell* case, and on what is also unsettling, for many people, about pornography of the kind Flynt has made a fortune purveying; and the conflict he articulates is what accounts for the liberal backlash against *The People vs. Larry Flynt*. In celebrating the constitutional triumph, the movie seems oblivious of the cultural damage. The movie has an easy time of it by virtue of the fact that the plaintiff in *Hustler v. Falwell* was a man regarded by many Americans, and by most liberals, as a self-righteous and meddlesome proponent of illiberal policies—in other words, a slightly dangerous man. But Falwell's views and personality are irrelevant to the constitutional issues in his suit, and one can put what is at stake in those issues much more starkly by asking whether, if the butt of *Hustler*'s parody had been, say, Martin Luther King, Jr., Oliver Stone and Milos Forman would have made a movie about it.

The question the *Falwell* case poses (as Post analyzes it) is whether a principle of free speech can be devised which is firm enough to protect dissident and unpopular opinion but not so inflexible that it protects hatemongers and speech bullies along with it. Many intelligent people, in the years since *Hustler v. Falwell* was decided, have tried to formulate such a principle, although the task seems doomed by the impossibility of coming up with a general standard that would allow courts to parse unerringly the difference between hate speech and flag-burning, or between Larry Flynt and Robert Mapplethorpe. Protect one type of speech offensive to some and it is hard not to protect all. For people who have concluded that the social costs of a general protection are smaller than the social costs of a more elaborate and discriminating approach, *Hustler v. Falwell* (or even the hypothetical *Hustler v. King*) is an easy case.

But reduced to legal terms like this, the really significant things in most actual cases—the things that make the issues matter to us in the first place—tend to drop out, and this seems to be what has happened in *The People vs. Larry Flynt*. The anthropology of the story is a lot more interesting than the jurisprudence. For what is notable, as a cultural matter, about most speech cases is the symbiosis of the two sides. Orthodoxy depends upon heterodoxy, victimization requires persecution, good taste creates bad taste: the observation is perfectly obvious, but it is precisely what drops out in a legal analysis. In legal terms, Jerry Falwell and Larry Flynt represent opposed interests, each out to bring down, or at a minimum to chill, the other side. But in cultural terms, the Falwells and the Flynts are mutually reinforcing entities. They acquire their definitions from each other, and what is fascinating about them is not that they ended up in court together, but that they arose together, they fell together, and their worlds constantly interpenetrated one another—were, at bottom, the same world.

3

The first issue of *Hustler* appeared in 1974. The magazine became successful, and world famous, in 1975, when it published a five-page photo spread of Jacqueline Kennedy Onassis in the nude. The pictures had been taken by an Italian paparazzo, with a telephoto lens, who had staked out the Greek island of Skorpios, where the Onassises had a house. They had been offered first to *Playboy* and *Penthouse*, the established magazines in the field, but *Playboy* and *Penthouse* turned them down (exercising scruples they would soon find good reasons to abandon). Flynt bought them, he claims in his autobiography, for $18,000, and the issue of *Hustler* in which they appeared sold a million copies off the newsstand in a matter of days. It was the perfect combination of titillation and personal violation, and once Flynt got his hands on the formula, he never let go.

Now, the distinctive thing about *Hustler* is that it was not *Play-*

boy. This is a point that gets made in *The People vs. Larry Flynt*, but made in the wrong way. The filmmakers stress the fact, which is undoubtedly correct, that Flynt set out to create a magazine for downscale readers. *Playboy* was a self-proclaimed lifestyle magazine. It accompanied its photographs of partially clad and unclad women with articles on fashion, high-end audio equipment, and expensive cars, and with fiction by big-name writers like John Updike and interviews with noteworthy figures like Buckminster Fuller. Flynt's initial insight was that the typical consumer of nudie pictorials was probably not realistically in the market for high-end audio products and did not have much interest in the views of Buckminster Fuller. So he set his sights on the sort of reader for whom solemn interviews with noteworthy figures represented the height of pretension—the sort of reader who would get more pleasure from seeing such people lampooned than from reading their interviews. *Playboy* would have interviewed Jerry Falwell; *Hustler* ran a Campari ad parody.

All very fine and democratic, but it leaves out a more significant point of contrast, and that has to do with the partially clad and unclad women. *Playboy* published its first issue in 1953, and in spite of its liberated attitude toward sex, it was, in its attitude toward women, very much a magazine of that decade. *Playboy* women were naked, but they were in every other respect as inaccessible and chaste as nuns. They were women who had been somehow reduced to flesh and elevated to sanctity at the same time. They represented some fantasy of fifties bachelorhood: upstanding, clean, and miraculously free of guilt. They had perfect breasts in the same sense that they had perfect teeth. There was no suggestion that they had any sexual interests of their own.

The mass-market pornography of the so-called "sexual revolution," the pornography that emerged in the late sixties and early seventies and flooded into bookstores, newsstands, movie theaters, and ultimately video outlets, was based on a different premise. It has become common to talk about pornography as the representation of male dominance and female submission, as sending the "message" that women were put on earth for the sexual gratification of men.

This is the way it is described, for example, by Catharine MacKin-non and other feminists who advocate censorship, and the descrip-tion tends to be accepted even by people who reject MacKinnon's legal arguments. But mass-market pornography was not based, in the beginning, anyway, on the image of the sex-driven male. It was based on the image of the sex-driven female. The pop ideology of sexual liberation was that, contrary to the lesson taught by centuries of moral conditioning, women enjoyed sex as much as men, and in the same way as men were imagined to enjoy it—that is, actively, promiscuously, and without guilt. Most of the pornographic films of the era that achieved the status of cultural chic were about women in search of sexual pleasure: *I Am Curious (Yellow)* (1968), *Deep Throat* (1972), *The Devil in Miss Jones* (1973), and the soft-core *Em-manuelle* films, which began in 1974.

These movies were produced entirely for the delectation of men, of course, and when Linda Marciano, the star of *Deep Throat*, emerged a decade later to reveal that she had performed in that film under duress, she exposed rather dramatically the extent to which the promiscuous woman of the sexual revolution, despite all the popular rhetoric about sexual equality and "no double standard," was just another male fantasy. In the early seventies, though, when Flynt was entering the sex business as the owner of a striptease club in Dayton, that rhetoric was at its height. Commercial sex—strip-tease clubs and pornographic movies and magazines—was under-stood in many minds as the natural consequence of the frank acknowledgment that men and women both enjoy sex. This is the view of the sexual revolution adhered to by the makers of *The People vs. Larry Flynt*—that Flynt was just being honest about a subject made shameful by prudes and hypocrites. And it is why they went out of their way to remake Althea Flynt.

Who the real Althea was is probably beyond recovering. The Althea of Flynt's autobiography is the one woman he meets with whom he can share something *besides* sex, and he makes it rather clear that good sex was not the basis of their relationship. But good sex is the basis of their relationship in Forman's movie, which imag-ines Althea as the very type of the female sexual athlete and aggressor of sexual-revolution mythology. That Larry and Althea are sexual equals—that equality is precisely the lesson Althea comes into Larry's life to teach him—is emphasized in a number of scenes, most notably one (not in the screenplay) in which Larry smacks Althea, early in their relationship, and she warns him *never* to hit her again. But in fact, the real Althea admitted that Flynt beat her, and she was once quoted in *Hustler* explaining that "I don't see anything wrong with a man striking a woman. In fact, many women are turned on by it."[10]

Getting this wrong means missing the whole point of *Hustler*'s accomplishment. *Hustler* was not, in the tradition of *Playboy*, about sex as play or about sex without moral hang-ups. It was about sex as a kind of violation. The nude photographs of Jacqueline Onassis epitomized the magazine's view of sex. When that issue of *Hustler* appeared, the governor of Ohio, Jim Rhodes, was caught buying a copy at a newsstand, and this indiscretion became widely reported, much to Flynt's delight. The episode is presented in the movie, where it is played as another proof of the fake prudery of official culture. Rhodes wants to see the pictures, but he is ashamed of it, and this is portrayed as an example of the sort of hypocrisy men like Larry Flynt dare to expose. But it is not hypocrisy. It is natural to want to see pictures of a famous woman naked, and it is also shameful, since the pictures violate her privacy in the most flagrant way. The itch to see the pictures is completely bound up with the sense that it's wrong, the sense that the itch itself is somehow personally debasing. Far from constituting another step toward a more honest and democratic sexuality, this association between sex and guilt, between (as Althea was made to say about being beaten) pleasure and indignity, was a throwback to the world before *Playboy*. Larry Flynt put the shame back into sex.

Jerry Falwell was on the same mission, and the parallel is less superficial than it may sound. Falwell's relation to the sexual revolution was, on a certain level, exactly the same as Flynt's: he, too, hoped to exploit the sense of sin and shame that the revolution had supposedly made obsolete. Falwell would have been no more imaginable without *Playboy*, and everything that followed from it, than

Flynt would have been. They were both sexual reactionaries. The intertwining of the world of televangelism and the world of sex magazines was, in fact, one of the most remarkable phenomena of the period covered in *The People vs. Larry Flynt*, and it is too bad that the filmmakers didn't find more to say about it.

Falwell emerged on the public stage when Jimmy Carter, then running for president, confessed in an interview in *Playboy* to having sometimes felt "lust in my heart." Before Carter's confession, Falwell had been known mostly in the neighborhood of his native Lynchburg, Virginia, where he had established an immensely successful ministry, at the Thomas Road Baptist Church, and where, in 1971, he had founded Liberty Baptist College. Most of his preaching had been directed against alcohol and drugs, but after seeing the national attention he attracted by his public criticism of Carter (who, of course, had identified himself as a born-again Christian), Falwell changed his targets to abortion, homosexuality, and pornography. It was an excellent career move.

Carter's election, in 1976, suggested to many people that outspoken Christianity was a way for even a Democrat to win elections, and in 1979, a group of conservative political and religious figures asked Falwell to head an organization named, by the conservative activist Paul Weyrich, the Moral Majority, whose mission was to mobilize Christian voters on behalf of Republican candidates. The Moral Majority took considerable credit (with what justification remains a matter of dispute) for the election of Ronald Reagan in 1980, and although Reagan was careful not to associate himself personally with Falwell, he was also careful not to dissociate himself publicly. So that when *Hustler* ran its ad parody, in 1983, it was not firing off a random attack on someone who had strayed accidentally into its line of fire. The ad was part of a campaign against Falwell, who had already been honored as *Hustler*'s "Asshole of the Month." For Falwell was not only the personification of the sort of officious sanctimoniousness *Hustler*'s readers were supposed to enjoy lampooning; he also was a man in a position politically to damage the commercial empire of Larry Flynt. Falwell and Flynt were each other's devils, but they were also each other's raisons d'être.

By 1983, Falwell had an empire of his own. He had, in fact, two

empires, a ministry and a political organization. The core congregation of Falwell's ministry was the church in Lynchburg, which had
seventeen thousand members in 1983 (up from thirty-five when Falwell took it over, in 1956). But Falwell also had a television program,
The Old Time Gospel Hour, which was carried weekly on 373 stations—more than any other televangelist of the time. By the early
eighties, the program claimed to have twenty-five million viewers,
and was bringing in a million dollars in contributions a week. Fund-
raising was, in fact, its main activity, so much so that, as Frances
Fitzgerald reported, five of every seven dollars raised was spent just
to keep the show going.[11] When the Moral Majority was formed, it
started its fund-raising drive using the television program's mailing
list, and brought in $2.2 million in the first year. The ministry's
newsletter, the *Journal Companion*, was turned into the political organization's newsletter, the *Moral Majority Report*, which was sent
to 840,000 homes with a readership estimated at three million.
More than three hundred radio stations broadcast Moral Majority
commentary daily. In 1983, the organization claimed four million
members, which is probably an exaggeration, but which indicates
the scale on which Falwell conceived of himself and his influence at
the time.

When the Campari ad appeared, in 1983, Falwell was quick to
sue, but he was also quick to turn the ad to financial account. He
sent out two mailings under the aegis of the Moral Majority to
members and "major donors," requesting funds to "defend his
mother's memory," and a third letter to 750,000 viewers of *The Old
Time Gospel Hour*. The mailing to the major donors—there were
26,900 of them—included copies of the ad, with eight offensive
words blacked out. The letters raised more than $700,000 in thirty
days. When Flynt learned of them, he countersued Falwell for copyright infringement—for reproducing the ad without permission
from *Hustler*. He lost this suit, but he made his point, which was, of
course, that Falwell was so far indifferent to the reputation of his
mother (who was, by the way, no longer alive) as to disseminate to
thousands of people who had never seen it the parody that traduced
her.[12]

Who received these appeals? Falwell's constituents, like the constituents of all the televangelists who flourished in the 1980s, were generally downscale. They were not well off, and they tended, in the words of an official of the National Council of Churches, which paid close attention to the phenomenon, "to be alienated from mainline America. They feel they are on the short end of things, that they haven't gotten what others have."[13] The profile of Falwell's audience, in other words, apart from the obvious difference, was remarkably parallel to the profile of *Hustler*'s audience—a circumstance beautifully illuminated by an event which took place while Flynt and Falwell were in the midst of their legal war over the Campari ad.

In 1986, Alan Sears, the executive director of the Meese Commission, which had been set up at the direction of President Reagan to examine the issue of pornography, wrote a letter, on Justice Department stationery, to twenty-three companies accusing them of being "major players in the game of pornography." The letter gave the companies three weeks to respond, with the implicit threat that they would somehow be exposed in the commission's final report if they did not. Among these companies were 7-Eleven; Rite-Aid, the drugstore chain; and Kmart, which owned Waldenbooks. All were accused (Sears based his letter on testimony before the commission by another fundamentalist crusader, the Reverend Donald Wildmon) of retailing *Playboy*, *Penthouse*, and other sexually explicit magazines. The effect on the magazines was devastating. 7-Eleven convenience stores, which are not ordinarily the source of goods for upscale consumers, were in fact the major outlet for *Penthouse*, and they sold 20 percent of all copies of *Playboy*. The companies buckled—since, clearly, they were also patronized by many churchgoing, fundamentalist shoppers who regarded pornography as sinful, and who could be expected to be susceptible to calls for a boycott.

Although *Penthouse* and several other plaintiffs ultimately obtained a federal court ruling that Sears's letter constituted unlawful prior restraint, "the damage," as John Heidenry says, "had been done. The removal of *Playboy* and *Penthouse* from ten thousand stores across the country, including the mammoth 7-Eleven and Rite-Aid chains, sent the circulations of both magazines plummeting."[14] *Hustler* was one of the magazines affected. The incident, Heidenry also points out, was not an isolated incident of extremist pressure on mainstream taste. It reflected a shift in mainstream tolerance of pornography as well. In 1986, *Time* magazine reported that 63 percent of women and 47 percent of men now believed that pornography led men to commit rape.

But the demise of the culture of anything-goes sexuality coincided with the demise of the culture of televangelism, and by the end of 1987, when *Hustler v. Falwell* was finally argued before the Supreme Court, Falwell's empire had become as marginalized as Flynt's. The reason was the PTL scandal, which was, fittingly, played out in the twin worlds of religious broadcasting and adult magazines. The scandal began when Jim Bakker, the host, with his wife Tammy Faye, of the television program of the PTL (Praise the Lord) Club, was accused of having committed adultery by a church worker named Jessica Hahn, who claimed Bakker had deflowered her, and of having used several hundred thousand dollars of PTL money to purchase her silence. The ensuing inquiry into PTL's financial affairs disclosed a massive bilking scheme, and in the uproar, Bakker asked Falwell to take custody of his ministry. Falwell agreed, and his magnanimity proved his undoing. Falwell's constituency was Baptist; Bakker's was Pentecostal, and the suspicion quickly arose that Falwell was principally interested not in saving PTL but in dissolving it in the interests of folding its viewership—the program was said in 1987 to reach over twelve million homes—into his *Old Time Gospel Hour* ministry. Falwell denied the charge, but it was repeated continually, and the light thrown by Bakker's indictment and conviction on the whole practice of fund-raising through religious broadcasting (by 1987, *The Old Time Gospel Hour* was reported to be spending twenty-six minutes of every half-hour pleading for money) ended by crippling the national credibility of televangelists like Falwell.

Hahn, meanwhile, went on to pose twice for *Playboy*, the second time following plastic surgery subsidized by Hugh Hefner himself. (Her claim to have been a virgin when Bakker slept with her has been pretty thoroughly discredited.) In 1988, a year after Hahn's pic-

tures appeared in *Playboy*, *Penthouse* revealed that another prominent televangelist, Jimmy Swaggart, had paid a prostitute to pose for
him, in a hotel room, in provocative postures he told her he had
seen in adult magazines. And a year after that, *Penthouse* published
an interview with a protégé of Bakker's who claimed to have served
as his "male prostitute."

The sexually explicit magazine industry and the televangelist
fund-raising industry were, in short, working opposite sides of the
same street. They knew each other's business better than anyone
else in America did: they were fighting over the same socioeconomic constituency. So it is not surprising that when Falwell sued
Flynt over the Campari ad, the lawyer he chose to represent him
was Norman Roy Grutman, a man who had become famous as the
principal attorney for *Penthouse*. Falwell knew Grutman well. He
had met him back in 1981 when he was suing *Penthouse* for running
an interview with him without his permission. Grutman had attracted attention on that occasion by referring publicly to Falwell as
"Foulwell," but he won the case—and got a new client in the bargain. Flynt has, understandably, a good deal of fun with this irony in
An Unseemly Man, but the filmmakers, for some reason, never mention it. They may have felt it was the kind of detail that would spoil
the simplicity of the legal drama they wished to present, but it is a
detail that touches the heart of the cultural moment their movie is
about.

Laurie Anderson's
United States

Laurie Anderson was born in Chicago in 1947 and was raised in the suburb of Glen Ellyn. She entered Mills College, in California, in 1965, with the intention of becoming a doctor, but dropped out after a year and moved to New York City, where she enrolled at Barnard. She graduated with a degree in art history in 1969, studied for a year with Sol Lewitt and Carl Andre at the School of Visual Arts, and in 1972 received an M.F.A. from Columbia, where she majored in sculpture and studied with Meyer Schapiro and the philosopher Arthur Danto. Her career as a performance and mixed-media artist began the same year.

In 1978, Anderson heard the song "O Souverain," from Jules Massenet's opera *Le Cid* (1885), at a concert in Berkeley. The experience inspired her to write "O Superman," which, with the help of a five-hundred-dollar grant from the National Endowment for the Arts, was released as a single by 110 Records in 1981. "O Superman" went to number two on the British pop charts. It was a crossover hit that no one had anticipated—110 Records had pressed only a thousand copies, and lacked the capacity to meet the demand for more. The song's success led to a six-record contract between Anderson and Warner Bros. Records. The first of those albums was *Big Science*, released in 1982.

The Warner Bros. money enabled Anderson to complete and mount her mixed-media work *United States*, which she had been working on since 1979, and which included many of the songs on *Big Science*. *United States* opened at the Brooklyn Academy of Music on February 3, 1983. (I saw the second show, on February 5 and 6.) The work was divided into four parts, comprising seventy-eight separately titled segments, some of them musical and some spoken; and it took eight hours, split over two nights, to perform. Although it is Anderson's most famous work, it has been performed in its entirety only four times—twice in the Opera House at BAM, once at the Dominion Theatre in London, and once in Zurich, where it was done in one all-night, eight-hour set. No complete video of it exists.[1]

United States is often classified as performance art, but this can be misleading. The work was much more conventionally staged than performance art ordinarily is. Anderson used the proscenium for the traditional theatrical purpose—that is, to establish an unambiguous distinction between the performer and the audience, a distinction performance artists generally go to some lengths to blur. And she rigorously excluded the element that gives most performance art its edge, which is contingency. In performance art, a piece isn't performed; the performance is the piece. The work of art is whatever happens within the set of conditions the artist has laid down.

Anderson had created that kind of work many times before. In her *Institutional Dream Series* (1973), she had slept in public places (such as the beach at Coney Island in January; night court at 100 Centre Street, in New York City; and the women's bathroom in the Schermerhorn Library at Columbia). In *Duets on Ice* (1974–75), she had performed on the streets in the five boroughs of New York City and in Genoa, Italy, to whatever groups of passersby assembled. She told them personal anecdotes, accompanying herself on a "self-playing" violin—that is, an instrument that played prerecorded music when the bow was scraped across the strings. "The pre-recorded material was mostly of cowboy songs recorded on ninety-minute cassettes," as she described the piece. "I'd play along, but since it was a loop there was no definite way to end the concert. So the timing mechanism was a pair of skates with their blades frozen into blocks of ice. When the ice melted and I lost my balance, the concert was over."[2] The blocks of ice were the performance-art element: they made each performance time- and place-specific. In *United States*, though, Anderson was performing pieces she had already created, and some of which her audience knew from listening to "O Superman" and other tracks on *Big Science*. Anderson's appearance at BAM had a lot more in common with Barry Manilow at Wolf Trap than it did with Chris Burden at The Kitchen. *United States* was a concert.

Still, Anderson did come out of the performance art tradition, and *United States* was essentially an elaboration of that tradition's central insight, which is that the ground of expression is the body. This may seem a counterintuitive thing to say about a work famous for an ostentatious display of electronic hardware—vocoder, harmonizer, synclavier—and lots of visual effects. And most of the songs and stand-up routines Anderson delivered in *United States* were wan, ironic tales about daily life in the postindustrial—what we now call the digital—age, with repeated references to airplanes, televisions, petrochemicals, missiles, and outer space. The gadgets and the spaceships may have given people the idea that *United States* enacted a disaffection with creeping dehumanization, that it was a cri de coeur against the disenchantment of the world. But its effect on me was exactly the opposite. I took the point to be that the world *can't* be disenchanted, because enchantment is the mode in which human beings experience it. The trail of the human serpent (said William James) is over everything, even answering-machine beeps and aircraft safety instructions. Our electronics is no less an expression of ourselves than our poetry is.

One of the great evolutionary leaps in the history of modern entertainment was the invention of the microphone. The microphone is more than a convenience, and it is more than a prop; it is an ex-

tension of the body. It expands the space the performer can command by reducing that space to the dimensions of intimacy. It turns
the stadium into a bedroom; it murmurs softly into the ears of thousands. And then there is the object itself—this long, sleek, juiced-
up thing just begging to be caressed with sounds, to be kissed and
teased and masturbated. It is the instrument of vocal seduction and
its very image. That the microphone looks the way it does is no accident: the ghost of the body is hidden in the forms of everything we
create. Many images in *United States* were designed to make this
point: for example, an enormous blown-up photograph of an electric wall socket. It looked, twenty feet high, with its two vertical
slots and the little hole underneath, just like a face, frozen in an
expression of permanent astonishment, an electronic Mr. Potato
Head.

All the hardware in *United States* was prosthetic in just this way.
Anderson programmed her synthesizers with human voices (like the
breathy "hah hah hahs" in "O Superman"); she projected her own
silhouette onto a vast screen and made shadow puppets with her
hands. She inserted a miniature speaker into her mouth and manipulated the sound by moving her lips. She recorded her own voice on
a strip of audiotape, fixed the tape to a bow, and "played" it on a violin with a pick-up mounted on it in place of strings (the "self-
playing" instrument she had devised for *Duets on Ice*). She wired
her head and performed a drum solo on her skull. She turned herself, in short, into an instrument. She didn't sing the body electric.
She *was* the body electric.

The monologues in *United States* mostly expressed a mild neuro-
sis about living in a world filled with airplanes and answering machines; but the work itself exuded control. A petite androgyne, done
up in punk chic—black suit, red socks, Vaseline-spiked hair—and
manipulating her voice to sound, alternately, like a Midwestern in-
genue and a solemnly goofy Ronald Reagan, dominated the room
for eight hours. Contingency was banned for a reason: In two
evenings' worth of songs and stories about how things tend to go
wrong, nothing was supposed to go wrong. And the gamine persona
was plainly designed to point up a contrast: the more waiflike An-

derson seemed, the more mysterious and impressive was the control she exerted. The show was wired, and there was a woman in a punk hairdo throwing the switches. Feminism was not exactly the center of Anderson's material, but it was part of the message.

Well, as the song said, that was the time, and that was the record of the time. People like me, coming out of the sixties, once dreamed of a fusion between something like pop music and something like conceptual art. We longed for an expressive form that would combine the urgency and excitement of a musical concert with the cool detachment of an art without illusions. We wished for energy and imagination without pretension, for entertainment that did not pander and art that was not antagonistic to commercialism, merely indifferent to it. I suppose we hoped to strike such a balance in our own lives. Glimpses of what that sensibility might have been like were pretty rare. *United States* was one of them.

The Mind of Al Gore

I n the summer of 1992, after he was assured of the Democratic
nomination for president, Bill Clinton took a room at the Capitol
Hilton, in Washington, and set about the business of interviewing
potential running mates. Al Gore was then in his second term as a
senator from Tennessee. Gore had run for the Democratic presidential nomination himself four years earlier, on a platform (boiled
down to its crudest political elements) of electability. The basic argument of his campaign was that a Democrat could not win the
presidency unless he was a white Southerner. Gore lost the nomination, but he did not lose the argument. George Bush, a Connecticut
Yankee, defeated Michael Dukakis, the governor of Massachusetts,
by running as a Texan. The lesson was not lost on the Democrats.
Bill Clinton rose from the ashes of Michael Dukakis.[1]

According to the account in Bob Woodward's *The Agenda*,
Gore's vice-presidential interview lasted three hours. Afterward,
Clinton told his staff that he was pleased by their compatibility and
was inclined to offer Gore the spot. In the context of a transaction
usually governed by the political consideration known as "balance,"

this was not the obvious choice. Putting Gore on the ticket, the Bush campaign would say when the selection was announced, strengthened Clinton's chances in Arkansas. Why Gore? one of Clinton's advisers, Paul Begala, asked him. "I could die, that's why," Clinton said.

Well, that was one possibility. It has become a little hard to re-member, thanks to the short-term, not to say the micro-term, mind-set of his administration, in which every movement seems to be scripted by the morning's poll results, that Clinton ran for the presi-dency with the intention of doing something more than simply clinging to the office. But he did. He wished to change the DNA of the Democratic Party, to shed its associations with big government, interest-group politics, and agnosticism about "values." And in this matter he and Gore thought exactly alike. Their shared commit-ment to genetic engineering had led them, long before that summer, to enter into a mutual nonaggression pact. Clinton remained neu-tral in the 1988 primaries to help Gore's chances against Dukakis, and, according to Woodward, Clinton would have stayed out of the 1992 primaries as well if Gore had decided to run. In 1989, though, Gore's son was struck by a car and almost killed; the event led to a period of intense family introspection, and Gore was still not ready, three years later, to take on a national campaign. The door was opened for Clinton, and he walked through like a conqueror.

By choosing Gore as his running mate in 1992—by, in effect, doubling the Southernness of his candidacy—Clinton was casting himself off from the party of George McGovern, Walter Mondale, and Mario Cuomo. He was placing all his chips on the future. And he won the bet. The selection of Gore gave the campaign a huge bounce in the polls coming out of the convention, and it never looked back. As the Bush people had predicted, Gore helped deliver Arkansas; he also helped deliver California and Michigan. And in the end, the McGovernites went along, too. After all, they had no place else to go.

In short, Gore has always been Clinton's designated successor. He is the ideological heir, the legacy-bearer, the anointed's anointed. "I could die": if anything were to happen to Clinton, the genetic code would not be lost. Gore would know what to do. And if nothing happened to Clinton, if Clinton made it through his terms of office, then Gore would carry on the work for another eight years, and the Democratic Party would be saved for a whole generation. In accepting the vice-presidential nomination at the 1992 convention, Gore told the delegates that he finally had the job of his dreams: he was the warm-up act for Elvis. In his own mind, he must have been imagining the day when it would be said that Elvis had been the warm-up act for Al Gore.

Mortality does not seem to be the gravest threat right now to the grand design of Clinton and Gore. The gravest threat is what it has always been: Clinton. The trouble with Clinton is that he is, in the considered and no doubt heartfelt words of George Bush, a bullshit artist. A bullshit artist is not the same thing as a liar (though this may seem like the kind of distinction a bullshit artist would make). Clinton always sounds like he is trying to please everyone because he *is* always trying to please everyone. That is the basis of his approach to government. And since he can't always please everyone, he often finds himself obliged to warm the truth a little. This is not because he wishes to deceive you; it's because he wants you to know that his heart is in the right place. He cannot bear to be the bringer of bad news—which is why it is fully believable that he did not tell his wife the truth about Monica Lewinsky (or, for that matter, tell Monica Lewinsky the truth about his wife). He thinks that even though the situation may not be 100 percent copacetic right this minute, everything will be fine in the long run, so why cause unnecessary pain? Monica will be happy with her new job at *George*, where she will find another celebrity to flash her underwear at and forget all about Bill; Bill will spend more time with Hillary; Ken will self-destruct. He truly is the man from Hope.

It is the sour and rather pathetic irony of his career that Clinton is now in the position of having to defend himself against the charge that he is a liar by arguing that he is only a bullshit artist. He wasn't good (to paraphrase Lyle Lovett), but he had good intentions. The success of this argument will be politically determined. From the perspective of the grand design, though, the danger is that Clinton's personal weakness, his tendency to let his intentions vouch for his actions, will discredit his politics, which are the politics of compromise and coalition-building. Reaching out will come to seem indistinguishable from pandering, and the so-called Third Way—the path, which Clinton is credited with blazing and which most of Europe is now supposed to be trying to follow, between welfare-state liberalism and free-market conservatism—will look like an empty formula for political survival. And if Clinton goes down, can Gore rise from *his* ashes?

One morning in late September 1998, a few days after the day on which the House Judiciary Committee had made the nation a Rosh Hashanah gift of Clinton's grand jury testimony, I went to the White House to talk to a man now contemplating the fact that he was about to be handed, and possibly sooner rather than later, an unpleasantly limp baton.

The vice president's office shares a reception area with the president's, and on this morning members of the Congressional Black Caucus, led by Maxine Waters, were arriving to meet with Clinton. The Black Caucus had recently appointed itself the fairness referee in the president's impending struggle with Congress, and if they had been wearing mood badges that morning, every badge would have displayed the same message: Comfort Level Extremely High. The African-American public is almost united in its contempt for the charges Starr chose to bring against the president, and this has put the black congressional leadership in the unusual position of being able to take a stand on principle without giving up an inch of political ground. If the president pulls through, they will have earned many favors. If he falls, they will be there to pick up some of the pieces. Charles Rangel, the longtime Harlem congressman who sat on the House Judiciary Committee that voted articles of impeachment against Richard Nixon, was slapping backs and growling with genial pleasure, like a politician inside his own local clubhouse. The thought occurred that Charles Rangel always gives the impression of a politician inside his own local clubhouse. But the manner seemed to fit the moment.

Several nights earlier, Gore had introduced the president at a

black-tie dinner sponsored by the Congressional Black Caucus, and
I had watched him on C-SPAN, doing some homework on the
famously inscrutable Gore body language. He has, as a public
speaker, only two dials on the console: pace and volume. To convey
gravity, he slows down; to convey urgency, he gets louder. Clinton
purrs; Gore declaims. In his address to the Black Caucus, he ended
by listing, at about volume nine, the positions to which Clinton has
appointed African-Americans during his administration. It was, indeed, a long and impressive list, and it accomplished the desired
end of bringing the audience to their feet. When Clinton's turn at
the podium came, he was, by comparison, muted, long-winded, and
a little dry, as though the only thing on the minds of everyone in the
room must be the pros and cons of pending empowerment-zone legislation. "Just doing the job the American people elected me to do"
was the message implied by the performance. One could see the division of labor for the midterm campaign ahead.

Once we were inside the vice president's office and the door was
closed, the world of the Black Caucus and the Starr report seemed
shut out. The vice president said that he was glad to have the
chance to discuss serious subjects; so much of his time was being
taken up by what he called "all these political events."

Physically, what strikes you first about Gore is the solidity. He
has the frame of an athlete, but the upper body is heavy, and the
complexion is unexpectedly pale. The mask is, indeed, a mysterious
feature. He inflects with his face, rather than with his voice. He gri-
maces, as though he were putting a kind of facial English on the
words, and though the effect seems self-conscious, it brings out a
certain ruggedness. You see the muscular Gore, the superachiever,
the star quarterback who is also captain of the debating team and is
invited on Sunday afternoons to have tea with the dean. But in re-
pose the face sometimes goes completely flaccid, the eyes become
hooded, and you see the Vulcan side. The light for the hard drive is
on, but there is no message on the screen.

Like the face, the manner sends disparate signals. The initial impression is of mildness; the demeanor is formal, the aura is tepid.
The system has clearly been designed to avoid wasteful heat loss.

The second impression, though, is of a certain stubbornness, and a certain capacity, carefully walled off, for impatience. This is, after all, a man who ran for president when he was forty, something that requires not only unusual self-discipline (not to mention self-importance), but an unusual willingness to demand self-discipline of others. One imagines that Gore has trained himself so well to live within the narrow definition of what a politician must be today in order to survive that he has little tolerance for ordinary fecklessness. He could, by his appearance, be the head of an extremely prosperous nondenominational church, a man of God who sits on the boards of corporations, and for whom a degree of personal rectitude that would be pretty much inconceivable for most of us is just part of the job description. When I explained that my assignment was to capture the essence of his thought, the vice president laughed self-deprecatingly. "I wish you luck," he said. But he did not seem displeased.

Still, I said, I wanted to know his answer to a political question first: Why has the Clinton-Gore administration been the object of so much animosity? It is, after all, basically a centrist, pro-business, pro-defense administration; it adopted a Republican welfare plan and it balanced the budget without losing the support of traditional Democratic constituencies. These were precisely the policies the new genome was supposed to produce. But the halo of electability had not been transformed into a halo of leadership ability. The Whitewater story broke in the *Times* even before Clinton had taken the oath of office, and his presidency has endured ever since a political and journalistic inquisition the essential effect of which, whatever the justifications, has been to place its legitimacy on permanent probation.

It's true that for people with a reputation for brains the Clintons are amazingly inept at (as editorial writers say) "getting the facts out." They apparently cannot bring themselves to admit that their actions are less than noble, even when their actions, like avoiding the draft or making a quick buck in the commodities market or lying about an affair, are merely human. Since their hearts are in the right place, what does it matter where their hands happen to be? The ar-

rogance is a little exasperating. But politically, Clinton is an accom-
modationist. There is no point of view he cannot share. Clarence
Thomas and Anita Hill, he informed the grand jury on August 17,
were both telling the truth. What is there in America that doesn't
want to be accommodated?

Gore's answer was striking for its dispassion. After all, the question of whether, if he inherits Clinton's legacy, he will also inherit
Clinton's enemies can never be far from his mind. He must, in his
man-of-God mode, be distressed at finding his own carefully tended
ambitions threatened by the moral negligence of his brother Bill. In
his star-quarterback mode, he must be ready to strangle the guy. But
he took a very, very long view of the situation.

He began, with great deliberation (throughout our conversation,
the speed dial was turned way down), by suggesting two reasons for
the present toxicity. The first is political. "I view our efforts as being rooted in a longer and larger Democratic tradition," he said.
"Franklin Roosevelt would have recognized the kind of outreach and
broad-based coalition building that we have engaged in. So would
John F. Kennedy." In those days, he said, the Democratic Party was
the dominant party in America, and that is the party he and Clinton
have been trying to resurrect. "The success of the 1990s version of
the Republican Party," he said, "really depends on a cartoon image of
the Democratic Party, rather than a rebuilding of the Democratic
Party at its best." The Republicans understand that if the new DNA
takes, they are doomed to minority status forever, so they cannot
merely oppose Clinton. They must deny him legitimacy.

The other poison, Gore suggested, is cultural. "There is a deep
well of cynicism in the culture today," he said. The country has suffered, over the last forty years, "a whole series of body blows to the
self-confidence necessary to self-governance." That government
doesn't work has become the premise of every political dispute, and
all the Republicans need to do to discredit the administration's policies is to drop their bucket into this well.

From one point of view, of course, this was an answer from
Mars. Surely one did not need to go back forty years to look for the
source of cynicism about politics; one could just go back to Monday.

If you were writing a book on cynicism, the sentence "It depends on what the meaning of 'is' is" would make an excellent epigraph. Still, Gore's analysis was a reminder that he and Clinton really do think of their mission as a generational one, and that they have to be understood in a generational context.

2

Clinton was born in 1946, Gore two years later. Both men essentially started running for office when they were in grade school. This meant that for both of them the romance of politics was represented not by Eugene McCarthy or Tom Hayden or Daniel Cohn-Bendit, but by John F. Kennedy. The photograph of Clinton shaking hands with Kennedy in the Rose Garden, taken just a few months before the assassination, is a well-advertised piece of Clintoniana. Gore's connections were much more personal. He is the only son of Senator Albert Gore, Sr., and he was introduced to Washington politics as a small child. The Kennedys were not just distant icons; they were, in effect, his dad's business partners. They came to the house.

So that Clinton and Gore are not, in the general sense, sixties Democrats; they are, much more specifically, Kennedy Democrats. For all their futurist-sounding talk about the New Democrats and the Third Way (a distinctly Toffleresque phrase), they are really trying to go backward, to reknit a raveled tradition. They think that the Democratic Party went down the wrong road after 1963, and persisted on it for almost thirty years. A national majority party transformed itself into a minority party. From 1963 to 1992 was the Interregnum. Clinton and Gore mean to be the Restoration.

Like most Kennedy Democrats, Clinton and Gore are defined by their antagonistic relation to Lyndon Johnson. Johnson's Great Society policies, in the view of many Kennedy Democrats, set an impossible standard for the role that government should play in the effort to achieve social progress, and helped to polarize the electorate, to the disadvantage of the Democratic Party. But those policies might have been successfully moderated. Johnson is the villain because of his prosecution of the war in Vietnam. It was the war that created the culture, as Gore had described it to me, of political enmity: it dug the "well of cynicism" about government, and it destroyed the Democratic Party. It gave us Nixon, Watergate, and the degradation of the public service ideal.

For Clinton and Gore, the issue was not just political; it was personal. To young men who had been grooming themselves for a political career on, as they imagined it, the Kennedy model, Johnson's war presented an impossible dilemma. It forced them to choose between duty to country and duty to conscience, and in the most concrete way: they had to face the draft. The draft was a crisis for both Clinton and Gore, and nothing shows up the contrast in their personalities better than the difference in their strategies for coping with it.

The prospect of the draft drove Clinton almost to despair. It seems to have been the only time in his life, as David Maraniss's biography, *First in His Class*, makes clear, when he lost his sense of bearings. A man whose deepest impulse is to demonstrate sympathy for every faction was suddenly obliged to alienate the affections of one faction completely. Clinton responded, typically, by juggling his options—which included a pledge to join the University of Arkansas ROTC—until the lottery was instituted, and his number placed him outside the pool of probable inductees. His famous letter to the commander of the ROTC unit, explaining that he was dropping that option, is a classic of Clinton's special art: it manages to praise the honor of those who were willing to fight and the honor of those who refused to fight with equal sincerity. Thomas and Hill were both telling the truth.

Gore's experience was much worse. Albert Gore, Sr., had emerged as an opponent of the war (as did Clinton's political mentor, Senator J. William Fulbright, of Arkansas), and when the antiwar insurgency within the Democratic Party failed, with the nomination and defeat of Hubert Humphrey in 1968, Al Jr. found himself with Clinton's dilemma, but with much higher stakes. His father was up for reelection in 1970, and an antiwar position was unpopular in Tennessee. If young Al refused to serve, he would almost certainly sink his father's candidacy; he also, according to the testimony of some of his Tennessee friends, felt guilty about, in effect, sending another man in his place if he sheltered himself from the draft. So in 1969, after graduating from Harvard, he enlisted. His father lost anyway. It was the end of his political career.

When Gore spoke to me about this period in his life, he emphasized a couple of things besides his father's defeat. One was the shock he had when he returned to Cambridge in 1970, before going overseas, and walked through Harvard Square in his Army uniform. It was, as he put it, "a Ralph Ellison experience." He was sneered at; people shouted epithets. "People I would have identified as those I agreed with on the way we saw the world all of a sudden, because my hair was in a buzz cut and I was in a uniform—it made all the difference in the world to them. Of course, it seems painfully obvious now. But in other ways it was really quite revelatory."

The second was the shock he had when he got to Vietnam. He had always seen the issue in black-and-white terms, he said. "The policy was misguided and wrong, the war was a mistake, et cetera, et cetera. When I actually went there and got to know some of the South Vietnamese, who were genuinely terrified of what would happen to them if they lost their freedom in a takeover by the North, my easy assumptions about the nature of the conflict were challenged by the reality of it. It was so much more subtle. I still think that the policy was a mistake, but I think that it was much more complicated than either the proponents or the opponents of that policy thought." The war as an issue split his generation; the war as a reality made a mockery of the domestic political debate about it.

Once Clinton had successfully steered (we will not say dodged) his way through his period of exposure to the draft, he sailed serenely off to Yale Law School and then to his first campaign for public office. He had not taken his eyes off the prize for a minute. Gore, on the other hand, needed to put himself back together before he could go on. He was in Vietnam for five months, serving as an Army journalist. When he returned to the United States, in 1971, he swore off public service forever. He vowed, as he recalled in a speech at his twenty-fifth Harvard reunion, in 1994, that "I would never, ever go into politics." He did not exactly drop out—he worked for five years as a reporter on the *Tennessean*, a Nashville pa-per—but he tuned out. He went to divinity school, at Vanderbilt, and quit; he went to law school and didn't finish. He spent five years looking for an alternative to the career for which he had been raised. He finally changed his mind about politics, by all accounts over-night ("My wife was very surprised by it," he said), and in 1976 he ran successfully for his father's old congressional seat. But his whole education had taught him the necessity of undoing the damage wrought by Lyndon Johnson.

Gore's response to the sixties was therefore much more genera-tionally typical than Clinton's was. Contrary to the usual under-standing, the baby boomers didn't create the culture of the sixties; they didn't even inspire it. They consumed it. In 1968, the climax of the decade politically, the oldest baby boomer in America was just turning twenty-two. To the extent that baby boomers participated in protests, took drugs, and practiced "free love," they were responding to slogans, tastes, and fads dreamed up and promulgated by people much older than they were.

When, at the end of the decade, that whole culture seemed to implode, baby boomers were left to patch together a culture of their own in a landscape littered with fragments. The establishment and the elite culture, the culture of "the best and the brightest," were discredited; but so were the radical alternatives. Mainstream poli-tics had produced Nixon, radical politics had produced the Weath-ermen, and the counterculture had produced Charles Manson. For people disillusioned or burned out by the sixties, there grew up, in the seventies, a culture of therapy and renewal. Our problems are not political (this culture urged); our problem is our whole way of being in the world. Conflict and contention are symptoms of wrong thinking; a new age demands new epistemologies. It was the time of Erich Fromm and Alvin Toffler. This is in many respects the culture that shaped Al Gore. Gore is, to a much greater degree than Clin-ton, a man molded by the current of popular ideas. If he were not so manifestly buttoned down, you might even say that he was trendy.

You know right away with Gore that his philosophical ideas were not worked up for him by speech writers. Asked which thinkers he had been influenced by in his brief career as a divinity student, he mentioned Reinhold Niebuhr, Maurice Merleau-Ponty, and Edmund Husserl. Would that be Merleau-Ponty's *Phenomenology of Perception*? Yes, he said, with a flicker (just a flicker) of excitement—did I know it? He had found the work helpful, he said, "in cultivating a capacity for a more refined introspection that gave me better questions that ultimately led to a renewed determination to become involved with the effort to make things better." It is a little hard to imagine having this conversation with George W. Bush.

The vice president, as it gradually emerged in our talk, is a holist, a post-postmodernist, and a goo-goo. Let us ponder these in sequence. Holism is the view that by dividing experience up into different categories—fact and value, science and religion, art and morals—we end up treating a universe that is a living, integrated whole as though it were a machine with detachable parts. We murder to dissect. Beneath appearances a single reality beautifully blooms, holists believe, but we have lost touch with it.

Gore lays the blame for these artificial divisions (his view is nothing if not long) on the scientific revolution. "Clearly one of the large changes under way in our civilization," he told me, "is that we're trying to escape from the narrow segmented emphasis on specialization that began some four hundred years ago with the scientific revolution, seducing the rest of the centers of thought in our civilization into looking at the world in very narrow slices, gaining the great benefits of using this approach to understand in intricate detail ever narrower slices of the world, but at a cost of ignoring the interconnections with the rest of the world."

The most dangerous of these divisions, Gore believes, is the division between the mind and the body, for which he holds responsible Descartes' theory that the mind can know truth solely by rational introspection. A "philosophical error," Gore had called this theory in his best-selling book on the environmental crisis, *Earth in the Balance*, published in 1992. "The Cartesian model of the disembodied intellect," he argues there, is responsible not only for our twentieth-century environmental problems—the destruction of the ozone layer, the elimination of plant and animal species, and global warming—but also for what he calls our whole "dysfunctional civiliza-tion." Cartesian thinking has cut us off from our feelings.

Feeling is an important category for Gore. "Feelings represent an essential link between mind and body or, to put it another way, the link between our intellect and the physical world," he says in *Earth in the Balance*. "Abstract thought is but one dimension of our awareness." Living for centuries in this artificial way has produced "a kind of psychic pain at the very root of the modern mind." Gore has, it must be said, a rather abstract way of condemning abstrac-tion: "Insisting on the supremacy of the neocortex exacts a high price," he explains in the book, "because the unnatural task of a dis-embodied mind is to somehow ignore the intense psychic pain that comes from the constant nagging awareness of what is missing: the experience of living in one's body as a fully integrated physical and mental being." He goes on at some length to explain our relation to modern civilization in the vocabulary of codependency, addiction, denial, and recovery.

The most common misperception of Gore is that he is a techie, a superrationalist out of touch with his inner child. Gore sometimes plays to this image by beginning public appearances with his fright-eningly convincing impersonation of himself as a block of wood. But one suspects that, like many sobersided and deliberate people, he is extremely brittle, and that it is the brittleness, rather than the self-importance, that accounts for the stubbornness. It took him five years to recover from Vietnam; his son's accident kept him out of presidential politics for almost three years. It also led him to write *Earth in the Balance*, and all the discussion in that book about ad-dictive behavior and dysfunctional families clearly arises—he as much as says so—out of a personal trauma.

When he talked in his office, he connected the sense of lost in-tegration—the "psychic pain at the root of the modern mind"—to the cynicism he believes is poisoning politics. "Those who are cyni-cal, those who are overly skeptical about self-government—some of their energy comes from that, too," he maintained. "And postmod-ernism, also a mistake, came about in reaction to that earlier em-phasis on overspecialization. There's a great desire now to find the

connections between different parts of our society, our civilization—science and religion being the two large subdivisions that
need to be reconnected." He recommended a recent book on the
subject, called *The Marriage of Sense and Soul*. Did I know *that* one?
"That's one of my new favorites," he said.

The Marriage of Sense and Soul (research reveals) is by Ken
Wilber, who lives in Boulder and has written twelve previous works,
including *Sex, Ecology, and Spirituality* and *A Brief History of Everything*. *The Marriage of Sense and Soul* is endorsed by Deepak
Chopra ("Ken Wilber is one of the most important pioneers in the
field of consciousness in this century. I regard him as my mentor"),
the pollster Daniel Yankelovitch, and Michael Lerner, the editor of
Tikkun. Wilber's idea is that modern civilization denies the spiritual
and emotional side of experience by exalting the rational and the
material. The result is what he calls the modernist "flatland," a
world shorn of depth and meaning.

Wilber uses the term "postmodernism" to refer to the rejection
of the claim that science is value-free and objective. He thinks the
basic impulse of postmodernism is right, but that postmodernists
have gone too far, and have produced a flatland of their own. Modernists reduced the universe to external facts, he explains; postmodernists reduce it to representations, to "chains of signifiers." They,
too, deny the universe depth and meaning. The good news, however, is that cutting-edge science does reveal the presence of spirit
in the universe, and this is evidently what has stirred the vice president. When Gore says that we are entering the "post-postmodernist
era," he means that we can now set about reintegrating science and
religion, and so put meaning back into our lives.

This brings us to the goo-goo. Goo-goo is shorthand for "good
government," and Gore's chief assignment in the first Clinton administration was the task of "reinventing government," a mission
launched under the acronym REGO. Gore reportedly had asked to
take charge of welfare reform, a politically more promising agenda,
but the Clintons wanted that for themselves (it eventually went, by
default, to Newt Gingrich), and Gore ended up with the less galva-
nizing project of making government more efficient. He set about it

with due deliberation, however, and in many ways REGO has come to represent the essence of his philosophy of government.

Prosaic as it sounds, reinventing government is the crucial element in the Clinton-Gore plan to restore the Democratic Party. Americans are cynical about government programs, they believe, because government agencies have become monsters of bureaucratic rigidity and inefficiency, socialist dinosaurs in an entrepreneurial society. To the extent that the Democratic Party stands for the virtue of public works, Clinton and Gore had to show that public works work. They had to make government, as a branch of the service economy, deliver. This was to be their answer to Republican antigovernment rhetoric, and their ticket to long-term electoral success. (This is why one hears so much about the Family and Medical Leave Act, which Gore was closely involved with, even though the law is now more than five years old, and even though it is a "government program" only in a metaphysical sense, since it involves no state expenditures: it is an easily understood and popular example of friendly government.)

In enacting REGO, Gore followed the policy bible of the movement, David Osborne and Ted Gaebler's *Reinventing Government: How the Entrepreneurial Spirit Is Transforming the Public Sector* (1992), which has enjoyed a large influence among New Democrats, but his own thinking on the subject is, as one might expect, more philosophically expansive. It springs from the unlikely marriage of business management theory and the Federalist Papers. In Gore's REGO, James Madison meets Peter Drucker.

The advertised purpose of REGO is to cut waste and to downsize the workforce, and to some extent these goals are being met. The Department of Agriculture's wool-and-mohair subsidy, for example, has now been eliminated! ("The subsidy is no longer needed, since wool is no longer a strategic commodity," the official report solemnly notes.) And the federal workforce has been reduced by 351,000 employees, making it the smallest since the Kennedy administration. But Gore's ambition is more far-reaching. It is to redesign the government workplace. It's all a matter of, as he likes to put it, the "information flow."

Gore's thinking about information derives from Toffler's work. (He was an early enthusiast of the author of *Future Shock*.) But his blueprint for the new workplace is the United States Constitution. The Constitution was designed, he explained to me, to maximize individual contributions to the business of self-government while minimizing the tendencies toward a war of all against all based on selfish interests. Representative democracy achieves this goal (this is Madison's argument in Federalist No. 10) by establishing mediating institutions, like the Congress, which allow representatives to resolve political disputes with an eye to the good of the whole while remaining responsive to local interests. "You could see our Constitution as a kind of software," he suggested (Gore, not Madison). It channels "the flow of insights from individual American citizens toward a system for collecting the ones that have the most inherent value, according to a democratic vote, and then basing the decisions of the country on what results."

Business management theory, Gore said, has finally caught up to this eighteenth-century insight (and here the slowness dial received an extra twist): "Just as our Founders labored to write a constitution that would take advantage of that insight by embedding it in an architecture that would make the most productive use of those things," cutting-edge managers "now try to set up systems that convince their employees that their insights are highly valued, encourage them to pay attention to what they're doing, holistically, encourage them to see the connections between what they're doing and the overall goals of the organization, and then they set up systems for collecting those insights, editing them, discarding the ones that don't make any sense, and implementing the ones that are good." In REGO, this theory produced the "reinvention lab," in which government employees are free to come up with ways to streamline their agency's delivery of services.

In a commencement address at MIT two years ago, Gore had used a different analogy. "The first computers," he explained to the graduates, "relied on a central processing unit surrounded by a field of memory. To find the right answer to a particular problem, the C.P.U. would send out to the memory to retrieve data, then bring it to the center for processing." This was inefficient. Then came the breakthrough known as "distributive intelligence," which distributes the processing function throughout the memory field, "in the form of smaller, separate processors, each co-located with the memory it processes." Now, when you ask a computer to perform a task, "all of the processors begin to work simultaneously and process a small quantity of information. Then all of the separate parts of the answer are sent simultaneously to the center where they are assembled. One trip. Less time and heat." (Just like Congress?)

It would not be too much to say that Gore is in love with this metaphor. He believes that it explains the superiority of constitutional democracies over centralized state systems, and the superiority of free markets over command-control economies. It is a market theory of society: if all the little decisions are processed correctly, an invisible hand will guide the progress of the whole. You could sum it up as classical liberal holism: what is optimal for one must be optimal for all. This conception of decision-making is one reason the vice president is such a fan of the Internet: it democratizes the flow of information.

Who are the enemies of such an approach? I asked, still eager, in my retrograde way, to uncover conflict. "Anything that interrupts the smooth operations of that organization," Gore answered. "The level of cynicism that we talked about earlier is an enemy of the country's ability to succeed because it disrupts the flow of ideas and pollutes the debate over genuine difference into a contest of demonization aimed at those who hold particular views." As Madison had argued, he said, "differences of mere opinion" can be a cause of social disintegration, when "people focus only on the differences and demonize those who disagree with them."

Gore stood up. We had barely scratched the surface, he said; he regretted not having more time—though we had talked uninterrupted for an hour. Back outside, in the reception area, members of the Congressional Black Caucus were filing out of the Oval Office; a group of Russians was filing in, all looking desperately in need of a cigarette. I left the White House grounds through the Northwest Gate, with its now unforgettable associations—this is where Monica Lewinsky threw a fit in front of the Secret Service after learning that the Big Creep was entertaining Eleanor Mondale in the Oval Office, that two-timer!—and suddenly the administration's problems began to seem a lot less metaphysical.

3

Although Gore has yoked himself to Clinton—"I have been by his side every step of the way," he proudly told Richard Berke, of the *New York Times*, last December—he has by far the more conservative instincts. In 1988, when the cold war was still on, he ran as the most hawkish of the Democratic candidates, and it is worth remembering that the Willie Horton issue, which came to symbolize the debacle of the Dukakis presidential campaign, was first broached, during the primaries, by Gore. (Gore raised the question of Massachusetts's prison furlough policy; the Bush campaign racialized the issue. The despicable campaigns run by Lee Atwater and James Baker in 1988 and by Baker again in 1992, when the Bush campaign tried to make it seem that Clinton was a traitor because he had gone to Moscow as a student in 1969, arguably bear a lot more responsibility for the degradation of national politics than Watergate. Nixon, after all, was punished.)

In the administration, Gore has been alert to prevent Clinton from veering too far to the left. The Clinton presidency began by impersonating the Democratic Party it was supposed to have displaced. It proposed policies (gays in the military, a fiscal stimulus package) and programs (health care reform) that are associated with a big and activist government, and the party was clobbered in the 1994 midterm elections. After the deluge, Gore reportedly was instrumental in getting Clinton back on the New Democrat platform of smaller, more decentralized, more entrepreneurial government— Government Lite. And in the summer of 1996, when the Republican Congress passed welfare reform legislation, with the notion that Clinton, under pressure from his electoral base, would veto it and hand Bob Dole a potentially winning issue in the presidential campaign, Gore is said to have urged Clinton to sign the bill. He did, and robbed Dole of every issue save one that he could hardly bring himself to raise—character.

But then Gore seems to have made a mistake. When it became clear, in the final weeks, that Dole could not win, Clinton had a choice of continuing to campaign for the national ticket, in the hope of winning a majority of the popular vote, or of campaigning instead for Democrats in local House races, in the hope of regaining the House. He decided to push up his own numbers. Clinton and Gore fell short of 50 percent in the popular vote, in part because the news of the Indonesian connection (remember that one?) dominated the news just before the election; and the Democrats fell short of retaking the House. As a consequence, Clinton faces impeachment proceedings in a House controlled by the rival party. According to Elizabeth Drew's book on the 1996 election, *Whatever It Takes*, Gore was one of the people behind the decision not to campaign in the House races. He apparently did not want his most likely primary rival in 2000, Dick Gephardt, to become the Speaker (a motive not entirely consistent with the ambition to restore the Democratic Party to dominance). The Democrats have another shot at the House this fall, but unless Clinton can perform political jujitsu on his opponents (which is not inconceivable; Clinton is a man who is lucky in his enemies), it is probably too late.

A Republican Congress will be able to drag out impeachment hearings well into next year—a year that was to have been Gore's chance to perform in more of the spotlight. There is also, of course, the impending investigation into the Democrats' fund-raising practices in the 1996 campaign, which will almost certainly look at Gore's role. And then there is the personality issue. Clinton's electoral success is due in part to his centrist politics, but in part to sheer salesmanship. Whenever he can get his face in front of the camera, his approval ratings go up. Gore does not have this particular magic. His charisma emission levels are unusually low.

Gore is more sophisticated about the media than his public style suggests. He wrote his senior thesis at Harvard on the impact of television on the presidency, concluding that because television loves one face over many faces its effect has been to increase the president's political power at the expense of Congress's. In his conversation with me, he described (using what he referred to, with obvious satisfaction, as an "arcane metaphor" involving the religions of India) the difficulty of conducting the business of government in a televisual culture. But understanding the problem has not helped him solve it. He continues to look programmed in a medium in which everyone is programmed not to look programmed. Still, there is one fundamental rule in electoral politics: somebody has to beat you. It will be hard for a candidate to get noticeably to Gore's right without looking like an extremist. And, to the extent that the electorate is fed up with Clinton, Gore will profit by the stylistic contrast. After Elvis came the Beatles. (Also, it's true, the Monkees.)

But can Gore campaign on a platform of nonhierarchical management structures and access to the information flow? The old Democratic Party was defined by its interest groups. The new Democratic Party of Clinton and Gore is supposed to be defined by its transcendence of interest group politics. Cooperative government is the ideal. Can you win elections by appealing to a constituency of the whole? Gore has been careful to preserve his connections with traditional Democratic constituencies. He is, for example, a fervent supporter of affirmative action. "Don't tell me that our persistent vulnerability to racism has suddenly disappeared, and that we now live in a color-blind society," he said in a sermonesque address to the NAACP last July. "We've left Egypt, but don't tell me we've arrived in Canaan." When he gets down to policy, though, he sticks to the Government Lite formula. In the same speech, he proposed using "voluntary tools, such as charter schools, magnet schools, and public school choice to seek more diversity," and spoke proudly of the administration's "E-rate" initiative—a special rate, offered to poor school districts, for connection to the Internet. This is not the language of Roosevelt.

But it is a mistake to assume that it is not interest group politics. Policies like those are aimed directly at a specific constituency: the so-called wired workers, people who use computers on the job, work in nonhierarchical organizations, and practice on-the-job problem solving—Gore's cyber-Madisonians. According to an analysis by Elaine Kamarck (who directed Gore's REGO program until last year) and William Galston in a new magazine called *Blueprint*, which is being published as a kind of policy forum to accompany the Gore presidential campaign, 37 percent of Californians are now classified as "wired workers." They are socially liberal, fiscally conservative, and market-friendly. If holism means that what is good for you must be good for everybody, then they are probably holists, too. Gore speaks their tongue.

Whether he can rouse them to leave their screen-savers on for a few hours and actually go out and vote is another question. For Gore is a peculiar politician. He thinks long (holding Descartes responsible for the destruction of the rain forest, for example), but he plays a short game (jockeying to deny Gephardt field position in the race in 2000). He is a man whose philosophy is fuzzy but whose affect is rectilinear. And he maintains an abstract faith in process and flow, even though his administration is now facing disaster in part because of the intersection of an unfettered legal inquiry with an unguided information economy. Clinton and Gore don't need more process. Process is precisely what is killing these guys.

Gore's faith in process (in "the smooth operations of the organization") belongs, like his holism, to the mild, ecumenist side of his personality; but this is not, one comes to feel, what drives him. Professing a belief in processes is a way of masking the brute reality of politics, which is will. When we approve of a political or a judicial outcome, we tend to say that "the system worked." But it wasn't the system that drove Nixon from office or that denied Robert Bork a seat on the Supreme Court. Those things happened because people committed themselves, against the normal flow of political traffic, to making them happen. Politics is a battle *against* process, just as life is. It is a war against the tendency of things to take their natural course. That's why we care (when we do care) about politicians: because they offer to turn the tide of events in directions we favor. And we don't mind if they make a few enemies while they're at it. We want our team in charge. I'm pretty sure Al Gore knows the feeling.

The Reluctant Memorialist:
Maya Lin

I

One afternoon this winter, Maya Lin walked with me from SoHo, where she has her studio, across Canal Street and down Church Street to the place where the World Trade Center once stood.[1] Lin is a friendly, unpretentious woman. She is slight—she stands a little under five-three and weighs just over a hundred pounds—and though she is forty-two, she could pass for twenty. She dresses, on most days, like a college student who woke up late for class—corduroys, a turtleneck, and a hairband. She takes unexpectedly long strides, however. It's hard to keep up with her.

Lin did not especially want to visit the World Trade Center site with me. Within forty-eight hours of the September 11 attacks, calls and faxes had started coming in to her studio. Would Lin comment on the destruction of the World Trade Center? Would she write an op-ed piece about it? Would she be quoted in a magazine story on the New York City skyline? Would she provide remarks for an article about rebuilding downtown, prepare a sketch of a memorial for *The Early Show* with Bryant Gumbel, join a panel on the meaning of memorialization, submit to an interview with Barbara Walters? It is not her favorite kind of attention.

"I have fought very, very hard to get past being known as the Monument Maker," she told me shortly before we decided to take our walk. The Vietnam Veterans Memorial, dedicated twenty years ago, is the work with which Lin's name will be forever associated. In a career that, since then, has included houses, apartments, gardens, sculpture, landscape architecture, public art, a library, a museum, a line of furniture, a skating rink, clothing, two chapels, and a bakery, she has designed two other well-received memorials: the Civil Rights Memorial, in Montgomery, Alabama, in 1989, and the Women's Table, commemorating the admission of female students to Yale, in 1993. But two years ago, in *Boundaries*, a book in which she reviewed her major works, she announced that she was retiring from the monument business.[2] She had only one more memorial she wanted to make, she said: a work about the extinction of plant and animal species. Then came September 11, and although she declined the requests for articles, sketches, and interviews, she couldn't get the problem of a memorial out of her head. "Extinction is the last of my memorials," she told me. "But I cannot stop thinking about the World Trade Center. I just can't."

On September 11, Lin was in Colorado, where she and her husband, Daniel Wolf, spend the summers with their two young daughters. She woke up a little before the second tower was hit, and she called her brother, Tan, who lives on the Bowery, to see if he was all right. Tan had been watching the towers burn from the roof of his building. Lin and her husband returned to New York that weekend, and went to dinner at a restaurant in Tribeca, as many people were doing to help support businesses downtown. At some point, she noticed that her hand, which she had rubbed inadvertently against a wall, was smeared with ash. It was a while before she could bring herself to wash it off.

Lin thought about trying to get access to Ground Zero in those first few weeks, when people with connections were being issued hardhats and let into the site, but she decided not to. "I didn't want to be a tourist," she told me. She saw the ruins for the first time later in the fall, when they were still smoldering, from an office in the building at One Liberty Plaza. She could see the palm trees in the Winter Garden of the World Financial Center, all dead from the smoke. When the public viewing platforms went up, though, her instinct was to avoid the place. It's not that she deprecated people's desire to see the site. You can hardly be a builder of successful memorials and have no sympathy for the need to gaze on places of sadness and destruction. There is nothing at most Civil War battlefields today except grass, trees, and the occasional plaque; they are visually indistinguishable from a dozen nearby spaces that just happen not to be Civil War battlefields. But every year thousands of people travel miles to stand in them and brood. What distressed Lin about the Trade Center site was the prefabricated quality of the experience—the tickets people had to get, the lines they stood in, the memorabilia being hawked on the sidewalks. Spontaneity is important to her—emotions that mean something should somehow surprise you—and she felt that the lines and the souvenirs regimented people's response.

There was a five-minute wait when we arrived at the platform. It was chilly, the sidewalks were congested, and it was obvious that Lin had no inclination to stand in line. The other side of her general pleasantness is that you quickly know when she is not so pleased. She doesn't say much; she just, very politely, shuts off. We turned around, and ten minutes later we were sitting in a café on Broome Street. Lin ordered a cup of tea, and started talking. Something about being near the Trade Center site seemed to lift an inhibition, because a few days later she called to say that she couldn't believe she had talked so much. What she meant was that she couldn't believe she had talked so much about the two subjects that she had made up her mind to discuss as little as possible: the World Trade Center and the Vietnam Memorial.

September 11 turned a page in every New Yorker's life. It is a permanent before-and-after moment. For Lin, it also happened to coincide with a transitional period in her career. A number of large-scale

projects were finishing up, and she felt that she had finally succeeded in defining herself as something more than the designer of
the Vietnam Memorial. That was the reason she had written *Boundaries*. But she wasn't quite ready to begin the next phase.

Lin's work is self-consciously beautiful, because she is obsessed
with harmony—how we fit into the world and how the world shapes
us. "Site-specificity" is a cliché in contemporary art and architecture, but, if it is an instinctive mode for any artist, it is for Lin. Her
impulse is not to impose form; it is to evoke form out of what is
given—the landscape, the building, the light, the natural materials
at hand. This impulse expresses itself in work that is simple, grace-
ful, and, in its detachment, a little Zen.

But Lin is not a Zen-like person. She is a worrier. She worries
that people think she's abrasive, and she worries that she comes
across as someone who doesn't know what she's doing. She thinks
that she is too self-absorbed ("People would be amazed at how part
of me has lived like the ostrich, with its head in the sand," she said
to me once, when I asked about her life outside work), but distrac-
tions make her nervous. The polished, stripped-down, carefully sit-
uated work that she creates is the product of a permanently anxious
sensibility. If you saw that a smear on your hand was ash, you would
probably take note of it, but you would not be spooked by it. Lin was
spooked by it, because the other side of her aesthetic is an apprehension of disaster. Her work is about order, harmony, and serenity,
but it is also about what order and harmony are created to defy—
waste, damage, loss, solitude, death. Her inability to speak of her
work in those terms is probably a condition of her compulsion to
make it.

2

If you ask Maya Lin what type of artist she is, one of the things she
will say is "Midwestern." She was born in Athens, Ohio, twenty
miles from West Virginia, on the fringes of the Appalachians. Although her architecture shows Scandinavian and Asian influences
(she studied in Denmark and Japan), almost all the rest of her

work—the memorials, the sculpture, the landscape art, the installations—takes its inspiration from the hills, stones, and streams of southeastern Ohio.

Athens is the home of Ohio University, where Lin's mother (who still lives there) taught English and Asian literature, and where Lin's father (who died in 1989) was the dean of the college of fine arts. Through sixth grade, Lin went to the university's laboratory school, Putnam—a place where, in the progressive tradition of university laboratory schools, the children were encouraged to pursue their own interests. "By second or third grade, I was doing my own thing," she says. "I still resent being told what to do in any way, shape, or form. I'm sure it's clinical." After Putnam, she went to public school, where she was first in her class.

Athens, she says, was idyllic. Still, she felt out of place. There are two forms of adolescent alienation: the kind where you reject your family and embrace your peers, and the kind where the sentiments run the other way. Lin's was the second type. She never had a close friend after sixth grade; she didn't wear makeup or go to the prom. "I was pretty much isolated by the time I got to high school," she told me one day when we were sitting in the back of her studio, in a space she reserves for her art projects. There was a model behind her for what will eventually be a room-sized sculpture based on the contours of the ocean floor (which look a lot like the hills of southeastern Ohio). "I didn't get it. I never listened to, like, the Beatles. I was sort of in my own little world, and didn't realize there was any other world.

"I think some kids are just that way," she said. "I think it was also the way my parents felt in Athens." Lin is descended from two highly accomplished Chinese families.[3] Her paternal grandfather, Lin Changmin, was a scholar, poet, and diplomat whose daughter Lin Huiyin, Maya Lin's aunt, married Liang Sicheng, the son of the prominent political reform leader Liang Qichao. The couple were educated at the University of Pennsylvania, in the 1920s, and when they returned to China they dedicated themselves to recording and preserving China's architectural heritage. Liang and Lin were also designers of some eminence. Liang was involved in planning the

United Nations headquarters, in New York, in 1947. After the Communists took over, he and Lin helped to design the new national flag and the Monument to the People's Heroes, in the center of Tiananmen Square.[4] Maya Lin's mother, Ming-Hui, known as Julia, is the daughter of a prominent Shanghai eye specialist who received his medical education at Penn. Both of Julia's grandmothers were doctors; one of them was trained at Johns Hopkins.

Lin's parents left China as the Communists were coming to power. Her father, Huan, called Henry, got out fairly easily. He had been an administrator at Fuzhou Christian University, and he left in 1948 for the University of Washington, on a scholarship to study education. Julia, though, had an odyssey. Her father used his American connections to get her admitted, as a junior, to Smith College, but the telegram informing her that she had been offered a scholarship arrived the day the Communists marched into Shanghai, in May of 1949. She was smuggled out of Shanghai on a junk used to transport dried fish; her passport, visa, letter of acceptance, and ten dollars were sewn into the collar of her dress and her slippers. It took her a month to get to Hong Kong; she didn't make it to Smith until October. She met Henry Lin at the University of Washington, where she went for graduate work, in 1951. Her father lost his practice in the Cultural Revolution, and he died in 1975. She never saw him again.

When Maya Lin was growing up, her parents rarely talked about China. Neither she nor her brother speaks Chinese, and she thinks it's funny that she holds her chopsticks incorrectly (though she does favor Chinese food). She didn't know the story of her mother's escape until Julia took her and Tan to Shanghai, in 1985. She didn't know that her relatives had designed the Monument to the People's Heroes—that there is, so to speak, monument-making in her genes—until I mentioned it to her last winter. She did not have a sense of dispossession instilled in her. It was subtler than that; she was brought up by people who had been dispossesed, and who were determined that she and her brother should never know the experience.

She did understand that they were cut off from the rest of the family, and she appreciates the damage to her parents' lives more clearly now. "The home they knew was completely modified and changed by history," she said to me. "There wasn't a place of nostalgia to go back to. I saw it in my father's face after Tiananmen Square." (The pro-democracy demonstrations there were suppressed in the spring of 1989.) "He knew that China wouldn't even begin to return to an open-door policy in his lifetime. It was extremely upsetting. I still can go home, to the house I grew up in, and I know where some of my toys still are, and my dresses. And to wipe it out, to leave home at the age of eighteen or twenty . . ."

After high school, Lin went to Yale. She loved it. "I didn't have an adjustment problem," she told me when I asked her what it was like to go from Athens to the gritty city of New Haven in 1977. "In a strange way, I found kids that were just like me, and for the first time I felt that I fit in." She started out in the sciences, with the thought that she would become a field zoologist. When she learned that Yale's program involved vivisection, she quickly abandoned that idea. She didn't know, at first, what to do instead; but she loved art and she loved math—so, she explained, architecture seemed perfect.

Lin didn't take any architecture courses in her first two years at Yale, but when she finally began the program, she said, "I just focused, and I did nothing but. I would schedule my classes so they met once a week, and then I would pull all-nighters, like every other unhealthy little architecture student." One semester, she never went to the library. She simply obsessed about her buildings, and that has been her practice ever since.

After her design for the Vietnam Veterans Memorial was chosen, in 1981, she spent a year in Washington overseeing its development, taught at Exeter for a summer, and then entered the Harvard Graduate School of Design. She dropped out after less than a semester, because it was too difficult to deal with the issues surrounding the construction of the memorial and do her schoolwork at the same time. The next fall, she went back to Yale. She took her degree from the School of Architecture in 1986, and received an honorary doctorate from Yale in 1987. She has remained devoted to the university.

Last December, Yale's president, Richard Levin, asked Lin if she would be willing to stand for election as an alumni fellow of the Yale Corporation. Another Yale graduate, a New Haven pastor named the Reverend W. David Lee, had already put himself forward as a candidate representing the interests of the unions, from which he had accepted donations, and the community. Lin declined to campaign personally against Lee. She believes that it's inappropriate to have an agenda when you serve on a board, but she was not happy to find herself cast as the alternative to reform. (Alumni and former Yale administrators did campaign against Lee, though, and Lin ended up defeating him handily, in an election in which three times the usual number of alumni voted.)

3

"It was miserable," Lin said when I first asked her about her year in Washington. "It was beyond miserable." There is still indignation in her voice when she gets on the subject of the building of the Vietnam Veterans Memorial. She hates Washington, and has rarely been back since her work was finished. "I think it is actually a miracle that the piece ever got built," Lin wrote about the memorial in *Boundaries*. When art and politics collide, it is usually the art that gets totaled; that time, against all the odds, it didn't.

Still, beating the odds is not the same as a miracle. For a miracle, there is no explanation, and, except for one element, the Vietnam Memorial is explicable. There was a need to honor the soldiers who had gone to Vietnam; and there was a flourishing contemporary art movement, known as land art, that supplied the formal language for the piece that Lin designed. The people who planned the memorial—the Vietnam Veterans Memorial Fund and the arts professionals it hired to run the design competition—had specified in advance many of the features for which Lin's work is admired. They envisioned a mostly horizontal, contemplative work that did not disrupt the landscape of Constitution Gardens, the area in the Mall designated as the site. The competition guidelines stipulated that the monument "make no political statement regarding war and its conduct," and that it include the names of all 57,661 Americans who died in the war. (More names have been added since.) Lin's design was the unanimous choice of the competition jurors in part because it seemed so uncannily to fit the criteria the planners had in mind. What did seem to come out of the blue was the person behind Entry #1026 in the design competition, Maya Lin herself. Nobody had quite envisioned her.

Lin's design was an assignment for an undergraduate class on funereal architecture, taught by F. Andrus Burr. Lin had become interested in funereal architecture during a trip to Denmark, during her junior year. (She has said that it was in Denmark that she first experienced racial prejudice: people thought she was an Eskimo.)[5] She ended up studying in an area in the northwest corner of Copenhagen, called Nørrebro, which includes an enormous cemetery, Assistens Kirkegård. Hans Christian Andersen, Søren Kierkegaard, and other famous Danes are buried there. In the summer, people use the grounds as a park, and Lin got interested in the way the space had been integrated into the life of the city. Wherever she traveled after that, she told me, "I would always visit the cemetery."

In the fall of 1980, the class learned about the competition for the Vietnam Memorial and decided to make it an assignment. The students agreed to meet in Washington during the Thanksgiving break to look at the site. Lin stopped on the way back from Ohio. Constitution Gardens was empty that day except for a few Frisbee players, and she says that the solution simply popped into her head: she would cut into the earth and, in effect, polish it. A scar, the memory of a wound. It may be that the Frisbee players reminded her of the Copenhagen cemetery she had studied, for her memorial is, essentially, a gravestone in a park.

When Lin returned to Yale, she modeled the piece in the dining hall, out of mashed potatoes. Her submission was a pastel drawing, with an essay explaining how people would respond to the work. She mailed the application just before the deadline, March 31, 1981. Lin learned during graduation week that her design had been chosen. She was twenty-one.

In 1981, Lin wore her hair down to her knees. She was a myopic grind so indifferent to the rest of the world that she often didn't bother to wear her glasses in class. "I grew up in a college town in the middle of Appalachia," she explained, "so I'm still wearing Frye boots, and wearing my hair really long, and everyone's thinking I'm some sixties hippie. I have no idea what that's about. I'm not cutting my hair because I'm a good Chinese daughter. I'm wearing Frye boots because I'm a fashion disaster. And they connected me with antiwar and sixties radicals." She was also, of course, a woman, and her parents were Asian. The veterans decided that the best move would be to get her off the stage as fast as possible and let the grownups take over. They misjudged their designer. "I'm fairly clueless," Lin told me; "I'm also really stubborn."

Many issues drove the controversy that followed the selection of Lin's design, but one was a translation problem. The arts professionals knew how to read Lin's drawing: they would have recognized the form, the siting, and the materials as standard elements in land-art pieces. Most of the veterans, on the other hand, had never heard of Robert Smithson or Richard Serra (neither had Lin at the time, she claims, but she had surely absorbed some sense of the land-art aesthetic). They read Lin's pastel rendering as, at best, a weird shape. "First thing I thought of," said the man who conceived the campaign to build the memorial, Jan Scruggs, "was it looked like a bat."[6]

Scruggs was not a man of aesthetic bent. He had been an Army rifleman in Vietnam, and was working for the Labor Department when, in 1979, he saw Michael Cimino's *The Deer Hunter* and, after a night of solitary drinking, decided to devote himself to finding a way to honor Vietnam veterans. All he wanted was a memorial; he had little interest in a work of art. "Let's put the names on the Mall and call it a day" was his philosophy. He had no problem with Lin's design only as long as no one else did. When objections began, he was disposed to compromise.

The fiercest of the protesters was a veteran named Tom Carhart, who had been awarded two Purple Hearts. Carhart, too, had entered the design competition. He had no artistic training to speak of—he had gone to the library and checked out a book called *Anyone Can Sculpt*—but he believed that only a veteran could know what would constitute a proper memorial for veterans. He referred to Lin's wall as an "open urinal," and he is supposed to have suggested, for an inscription, the words "Designed by a gook." In an op-ed piece in the *Times*, he described Lin's memorial as "a black gash of shame." He rallied a number of supporters. The *National Review* referred to Lin's design as "Orwellian glop." Tom Wolfe and Phyllis Schlafly called it "a monument to Jane Fonda." Ross Perot said that it was "something for New York intellectuals."

Perot had given $160,000 to fund the design competition, and he became a leader (along with Henry Hyde and Pat Buchanan) of the anti-Lin forces. Lin met Perot while she was in Washington. "He came over to the architect's office." (She had arranged for a local firm, Cooper-Lecky, to be hired as the architect of record; she had, of course, no architecture degree herself.) "I was making the model. And he's, like"—she did a Perot impression—" 'Doncha just think they need a *parade*?' I said, 'Well, they really need more than a parade.' " (It is entertaining to imagine this face-off between two not-large persons with not-small egos.)

In the end, the veterans betrayed her. Frederick Hart, who had been an apprentice to the designer of the Iwo Jima memorial, Felix de Weldon, had set his heart on getting the commission for the Vietnam piece (though he had been an antiwar protester, and had once been tear-gassed in a demonstration). Hart had approached the fund before the competition began and proposed "a pavilion structure, with design influenced by elements of a Buddhist pagoda . . . containing two works of sculpture, one a realistic depiction of two soldiers and the second a more abstract form of Plexiglas with internal images." The veterans rejected this proposal, believing that an open competition would be more in the democratic spirit. In the competition, Hart finished third, with a design in collaboration with a landscape-architecture firm, EDAW. At first, opponents of Lin's design tried to get Hart and EDAW's substituted for hers, but EDAW declined to cooperate, so Hart and his supporters campaigned to add a representational sculpture to Lin's wall.

I asked Lin, while we were sitting in the café on Broome Street, if she had ever met Hart. "Yes, I did" was all she said at first. Well, was that unpleasant? "Yes, it was." She paused, and took a sip of tea. "He brought his wife in, and she just was glowering at me, it seemed. He said something like, 'Well, my statues right here will improve your piece.' I just couldn't believe someone could be that rude." Opponents of Lin's design had proposed that one of Hart's statues be placed at the apex of Lin's walls, the center of the memorial, with an American flag set above the wall ("like a putting green" was Lin's comment at the time). Interior Secretary James Watt held up a building permit until the fund agreed to add the flag and a sculpture. Ultimately, both—Hart's sculpture was a rendering of three larger-than-life servicemen—were placed three hundred feet from one end of the wall. Lin received a $20,000 prize; Hart was paid more than $300,000.

Lin learned about the compromise not from the veterans, and not even from Cooper-Lecky, a firm she had chosen over the veterans' objections. She learned about it from the press. "They could have said, 'Maya, we had to do this,'" she said, about the veterans. "They didn't have the stomach to tell me." After that, she felt that she could trust no one. "I was an untouchable in Washington," she said. "I remember trying to call Bush—he's a Yalie, maybe he can help me out. They wouldn't have anything to do with me."

She was befriended by the *Washington Post*'s architecture critic, Wolf Von Eckardt, who, with his friend Judith Martin (known to the world as Miss Manners), took Lin in. When Lin felt she was being rebuffed by the veterans, Von Eckardt got her story into the *Post*. She ended up admiring the group most people in Washington fear and loathe. "The reporters were great," she told me. "I always felt that you knew what you were going to get."

She also had to fight over the listing of the names. She had them arranged chronologically, but some veterans worried that this would make it difficult for visitors to find a name, and they insisted that the names be alphabetical. Lin finally prevailed when it was pointed out that more than six hundred people who died in Vietnam were named Smith. Seventeen were called James Jones. In her design, the names begin at the apex, starting with the year 1959, and run to the end of the right-hand wall and then back down from the left-hand side, ending at the apex again, with 1975. It is a circle, closed by the viewer. The wall is black granite, polished so that it will reflect. You look into the underground, where the dead are buried, and you see, behind their names, the ghost of your face.

Lin has a simple view of what the disputes boiled down to: she was the only one who understood that her design would work. She expresses no surprise that the memorial has been almost universally accepted as a success, even by some of its most obnoxious early critics. She always knew that she was right. When the wall was being constructed, the fund's project director, Robert Doubek, asked her what she thought people would do when they first saw it. "I think he wanted me to say, 'They're gonna love it,' " Lin told the *Times*, when she recounted the story. "And I said something like 'Well, I think they're going to be really moved by it.' What I didn't tell him is that they are probably going to cry and cry and cry."[7]

People say that Lin's memorial is a popularization of the edgier kind of public-art pieces that were being made elsewhere at the time. (Serra's notorious *Tilted Arc*, for example, also, basically, a wall in a public space, was installed in the plaza of the Federal Building in lower Manhattan in 1981. It was removed, after protests, in 1989.) People say that the idea of a contemplative memorial was already imagined by the organizers of the competition. And people say that the memorial transcends politics. These responses all miss the brilliance of what Lin did. The Vietnam Memorial is a piece about death for a culture in which people are constantly being told that life is the only thing that matters. It doesn't say that death is noble, which is what supporters of the war might like it to say, and it doesn't say that death is absurd, which is what critics of the war might like it to say. It only says that death is real, and that in a war, no matter what else it is about, people die. Lin has always said that she kept quiet about her politics while her work was being built, and she has kept quiet since. Maintaining that the memorial is apolitical is the civic thing to do: reconciliation is what we want memorials to promote. But the conservatives were not mistaken. The Vietnam Veterans Memorial is one of the great antiwar statements of all time.

There was talk at the time Lin's piece was built of closing the Mall to further memorials, but the National Park Service home page for the Vietnam Memorial describes it as consisting of "three components": Lin's wall, Hart's *Three Servicemen* (plus flagpole), and the Vietnam Women's Memorial, a sculpture of four figures, set three hundred feet from the opposite end of the wall from Hart's statue. The Women's Memorial, honoring "all women who served in Vietnam," was designed by Glenna Goodacre; it was dedicated in 1993, after years of lobbying. Lin thinks it's kitsch. Directly across from the Vietnam Memorial, on the other side of the reflecting pool, there is a Korean War Veterans Memorial—designed by Lin's old architect of record, Cooper-Lecky, and dedicated in 1995. Among its hodgepodge of elements is a long, polished black wall with faces etched into it, like reflections. It reads as a knockoff of Lin's design. "I can't go there," Lin said to me when I showed her a photograph. "I don't want to go there. It's painful. They cerebralize: it's, like, 'Oh, we'll fake the reflection.' You can't *fake* the reflection. It *is* the reflection." A huge Second World War memorial is next. The Mall has become a theme park.

4

The response is where Lin starts her work as a designer. She creates, essentially, backward. There is no image in her head in the beginning, only an imagined feeling. Often, she writes an essay explaining what the piece is supposed to do to the people who encounter it. She says that the form just comes to her, sometimes months later, fully developed, an egg that shows up on the doorstep one day. She rarely tinkers with it. She is, in other words, an artist of a rather pure and intuitive type.

This makes her an outsider in the world of architecture. Her work is not witty or allusive or high-concept; it has no pop elements. She is not a modernist or a formalist, either; she does not create pieces whose elements are in dialogue only with themselves. She's accustomed to being an outsider, or to feeling like one, and although she frets about it a little, she obviously cultivates the feeling.

It gives her the edge (carefully veiled, most of the time) that she seems to require. In one of our conversations, she told me about a sculpture that she had been invited to create for the lobby of an office building designed by the architect Helmut Jahn, in Des Moines. She requested a site model of the lobby from Jahn's office. She received a model of the grounds, with the building represented by a Styrofoam box. The implication was that she was free to make something outside, but Jahn's building was off limits. "Here comes this solid box, like, 'Don't touch me,'" she said, "and so, of course, I had no choice. Upstairs, here's this two-story glass wall. It's not my style. So, if I ran water down the inside of it, I could very quietly subvert his entire space without ever creating architecture." She cracked the wall and put a stream inside. And how did Jahn take it? "He was fine," she said, quickly. Then she laughed. "I mean, we never really spoke," she said.

But Lin designs buildings, too, and one of her chronic anxieties is whether she is essentially an artist who practices architecture or an architect who makes art, and whether it matters. Frank Gehry, one of her teachers at Yale, told her to forget about the distinction and just make things, "the best advice—actually, the only advice—I've ever been given from the architectural world," she has said.[8] It doesn't seem to have solved the problem, though. She admires Gehry's work, but she says that the person who inspired her was Richard Serra, whom Gehry brought in to critique student work. "Richard was amazing," she said. "I went through a very bleak graduate school, where I didn't get that much food for what I was after, and that was amazing—that one moment, where there's Richard, giving us a crit."

One of the few shows she has been to since her children were born (her older daughter is four) was Serra's, last fall, at the Gagosian Gallery, in Chelsea. The exhibition drew enthusiastic crowds and for some New Yorkers marked the spiritual reopening of downtown. Serra's huge pieces, *Torqued Spirals*, which the viewer walks into by following a dauntingly high, tilting steel wall that spirals inward, she loved for their massiveness and their sense of surprise. The artists she identifies with are all men who work on a large

scale: Serra, Smithson, Michael Heizer, James Turrell—people who
make roads in the desert and turn canyons into works of art. Compared with their work, Lin's is contemplative and understated. But
she dreams of bigness. "I want to find two or three of the most toxic
sites in the world," she once said to me, "and then I could become
an artist."

Gehry is probably right that it's pointless to worry about whether
one creates as an artist or as an architect, but if you had to put Lin
in either category you would call her an artist. One of the things
driving her since she left Yale has been her need to "prove" that she
can do architecture; she now feels that she has made enough buildings to settle that question. It is not clear who, exactly, was putting
her to the test, and it probably doesn't matter. There is a kind of person whose indifference to what the rest of the world thinks is a spur
to accomplishment: she will teach all these people in whose opinion
she has no interest to have a good opinion of her. It's a kind of
Method acting. It gives a person her motivation. As Lin talked about
her future work, it became clear that the artistic impulse—the impulse to make objects and place them in the world, rather than to
erect usable structures—was dominant again.

Lin has had two shows of what she calls her "studio sculpture":
Public/Private (1993) and *Topologies* (1997–98). One of the pieces,
Topographic Landscape (1997), is a large wooden field constructed of
planks cut in undulating shapes and pressed together, so that the result looks like a landscape of hills seen from an airplane. It is sometimes exhibited with a work called *Avalanche*, which is composed
from fourteen tons of broken glass, raked into a mountainous pile in
a corner of the gallery, and by several wall-mounted works that were
also created by shattering thick panes of glass. Lin's biggest broken-
glass piece is called *Groundswell*, created for the Wexner Center for
the Arts, at Ohio State University: it uses forty-three tons of glass,
raked into mounds. It is easy to appreciate these works as environmental installations (which is how Lin presents them): natural materials shaped in topological contours. It takes a little longer to see
that they are also refinements on destruction—just as it takes a
while to see that the Vietnam Memorial is made by repairing a tear

in the earth. The paradox of land art is that it is programmatically environmentalist and deferential to natural forms but is also an intrusion into the natural world of the most aggressive kind. It doesn't simply stick human forms on top of natural ones; it reshapes nature itself. A certain degree of ego is needed to make it.

In late spring, Lin told me that she was suddenly immersed in new projects again. She has started her long-deferred memorial to extinct species—a many-sited, global project. She has accepted a commission to create environmental art in Yellowstone National Park: she will try to put Old Faithful, which is now treated as an amusement-park attraction, back into its natural setting. And she is making a work in the Pacific Northwest connected with the bicentennial of the Lewis and Clark expedition. The work, intended to commemorate the expedition from an environmentalist point of view, will be about the land that was there before Lewis and Clark arrived, about the continent we have lost.

5

"I am starting to talk quietly to various parties involved with the World Trade Center site, from people on the architectural and planning end to some groups of victims' families," Lin told me in June. "I'm just offering advice about what can be learned from the Vietnam Memorial." In spite of her reluctance to associate herself publicly with the memorialization of September 11, she had, in fact, been taking calls from officials seeking her advice on the matter since shortly after the attacks. This spring, as the plans for the site started running on a very fast track—six master plans will be presented by the architectural and planning firm Beyer Blinder Belle this month, when the process for the selection of a memorial design is also scheduled to be announced—Lin began to have more frequent consultations with some of the parties to the redevelopment. She is not involved in the process as a potential designer, she told me; she's just someone whose experience, she thinks, might be helpful.

Lin's chief fear is that there is no unified vision for the redevel-

opment, and that the final plan will be an accretion of accommoda-
tions of every group that feels it has a stake in the site—the Port Authority, the landlords, the Community Board, local residents and
businesses, victims' families, firemen, policemen, and so on. In the
case of a memorial, she understands that it will be impossible to in-
sulate the design process from the victims' families, but she hopes
that when their need has been articulated, the competition will be
run by arts professionals, as it was for the Vietnam Memorial.

Lin is reticent about her own ideas for the site. The city has already been through two stages of memorialization, each successful,
she feels, in giving form to feeling: the candles and flowers and
heartbreaking "Missing" posters that appeared all over town in the
weeks immediately following the attacks; and the Tribute in
Light—the twin pillars of light that shone at the site this spring. "I
think they're really magical," she told me when the lights went up.
She was sorry to see them turned off after a month. But she was
talking one day to a woman whose husband had died in the attack,
and who complained about the lights: "We—we, the victims—don't
think it does that much."

"It's this 'we' thing," Lin told me. "There's this authority that's
going to say, 'This is mine first, then it's going to be yours, then it's
going to be yours.' " That is what happened, she believes, with the
Vietnam Memorial: some of the veterans couldn't relinquish what
they regarded as their moral ownership of the piece. Lin thinks that
the destruction of the Trade Center wounded everyone who
watched it. "At some level, we all shared it," she said, "and that has
never happened before in history. I hope that is really taken into
account."

There is another challenge facing whoever designs a World
Trade Center memorial, even if it is Maya Lin, and that is the legacy
of Maya Lin. The Vietnam Memorial changed the popular understanding of what a memorial should be, and it thus set the bar very
high for future memorialists. Now we expect that a memorial will be
interactive, and that it will visibly move the viewer. If it doesn't
make you cry, then it isn't working. It is Lin's strange gift—strange
in a person admittedly so self-absorbed—to know how people will

react to her art. She knew that visitors to the Vietnam Memorial would find it impossible not to touch the names chiseled into the wall. When she was an undergraduate, the names of Yale alumni who had died in Vietnam were being carved on a wall in Woolsey Hall, and she remembered that she couldn't walk past without touching them. At the Vietnam Memorial, you are also touching the shadow of your own hand, coming out of the darkness.

Lin believes that what enables her to create works that people respond to emotionally is her own emotional detachment, and that what enables her to address political subjects effectively is her apolitical posture. She has emotions and politics, obviously, but making art, for her, requires shutting those parts of herself down. A lot of contemporary culture seems to take the form of the opinion piece: you read the first paragraph—sometimes you read just the title— and you don't have to continue, because you know exactly what is going to be said. Everything is broken down into points of view, positions on a curve. If you're off the curve, or if you pay no attention to the curve, no one seems to know how to understand you, which is one reason that Lin has no interest in her own celebrity. She doesn't want to represent a point of view; she wants to make things.

In March, Lin attended the dedication of one of her installations, a winter garden in the lobby of the American Express Client Services Center in downtown Minneapolis. It is not a prepossessing site. The building is on a strip of large office structures; directly across the busy street is a large parking lot. The garden is inside a three-story glass box in the front of the lobby, visible from the street. Lin has turned part of the exterior wall into a waterfall, which freezes in the winter, changing the view out from the lobby and the view in from the street. There are trees, and stone benches, which are echoed in the landscaping Lin has designed outside the building. The distinctive feature of Lin's garden is the floor, which has been warped so that it has the contours of a hill (or a burial mound). The floorboards are the same as you would find in a bowling alley— that is, they read as level—but they have been curved to create rises and dips.

I arrived early for the dedication, and the floor was roped off. I wandered around looking at it from inside and outside the building. It was not especially impressive—a curved surface with a few trees and benches. Eventually, Lin showed up, there were speeches, and the rope was cut and we went onto the floor. It felt, weirdly, like walking in the woods, where each step is registered differently in the body—a little higher or a little lower than the eye picks up from the terrain. You experienced the floor through your bones. I asked her what she thought of the work. "I want a bigger floor," she said.

At noon the next day, Lin gave a presentation about the new winter garden to American Express employees in the cafeteria. There was a big turnout, and the audience listened intently. Lin showed slides, and explained how the work was related to some of her other pieces (like *Topographic Landscape*) that use similar shapes. There were questions. One was from a woman who asked Lin if she could tell them how she designed the Vietnam Memorial. Lin laughed. "No," she said. "Not today."

JULY 1, 2002

NOTES

Notes

WILLIAM JAMES AND THE CASE OF THE EPILEPTIC PATIENT

1. William James, *The Varieties of Religious Experience*, ed. Frederick H. Burkhardt (Cambridge, Mass.: Harvard University Press, 1985), 407.

2. James, *Varieties of Religious Experience*, 134–35.

3. William James to Frank Abauzit, June 1, 1904; quoted in "Appendix VI," in *Varieties of Religious Experience*, 508.

4. Quoted in *The Letters of William James*, ed. Henry James (Boston: Atlantic Monthly Press, 1920), vol. 1, 147–48 (my interpolations). The diary is in the William James Papers, Houghton Library, Harvard University.

5. *Letters of William James*, vol. 1, 147.

6. Ralph Barton Perry, *The Thought and Character of William James* (Boston: Little, Brown, 1935), vol. 1, 322, 324; vol. 2, 675.

7. Jacques Barzun, *A Stroll with William James* (New York: Harper & Row, 1983), 313.

8. Howard M. Feinstein, "The 'Crisis' of William James: A Revisionist View," *Psychohistory Review* 10 (1981): 80.

9. Henry James, Sr., to Henry James, n.d.; quoted in Jane Maher, *Biography of Broken Fortunes: Wilkie and Bob, Brothers of William, Henry, and Alice James* (Hamden, Conn.: Archon Books, 1986), 119.

10. Richard Poirier makes a case for this way of understanding the relative value of the two episodes in *The Renewal of Literature: Emersonian Reflections* (New York: Random House, 1987), 47–66. He relies on Feinstein's chronology, but his analysis does not, in fact, require it.

11. William James to Robertson James, April 17, 1870, *The Correspondence of William James*, ed. Ignas K. Skrupskelis and Elizabeth M. Berkeley (Charlottesville: University Press of Virginia, 1992–), vol. 4, 405.

12. William James to Robertson James, April 26, 1874, *Correspondence of William James*, vol. 4, 489.

13. William James to Charles Renouvier, November 2, 1872, *Correspondence of William James*, vol. 4, 430 (my translation).

14. William James to Robertson James, December 20, 1872, *Correspondence of William James*, vol. 4, 432.

15. Henry James, Sr., to Henry James, March 18, 1873, *Letters of William James*, vol. 1, 169. Reading Wordsworth had been John Stuart Mill's therapy for his youthful depression, as James probably knew, since it is a prominent episode in Mill's *Autobiography*.

16. Miscellaneous notes, William James Papers, Houghton Library, Harvard University, bMS Am 1092.9 (4473). Quoted by permission of the Houghton Library and Bay James.

17. Robert J. Richards, "The Personal Equation in Science: William James's Psychological and Moral Uses of Darwinian Theory," *Harvard Library Bulletin* 30 (1980): 392 n20; a longer version of this article appears in Richards's *Darwin and the Emergence of Evolutionary Theories of Mind and Behavior* (Chicago: University of Chicago Press, 1987), 409–50. Anderson's dissertation, "William James's Depressive Period (1867–1872) and the Origins of His Creativity: A Psychobiographical Study," was written at the University of Chicago. He published an article on the subject, " 'The Worst Kind of Melancholy': William James in 1869," in the same issue of the *Harvard Library Bulletin*, 369–86. Alfred Kazin reports Murray's remark in *God and the American Writer* (New York: Knopf, 1997), 165. Kazin's chapter on James first appeared in the *Princeton University Chronicle* in 1993.

18. I am grateful to Richard Lewontin and Leon Eisenberg for their assistance in making this inquiry. Eugene Taylor also attributes the denial of access to the James estate, rather than to the hospital; see Eugene Taylor, *William James on Exceptional Mental States: The 1896 Lowell Lectures* (Amherst: University of Massachusetts Press, 1984), 200 n19.

19. See Abraham Myerson and Rosalie Boyle, "The Incidence of Manic-Depressive Psychosis in Certain Socially Important Families," *American Journal of Psychiatry*, July 1941, 19. I am grateful to Kay Redfield Jamison for pointing this article out to me.

20. Henry James, *Notes of a Son and Brother* (London: Macmillan, 1914), 254, 256.

21. R. W. B. Lewis, *The Jameses: A Family Narrative* (New York: Farrar, Straus and Giroux, 1991), 188.

22. Cushing Strout, "William James and the Twice-Born Sick Soul," *Daedalus* 97 (1968): 1067. Strout later said that he had been given the idea about James and masturbation by Erik Erikson; see "The Strange Case of William James: An Exchange," *New York Review of Books*, April 8, 1999, 76.

23. Sander L. Gilman, *Disease and Representation: Images of Illness from Madness to AIDS* (Ithaca: Cornell University Press, 1988), 74–78.

24. See Gary Scharnhorst, *A Literary Biography of William Rounseville Alger (1822–1905): A Neglected Member of the Concord Circle* (Lewiston, N.Y.: Edwin Mellen, 1990), 123–26. Oddly enough, Scharnhorst, too, took Henry James's word for it that the Alger mentioned in the letter quoted in *Notes of a Son and*

Brother was Horatio, and he constructed a complicated theory that Horatio was a ghostwriter on the biography of Forrest. See Gary Scharnhorst, "A Note on the Life of Alger's *Life of Edwin Forrest*," *Theatre Studies* 23 (1976–77): 53–55; and Gary Scharnhorst and Jack Bales, *The Lost Life of Horatio Alger, Jr.* (Bloomington: Indiana University Press, 1985), in which the Brewster incident is discussed.

25. Henry Maudsley, *Body and Mind: An Inquiry into Their Connection and Mutual Influence, Specifically in Reference to Mental Disorders* (London: Macmillan, 1870), 86.

26. Alexander Bain, *The Emotions and the Will* (1859), 4th ed. (London: Longmans, Green, 1899), 443, 441–42.

27. Miscellaneous notes, William James Papers, bMS Am 1092.9 (4473). Quoted by permission of the Houghton Library and Bay James. Perry quoted from the Pomfret notes, but he deleted, without ellipsis, the sentences containing the references to B.W. James sometimes seems to have used a note pad, rather than his diary notebook, to record his thoughts during the period from 1870 to 1873; a few sheets survive, though they are almost never mentioned in works on James. Only one other page, besides the 1869 and the October 21, 1872, notes I have already referred to, is dated (May 16, 1873); none contains pertinent biographical information. In a letter to his wife, in which several of the notes are enclosed, James refers to them as having been written during his "pessimistic crisis."

28. Henry James to Mary James, November 21, 1869, Henry James, *Letters: Volume 1, 1843–1875,* ed. Leon Edel (Cambridge, Mass.: Harvard University Press, 1974), 172–73.

29. The editors of *The Correspondence of William James*, noting this gap, claim that an additional letter does survive from this period, a note to John Gray dated January 4, 1872. But since the note congratulates Gray on his engagement, and the marriage took place in June 1873, James probably (as often happens around the turn of the year) misdated it. He also mentions that his brother Wilkie, who, like Robertson, lived in Milwaukee, was visiting the James home in Cambridge. That visit took place around New Year's Day 1873. It is worth noting that James suffered from eye trouble all his adult life, and was often unable to write. After he married, his wife transcribed many of his letters from his dictation. There is some evidence that his eye problems were particularly severe during the period from which we have no letters.

30. Henry James, *Society the Redeemed Form of Man, and the Earnest of God's Omnipotence in Human Nature* (Boston: Houghton, Osgood, 1879), 43.

31. William James, Notebook Y, 1866–67 Medical School Notes, Francis A. Countway Library of Medicine, Harvard Medical School. Quoted by permission of the Countway Library and Bay James.

32. Dickinson Sargeant Miller, "A Memory of William James" (1917), in *William James Remembered*, ed. Linda Simon (Lincoln: University of Nebraska Press, 1996), 128.

33. Mary James to Henry James, July 1, 1873, March 17, 1874, and July 6, 1874, quoted in Gay Wilson Allen, *William James: A Biography* (New York: Viking, 1967), 183, 190; Henry James to Mary James, July 4, 1880, Henry James, *Letters:*

Volume 2, 1875–1883, ed. Leon Edel (Cambridge, Mass.: Harvard University Press, 1975), 292.

34. William James to Charles Renouvier, October 23, 1882; quoted in Perry, *Thought and Character of William James*, vol. 1, 683.

35. William James to Alice Howe Gibbens James, March 4, 1888, *Correspondence of William James*, vol. 6, 338.

36. William James to Frederic W. H. Myers, December 17, 1893; quoted in Allen, *William James*, 368.

37. William James to Henry James, January 1, 1901, *Correspondence of William James*, vol. 3, 153–54.

38. William James, "Introduction to *The Literary Remains of the Late Henry James*" (1884), *Essays on Religion and Morality*, ed. Frederick H. Burkhardt (Cambridge, Mass.: Harvard University Press, 1982), 61–63.

39. William James to James H. Leuba, April 17, 1904; quoted in Perry, *Thought and Character of William James*, vol. 2, 350.

40. William James, Diary, William James Papers, bMS Am 1092.9 (4450). Quoted by permission of the Houghton Library and Bay James.

41. Gertrude Stein, *The Autobiography of Alice B. Toklas* (1946), *Selected Writings of Gertrude Stein*, ed. Carl Van Vechten (New York: Vintage, 1972), 74–75.

42. John Jay Chapman, "William James" (1915), in *William James Remembered*, 56.

THE PRINCIPLES OF OLIVER WENDELL HOLMES

1. Mark DeWolfe Howe, *Justice Oliver Wendell Holmes: The Shaping Years, 1841–1870* (Cambridge, Mass.: Harvard University Press, 1957), 2. The other biographies relied on in this essay are: Howe, *Justice Oliver Wendell Holmes: The Proving Years, 1870–1882* (Cambridge, Mass.: Harvard University Press, 1963); Sheldon Novick, *Honorable Justice: The Life of Oliver Wendell Holmes* (Boston: Little Brown, 1989); Liva Baker, *The Justice from Beacon Hill: The Life and Times of Oliver Wendell Holmes* (New York: HarperCollins, 1991); and G. Edward White, *Justice Oliver Wendell Holmes: Law and the Inner Self* (New York: Oxford University Press, 1993). Portions of this essay also appear in my book *The Metaphysical Club* (New York: Farrar, Straus and Giroux, 2001).

2. John Pollock, quoted in Baker, *The Justice from Beacon Hill*, 235.

3. See Baker, *The Justice from Beacon Hill*, 245.

4. Oliver Wendell Holmes, "Codes, and the Arrangement of the Law" (1870), *The Collected Works of Justice Holmes: Complete Public Writings and Selected Judicial Opinions of Oliver Wendell Holmes*, ed. Sheldon M. Novick (Chicago: University of Chicago Press, 1995–), vol. 1, 212.

5. *Lochner v. New York*, 198 U.S. 45, 76 (1905).

6. Novick, *Honorable Justice*, xvii.

7. An excellent one-volume reader of Holmes's articles, opinions, letters, and speeches is *The Essential Holmes: Selections from the Letters, Speeches, Judicial*

Opinions, and Other Writings of Oliver Wendell Holmes, Jr., ed. Richard A. Posner (Chicago: University of Chicago Press, 1992). Posner confines his introductory remarks to twenty-two pages.

8. Oliver Wendell Holmes to Frederick Pollock, April 10, 1881, *Holmes-Pollock Letters: The Correspondence of Mr. Justice Holmes and Sir Frederick Pollock, 1874–1932*, ed. Mark DeWolfe Howe (Cambridge, Mass.: Harvard University Press, 1941), vol. 1, 17.

9. Oliver Wendell Holmes, *The Common Law* (1881), *Collected Works of Justice Holmes*, vol. 3, 115.

10. Holmes, *The Common Law, Collected Works of Justice Holmes*, vol. 3, 115.

11. Oliver Wendell Holmes to Elmer Gertz, March 1, 1899; quoted in Baker, *The Justice from Beacon Hill*, 172–73.

12. Oliver Wendell Holmes, review of *The Law Magazine and Review* (1872), *Collected Works of Justice Holmes*, vol. 1, 295.

13. Oliver Wendell Holmes, "The Path of the Law" (1897), *Collected Works of Justice Holmes*, vol. 3, 393.

14. Morton J. Horwitz, *The Transformation of American Law, 1870–1960: The Crisis of Legal Orthodoxy* (New York: Oxford University Press, 1992), 125.

15. Holmes, review of *The Law Magazine and Review, Collected Works of Justice Holmes*, vol. 1, 295.

16. See, for example, Horwitz, *Transformation of American Law*, 109–143; David Rosenberg, *The Hidden Holmes: His Theory of Torts in History* (Cambridge, Mass.: Harvard University Press, 1995); and Thomas C. Grey, "Accidental Torts," *Vanderbilt Law Review* 54 (2001): 1225–84.

17. Holmes, *The Common Law, Collected Works of Justice Holmes*, vol. 3, 115.

18. Holmes, *The Common Law, Collected Works of Justice Holmes*, vol. 3, 191.

19. Holmes, *The Common Law, Collected Works of Justice Holmes*, vol. 3, 191.

20. Holmes, *The Common Law, Collected Works of Justice Holmes*, vol. 3, 191.

21. Oliver Wendell Holmes, "Trespass and Negligence" (1880), *Collected Works of Justice Holmes*, vol. 3, 91.

22. Holmes, *The Common Law, Collected Works of Justice Holmes*, vol. 3, 194.

23. Holmes, "The Path of the Law," *Collected Works of Justice Holmes*, vol. 3, 399.

24. *Baltimore & Ohio Railroad v. Goodman*, 275 U.S. 66, 70 (1927).

25. Oliver Wendell Holmes, "Address" (1912), *Collected Works of Justice Holmes*, vol. 3, 541.

26. Oliver Wendell Holmes to Ethel Scott, November 19, 1915; quoted in Baker, *The Justice from Beacon Hill*, 623.

27. Oliver Wendell Holmes, "Privilege, Malice, and Intent," *Collected Works of Justice Holmes*, vol. 3, 373.

28. Oliver Wendell Holmes, "Natural Law" (1918), *Collected Works of Justice Holmes*, vol. 3, 447.

29. *Lochner v. New York*, 198 U.S. 45, 76 (1905).

30. *Schenck v. United States*, 249 U.S. 47, 52 (1919).

31. Quoted in Gerald Gunther, *Learned Hand: The Man and the Judge* (New York: Knopf, 1994), 162.

32. *Masses Publishing Co. v. Patten*, 244 Federal Reporter, 535, 540 (S.D.N.Y. 1917).

33. See Gerald Gunther, "Learned Hand and the Origins of Modern First Amendment Doctrine: Some Fragments of History," *Stanford Law Review* 27 (1975): 719–73.

34. Oliver Wendell Holmes to Learned Hand, April 3, 1919; quoted in Gunther, "Learned Hand and the Origins of Modern First Amendment Doctrine," 760.

35. *Gitlow v. New York*, 268 U.S. 652, 673 (1925).

36. *Abrams v. United States*, 250 U.S. 616, 630 (1919).

37. Oliver Wendell Holmes to Harold Laski, May 12, 1927; quoted in Baker, *The Justice from Beacon Hill*, 603.

38. Oliver Wendell Holmes to Lewis Einstein, October 28, 1912, *The Holmes-Einstein Letters: Correspondence of Mr. Justice Holmes and Lewis Einstein, 1903–1935*, ed. James Bishop Peabody (New York: St. Martin's, 1964), 74.

39. *Buck v. Bell*, 274 U.S. 200, 207 (1927).

40. Oliver Wendell Holmes to Frederick Pollock, September 1, 1910, *Holmes-Pollock Letters*, vol. 1, 167.

T. S. ELIOT AND THE JEWS

1. Anthony Julius, *T. S. Eliot, Anti-Semitism, and Literary Form* (Cambridge: Cambridge University Press, 1995), 173.

2. Julius, following other writers, asserts that "jew" in these lines is lowercase in all editions of Eliot's poetry until 1962 and uppercase thereafter; but my edition of *The Complete Poems and Plays, 1909–1950* (New York: Harcourt, Brace & World, 1971) retains the lowercase spelling. The British edition (which uses the upper case) is *Collected Poems, 1909–1962*. Used by permission of Faber and Faber Ltd.

3. T. S. Eliot, *After Strange Gods: A Primer of Modern Heresy* (New York: Harcourt, Brace, 1934), 20.

4. It's only fair to Ricks to point out, against Julius's general criticism, that he does find an unthematized anti-Semitism in some of Eliot's poems, and that he recognizes the difficulty of bracketing the anti-Semitism in any consideration of Eliot's work. "It is better," he says, "not only as ultimately more complimentary to the best in Eliot but also as more illuminating of the poems and the depth of their life, to acknowledge that in so far as Eliot's poems are tinged with anti-Semitism, this—though lamentable—is not easily or neatly to be severed from things for which the poetry is not to be deplored or forgiven but actively praised" (*T. S. Eliot and Prejudice* [Berkeley: University of California Press, 1988], 72). Presumably Julius would object to this as a continuing effort to argue that the anti-

Semitism is to be deplored not only because it is offensive, but also because it is inherently unpoetical.

5. Julius, *T. S. Eliot, Anti-Semitism, and Literary Form*, 218.

6. T. S. Eliot, *The Sacred Wood: Essays on Poetry and Criticism*, 2d ed. (London: Methuen, 1928), 5.

7. T. S. Eliot, *A Sermon Preached in Magdalene College Chapel* (Cambridge: Cambridge University Press, 1948), 5.

8. Henri Bergson, *An Introduction to Metaphysics*, trans. T. E. Hulme, 2d ed. (Indianapolis: Bobbs-Merrill, 1955), 27–28. The essay was first published in *Revue de métaphysique et de morale* in January 1903; Hulme's translation was published in London in 1913.

9. T. S. Eliot to Conrad Aiken, September 30, 1914, *The Letters of T. S. Eliot, Volume 1, 1898–1922*, ed. Valerie Eliot (San Diego: Harcourt Brace Jovanovich, 1988), 59.

10. T. E. Hulme, "Searchers after Reality—Haldane," *New Age* 5 (August 19, 1909): 316.

11. T. S. Eliot, "The Metaphysical Poets," *Selected Essays*, new ed. (New York: Harcourt, Brace and World, 1950), 248.

12. Charles Maurras, *L'Avenir de l'intelligence* (Paris: Flammarion, 1927), 16–17 (my translation).

13. Maurras, *L'Avenir de l'intelligence*, 208.

14. Maurras, *L'Avenir de l'intelligence*, 220.

15. Pierre Lasserre, *Le Romantisme français: essais sur la révolution dans les sentiments et dans les idées aux XIXième siècle*, nouvelle édition (Paris: Mercure de France, 1908), 155 (my translation).

16. Quoted in Ricks, *T. S. Eliot and Prejudice* (Berkeley: University of California Press, 1988), 13.

17. See Peter Ackroyd, *T. S. Eliot: A Life* (New York: Simon and Schuster, 1984), 42.

18. My account of the Bernstein demonstrations is drawn from Eugen Weber's *Action Française: Royalism and Reaction in Twentieth-Century France* (Stanford: Stanford University Press, 1962), 83–84; information about Maurras's articles is from Nancy Hargrove's "'Un Présent Parfait': Eliot and La Vie Parisienne, 1910–1911," in *T. S. Eliot at the Turn of the Century*, ed. Marianne Thormählen (Lund, Sweden: Lund University Press, 1994), 49. Eliot later nostalgically recalled witnessing one of the riots instigated by the *camelots* in 1910; see "A Commentary," *Criterion* 13 (April 1934): 453.

19. Michael H. Levenson, *A Genealogy of Modernism: A Study of English Literary Doctrine, 1908–1922* (Cambridge: Cambridge University Press, 1984), 80–102. Hulme's writings were eventually collected, by Karen Csengeri, in a chronologically correct edition, in which Csengeri notes the confusion caused by Read's edition. *The Collected Writings of T. E. Hulme* (Oxford: Oxford University Press, 1994).

20. The syllabi of Eliot's extension courses were first published by Ronald Schuchard, in "T. S. Eliot as Extension Lecturer, 1916–1919," *Review of English Studies*, n. s. 25 (1974): 163–73, 292–304. See also Schuchard, *Eliot's Dark Angel: Intersections of Life and Art* (New York: Oxford University Press, 1999), 26–32.

21. Julien Benda, *Belphegor*, trans. S. J. I. Lawson (New York: Payson and Clarke, 1929), 3.

22. Benda, *Belphegor*, 113.

23. Benda, *Belphegor*, 117. Benda was himself the son of a Jewish tradesman who had emigrated from Belgium.

24. Benda, *Belphegor*, 123.

25. Benda, *Belphegor*, 80–81.

26. T. S. Eliot to Scofield Thayer, August 10, 1920, *Letters*, 401.

27. *Criterion* 1 (April 1923): 242.

28. T. S. Eliot, "The Idealism of Julien Benda," *New Republic* 57 (December 12, 1928): 105.

29. T. S. Eliot, *For Lancelot Andrewes: Essays on Style and Order* (London: Faber and Faber, 1928), 7.

30. The *NRF* article was by Albert Thibaudet; Eliot subscribed to the magazine after returning to America in 1911. See Herbert Howarth, *Notes on Some Figures Behind T. S. Eliot* (Boston: Houghton Mifflin, 1964), 177.

31. T. E. Hulme, "A Tory Philosophy," *Commentator* 4 (April 3, 1912): 294.

32. See Paul Elmer More to Austin Warren, August 11, 1929, quoted in Arthur Hazard Dakin, *Paul Elmer More* (Princeton: Princeton University Press, 1960), 269 n1.

33. T. S. Eliot, "The *Action Française*, M. Maurras, and Mr. Ward," *Criterion* 7 (March 1928): 203.

34. T. S. Eliot, "Thoughts after Lambeth," *Selected Essays*, 342. During the war, after Maurras had become a supporter of Pétain, Eliot conceded that the pope's condemnation of the Action Française in 1926 was probably sounder than he had argued at the time. See the *Christian News-Letter*, August 28, 1940, 1–4. Eliot later deplored the imposition of Nuremberg-style laws on French Jews by the Vichy regime. His remarks on the subject (discussed by Julius) are in the *Christian News-Letter*, September 3, 1941, 1–4.

35. T. S. E[liot], "A Commentary," *Criterion* 2 (April 1924): 231.

36. T. S. Eliot, "Hamlet," *Selected Essays*, 124–25.

37. Ford Madox Hueffer, "From China to Peru," *Outlook* 35 (June 19, 1915): 800.

38. Kenneth Asher, *T. S. Eliot and Ideology* (Cambridge: Cambridge University Press, 1995), 2–3.

39. Richard Wollheim, *On Art and the Mind* (Cambridge, Mass.: Harvard University Press, 1974), 249.

40. Review of *The Yellow Spot*, *Criterion* 15 (July 1936): 759–60. Belgion later published a strong attack on French anti-Semitism, mentioning Maurras and the Ac-

tion Française in particular, along with Georges Bernanos: see "French Chronicle," *Criterion* 18 (January 1939): 297–311.

41. T. S. E[liot], "A Commentary," *Criterion* 18 (1938): 59.

42. Viscount Lymington, *Famine in England* (London: H. F. and G. Witherby, 1938), 208.

43. Lymington, *Famine in England*, 43.

44. A. H. Lane, *The Alien Menace: A Statement of the Case*, 4th ed. (London: Boswell, 1933), 20.

45. Gerard Wallop, Earl of Portsmouth, *A Knot of Roots: An Autobiography* (New York: New American Library, 1965), 151.

46. Ezra Pound, "Patria Mia, II," *New Age* 11 (September 12, 1912): 466. Readers of "Patria Mia" in Pound's *Selected Prose 1909–1965*, edited by William Cookson (New York: New Directions, 1973) will not find this sentence. Cookson chose to reprint a later version.

47. John Quinn to T. S. Eliot, June 30, 1919; T. S. Eliot to John Quinn, March 12, 1923. The letters are in the Quinn collection at the New York Public Library. They have not been published. Eliot's letters are being brought out by his widow. The first volume, including letters up to 1922, was published in 1988; no subsequent volume has appeared. Carole Seymour-Jones, in her biography of Eliot's first wife, *Painted Shadow: The Life of Vivienne Eliot* (New York: Doubleday, 2002), reported that there are anti-Semitic statements in letters by Eliot to Pound still in the archives (see p. 496).

48. T. S. Eliot, "Trois écrivains anglais," *Aspects de la France et du Monde*, April 25, 1948, 6.

49. Asher, *T. S. Eliot and Ideology*, 97.

RICHARD WRIGHT: THE HAMMER AND THE NAIL

1. Richard Wright, "How Bigger Was Born" (1940), *Early Works*, ed. Arnold Rampersad (New York: Library of America, 1991), 874. On Wright's life, see Addison Gayle, *Richard Wright: Ordeal of a Native Son* (Garden City, N.Y.: Doubleday, 1980); Michel Fabre, *The Unfinished Quest of Richard Wright*, trans. Isabel Barzun (Urbana: University of Illinois Press, 1993); and Hazel Rowley, *Richard Wright: The Life and Times* (New York: Holt, 2001).

2. Louella Parsons quoted in Donald Bogle, *Blacks in American Films and Television: An Illustrated Encyclopedia* (New York: Simon and Schuster, 1988), 416–17; and see Mason Wiley and Damien Bona, *Inside Oscar: An Unofficial History of the Academy Awards* (New York: Ballantine, 1986). Other accounts of McDaniel's Oscar night indicate that she sat for part of the evening at David O. Selznick's table: see Carlton Jackson, *Hattie: The Life of Hattie McDaniel* (Lanham, Md.: Madison Books, 1990).

3. Irving Howe, "Black Boys and Native Sons" (1963), *Selected Writings, 1950–1990* (San Diego: Harcourt Brace Jovanovich, 1990), 121.

4. Richard Wright, *Native Son* (1940), *Early Works*, 731.

5. Quoted in "Note on the Texts," in Wright, *Early Works*, 912.

6. Wright, *Native Son*, *Early Works*, 476.

7. Wright, "How Bigger Was Born," *Early Works*, 862–63.

8. Wright, "How Bigger Was Born," *Early Works*, 881.

9. Wright, *Native Son*, *Early Works*, 706.

10. Keneth Kinnamon, Introduction to *New Essays on Native Son*, ed. Kinnamon (Cambridge: Cambridge University Press, 1990), 5–6. Wright mentions these articles on Nixon as a source in "How Bigger Was Born."

11. Wright, *Native Son*, *Early Works*, 849.

12. John M. Reilly, "Giving Bigger a Voice: The Politics of Narrative in Native Son," in Kinnamon, ed., *New Essays on Native Son*, 60.

13. Richard Wright, *Black Boy* (1945), *Later Works*, ed. Arnold Rampersad (New York: Library of America, 1991), 258–60.

14. James Baldwin, "Many Thousands Gone," *Notes of a Native Son* (1955), *Collected Essays*, ed. Toni Morrison (New York: Library of America, 1998), 27.

15. Wright, *Black Boy*, *Later Works*, 235.

THE LONG SHADOW OF JAMES B. CONANT

1. James Hershberg, *James B. Conant: Harvard to Hiroshima and the Making of the Nuclear Age* (New York: Knopf, 1993), 222. Unless otherwise noted, information about Conant's life and his activities during the war is drawn from this source.

2. Interim Committee minutes, May 31, 1945; quoted in Hershberg, *James B. Conant*, 225.

3. Hershberg is the first historian to have uncovered this story.

4. James B. Conant to Harvey H. Bundy, September 23, 1946; quoted in Hershberg, *James B. Conant*, 293.

5. Henry L. Stimson to Felix Frankfurter, December 12, 1946; quoted in Hershberg, *James B. Conant*, 295.

6. James B. Conant to McGeorge Bundy, November 30, 1946; quoted in Hershberg, *James B. Conant*, 297.

7. Henry L. Stimson, "The Decision to Use the Atomic Bomb," *Harper's* (February 1947), 106.

8. In his history of nuclear policy, published in 1988, McGeorge Bundy referred briefly to his own role as "scribe" in Stimson's article, which he by then felt made the deliberations appear more thorough than they were; but he does not mention Conant's involvement. He also does not present a rationale, official or otherwise, for the Nagasaki bomb. It is sometimes stressed that the question of the number of targets was not submitted to the purview of the Interim Committee; but it must have been within the purview of someone. Whether intended as such or not, that was the terror bomb, for it suggested a willingness to use the

weapon without compunction: it was not in any sense a "demonstration," since the demonstration had already been made at Hiroshima. See *Danger and Survival: Choices about the Bomb in the First Fifty Years* (New York: Random House, 1988).

9. Hershberg, *James B. Conant*, 299.

10. Sigmund Diamond, *Compromised Campus: The Collaboration of Universities with the Intelligence Community* (New York: Oxford University Press, 1992).

11. SAC Boston to FBI Director, February 9, 1949; quoted in Diamond, *Compromised Campus*, 47.

12. Diamond, *Compromised Campus*, 112.

13. Hershberg, *James B. Conant*, 520.

14. Quoted in Hershberg, *James B. Conant*, 755.

15. See Nicholas Lemann, *The Big Test: The Secret History of the American Meritocracy* (New York: Farrar, Straus and Giroux, 1999); and Morton Keller and Phyllis Keller, *Making Harvard Modern: The Rise of America's University* (New York: Oxford University Press, 2001), 13–169.

16. James B. Conant, "Wanted: American Radicals," *Atlantic Monthly* 171 (May 1943): 43.

17. James B. Conant, *Slums and Suburbs* (New York: McGraw-Hill, 1961), 34.

18. W. B. Carnochan, *The Battleground of the Curriculum: Liberal Education and American Experience* (Stanford: Stanford University Press, 1993), 93.

19. *General Education in a Free Society: Report of the Harvard Committee* (Cambridge, Mass.: Harvard University Press, 1945), 102. "The root argument for using, wherever possible, great works in literature courses," the report explains, "is briefly this: ours is at present a centrifugal culture in extreme need of unifying forces" (108). Elsewhere, the authors note that "open-mindedness without belief is apt to lead to the opposite extreme of fanaticism" (78). Specifically, the report calls for general courses in three areas: humanities, social science (also a "great texts" course), and natural science. One chapter is devoted to the secondary school curriculum, and proposes a program of general instruction; another is concerned with Harvard's curriculum, and recommends a more qualified mix of core courses and distribution requirements. The obstacle to core requirements (as opposed to distribution requirements) at the college level is always the reluctance of the disciplines to participate in general instruction, which is implicitly "interdisciplinary" and nonprofessionalized.

20. "The President's Commission on Higher Education," in *American Higher Education: A Documentary History*, ed. Richard Hofstadter and Wilson Smith (Chicago: University of Chicago Press, 1961), 2: 989–90.

21. Roger Geiger, "The Ten Generations of American Higher Education," in *American Higher Education in the Twenty-First Century: Social, Political, and Economic Challenges*, ed. Philip G. Altbach, Robert O. Berdahl, and Patricia J. Gumport (Baltimore: Johns Hopkins University Press, 1999), 61.

22. U.S. Bureau of the Census, *Historical Statistics of the United States, Colonial Times to 1970* (Washington, D.C., 1975), 1: 382, 387; Walter P. Metzger, "The Academic Profession in the United States," in *The Academic Profession: National, Disciplinary, and Institutional Settings*, ed. Burton R. Clark (Berkeley: University of California Press, 1987), 124.

23. Geiger, "Ten Generations," 62.

24. Elizabeth A. Duffy and Idana Goldberg, *Crafting a Class: College Admissions and Financial Aid, 1955–1994* (Princeton: Princeton University Press, 1998), 22. See also Marvin Lazerson, "The Disappointments of Success: Higher Education After World War II," *Annals of the American Academy of Political and Social Science* 559 (1998): 72.

25. This is the conclusion of Duffy and Goldberg's *Crafting a Class*, a study of admissions policy at sixteen Ohio and Massachusetts liberal arts colleges.

26. National Center for Education Statistics, "Total Fall Enrollment in Institutions of Higher Education, by Attendance Status, Sex of Student, and Control of Institution: 1947 to 1997," "Enrollment of Persons 14 to 34 Years of Age in Institutions of Higher Education, by Race/Ethnicity, Sex, and Year of College: October 1965 to October 1998," *Digest of Education Statistics* (Washington, D.C., 1999).

27. Statistic calculated from tables in the *Chronicle of Higher Education*, "Almanac Issue, 1995–96" (Washington, D.C., 1996).

28. Martin J. Finkelstein, Robert K. Seal, and Jack H. Schuster, *The New Academic Generation: A Profession in Transformation* (Baltimore: Johns Hopkins University Press, 1998), 26–32.

29. National Center for Education Statistics, "Doctor's Degrees Conferred by Institutions of Higher Education, by Racial/Ethnic Group and Sex of Student: 1976–77 to 1996–97," *Digest of Education Statistics*, 1999.

30. *Regents of the University of California v. Bakke*, 438 U.S. 265 (1978).

31. The landmark study identifying these changes is Ernest L. Boyer, *Scholarship Reconsidered: Priorities of the Professoriate* (San Francisco: Carnegie Foundation for the Advancement of Teaching, 1990); see also Bruce Kimball, *The Condition of American Liberal Education: Pragmatism and a Changing Tradition* (New York: College Entrance Examinations Board, 1995). On the etiology of these changes, see Louis Menand, *The Marketplace of Ideas* (New York: American Council of Learned Societies, 2001).

32. James B. Conant, *Education in a Divided World: The Function of the Public Schools in Our Unique Society* (Cambridge, Mass.: Harvard University Press, 1948), 232.

THE LAST EMPEROR: WILLIAM S. PALEY

1. Sally Bedell Smith, *In All His Glory: The Life of William S. Paley* (New York: Simon and Schuster, 1990), 16. Information about Paley is drawn from this book.

2. See Erik Barnouw, *A History of Broadcasting in the United States*, 3 vols. (New York: Oxford University Press, 1966–70), published in a one-volume abridgment

as *Tube of Plenty: The Evolution of American Television* (New York: Oxford University Press, 1975); and, especially, for the analysis that follows, J. Fred MacDonald, *One Nation Under Television: The Rise and Decline of Network TV* (New York: Pantheon, 1990). On the emergence of the postnetwork world, see Ken Auletta, *Three Blind Mice: How the TV Networks Lost Their Way* (New York: Random House, 1991).

3. For these examples, see MacDonald, *One Nation Under Television*, 107.

4. Smith, *In All His Glory*, 91.

5. MacDonald, *One Nation Under Television*, 129.

6. Smith, *In All His Glory*, 140.

A FRIEND WRITES: THE OLD *NEW YORKER*

1. Quoted in Ben Yagoda, *About Town: The "New Yorker" and the World It Made* (New York: Scribner, 2000), 339. Yagoda's is one of several studies of the magazine published since its DNA (both editorial and business) was changed with the appointment of Tina Brown as editor in 1992; see also Mary F. Corey, *World through a Monocle: "The New Yorker" at Midcentury* (Cambridge, Mass.: Harvard University Press, 1999); and Thomas Kunkel, *Genius in Disguise: Harold Ross of "The New Yorker"* (New York: Random House, 1995). There have also been several autobiographical accounts: Renata Adler, *Gone: The Last Days of "The New Yorker"* (New York: Simon and Schuster, 1999); Ved Mehta, *Remembering Mr. Shawn's "New Yorker": The Invisible Art of Editing* (Woodstock, N.Y.: Overlook Press, 1998); Lillian Ross, *Here but Not Here: A Love Story* (New York: Random House, 1998); and Alec Wilkinson, *My Mentor: A Young Man's Friendship with William Maxwell* (Boston: Houghton Mifflin, 2002).

2. Quoted in Linda H. Davis, *Onward and Upward: A Biography of Katharine White* (New York: Harper and Row, 1987), 239.

3. See Norman Mailer, *The Armies of the Night: History as a Novel, The Novel as History* (New York: New American Library, 1968), 26.

4. James Thurber, *The Years with Ross* (Boston: Little, Brown, 1959), 96.

5. See Michael Wood, "Pictures from an Institution," *New York Review of Books*, May 15, 1975, 13–14.

6. "Notes and Comment," *New Yorker*, July 6, 1968, 17.

7. "Notes and Comment," *New Yorker*, July 20, 1968, 25.

8. Robert Warshow, "E. B. White and the *New Yorker*" (1947), *The Immediate Experience: Movies, Comics, Theatre, and Other Aspects of Popular Culture* (Garden City, N.Y.: Doubleday, 1962), 106.

9. Gigi Mahon, *The Last Days of the "New Yorker"* (New York: McGraw-Hill, 1988), 81.

10. "Notes and Comment," *New Yorker*, April 22, 1985, 35–36.

NORMAN MAILER IN HIS TIME

1. Norman Mailer, *The Naked and the Dead* (New York: Henry Holt, 1948), 718.

2. Norman Mailer, "The White Negro" (1956), *Advertisements for Myself* (New York: Putnam, 1959), 347.

3. Peter Manso, *Mailer: His Life and Times* (New York: Simon and Schuster, 1985), 254. Manso's book is an oral history. More conventional biographies of Mailer are Hilary Mills, *Mailer: A Biography* (New York: Empire, 1982); and Mary V. Dearborn, *Mailer: A Biography* (Boston: Houghton Mifflin, 1999). Mailer has expressed disapproval of Manso's and Dearborn's books.

4. Mailer, "The White Negro," *Advertisements for Myself*, 355.

5. Mailer, "The White Negro," *Advertisements for Myself*, 351.

6. Norman Mailer, *Cannibals and Christians* (New York: Dial Press, 1966), 2.

7. Norman Mailer, *Of a Fire on the Moon* (Boston: Little, Brown, 1970), 131.

8. Norman Mailer, "By Heaven Inspired" (1992), *The Time of Our Time* (New York: Random House, 1998), 1104.

9. Norman Mailer, *Oswald's Tale: An American Mystery* (New York: Random House, 1995), 198.

10. Mailer, "A Review of *American Psycho*" (1991), *The Time of Our Time*, 1075, 1077.

11. Mailer, "A Review of *American Psycho*," *The Time of Our Time*, 1075.

12. Mailer, "Madonna" (1994), *The Time of Our Time*, 1131, 1127.

13. Norman Mailer, "Superman Comes to the Supermarket" (1960), *The Presidential Papers* (New York: Putnam, 1963), 45–46.

14. John Aldridge, "An Interview with Norman Mailer," *Partisan Review* 47 (1980): 182. Mailer discusses Capote's book in the interview.

15. Norman Mailer, *The Executioner's Song* (Boston: Little, Brown, 1979), 9.

LIFE IN THE STONE AGE

1. Robert Draper, *"Rolling Stone" Magazine: The Uncensored History* (New York: Doubleday, 1990), 255.

2. Draper, *"Rolling Stone" Magazine*, 131.

3. Draper, *"Rolling Stone" Magazine*, 127.

4. Draper, *"Rolling Stone" Magazine*, 20.

5. Draper, *"Rolling Stone" Magazine*, 131.

6. Peter Guralnick, "Elvis Presley," in *The Rolling Stone Illustrated History of Rock 'n' Roll*, ed. Jim Miller, rev. ed. (New York: Random House, 1980), 25.

7. Bill Wyman, *Stone Alone: The Story of a Rock 'n' Roll Band* (New York: Viking, 1990), 193.

8. Lester Bangs, "The Doors," in *The Rolling Stone Illustrated History of Rock 'n' Roll*, 280.

9. Simon Frith, *Sound Effects: Youth, Leisure, and the Politics of Rock 'n' Roll* (New York: Pantheon, 1981), 11.

10. "Playboy Interview: Timothy Leary," *Playboy* 13 (September 1966): 100, 102. Many of Leary's personal remarks about his use of LSD as an aphrodisiac were silently edited out of the version reprinted in *The Playboy Interview*, ed. G. Barry Golson (New York: Playboy Press, 1981).

11. Norman Mailer, *The Armies of the Night: History as a Novel, The Novel as History* (New York: New American Library, 1968), 5.

12. Thompson has been the subject of two biographies: E. Jean Carroll, *Hunter: The Strange and Savage Life of Hunter S. Thompson* (New York: Plume, 1993); and Peter O. Whitmer, *When the Going Gets Weird: The Twisted Life and Times of Hunter S. Thompson: A Very Unauthorized Biography* (New York: Hyperion, 1993). Two volumes of correspondence have been published, both edited by the historian Douglas Brinkley: *The Proud Highway: Saga of a Desperate Southern Gentleman, 1955–1967* (New York: Simon and Schuster, 1997); and *Fear and Loathing in America: The Brutal Odyssey of an Outlaw Journalist, 1968–1976* (New York: Simon and Schuster, 2000).

13. Gered Mankowitz, in A. E. Hotchner, *Blown Away: The Rolling Stones and the Death of the Sixties* (New York: Simon and Schuster, 1990), 158.

THE POPIST: PAULINE KAEL

1. Pauline Kael, "The Man from Dream City" (1975), *When the Lights Go Down* (New York: Holt, Rinehart and Winston, 1980), 6.

2. Pauline Kael, "Raising Kane," in Kael, Herman J. Mankiewicz, and Orson Welles, *The Citizen Kane Book* (Boston: Little, Brown, 1971), 14, 13.

3. Kael, "Raising Kane," 20.

4. Pauline Kael, *5001 Nights at the Movies: A Guide from A to Z* (New York: Holt, Rinehart and Winston, 1982), 160.

5. Kael, *5001 Nights at the Movies*, 383.

6. Pauline Kael, "Flesh" (1973), *Reeling* (Boston: Little, Brown, 1976), 94.

7. Pauline Kael, "Come-Dressed-As-the-Sick-Soul-of-Europe Parties," *I Lost It at the Movies: Film Writings 1954–1965* (Boston: Little, Brown, 1965), 176.

8. Pauline Kael, "Sugarland and Badlands" (1974), *Reeling*, 301.

9. See, on Kael's career generally, Phillip Lopate, *Totally, Tenderly, Tragically: Essays and Criticism from a Lifelong Love Affair with the Movies* (New York: Doubleday, 1998), 219–50.

10. Pauline Kael, "Notes on Evolving Heroes, Morals, Audiences" (1976), *When the Lights Go Down*, 195.

11. Pauline Kael, "Urban Gothic" (1971), *Deeper into Movies* (Boston: Little, Brown, 1973), 318–19.

12. Pauline Kael, "When the Saints Come Marching In" (1974), *Reeling*, 377.

13. Pauline Kael, "Saint Cop" (1972), *Deeper into Movies*, 388.

14. Pauline Kael, "Pods" (1978), *When the Lights Go Down*, 524.

15. Pauline Kael, "Portrait of the Artist as a Young Gadgeteer" (1981), *Taking It All In* (New York: Holt, Rinehart and Winston, 1984), 227.

16. Pauline Kael, "Love Hate" (1988), *Movie Love: Complete Reviews 1988–1991* (New York: Dutton, 1991), 48.

17. Pauline Kael, "The Sevens," *State of the Art* (New York: Dutton, 1985), 65.

18. Pauline Kael, "After Innocence" (1973), *Reeling*, 167.

19. Pauline Kael, "It's Only a Movie," in *Film Study in Higher Education*, ed. David C. Stewart (Washington, D.C.: American Council on Education, 1966), 143–44.

20. Pauline Kael, "Is There a Cure for Movie Criticism?" (1962), *I Lost It at the Movies*, 292.

21. Robert Warshow, "Author's Preface," *The Immediate Experience: Movies, Comics, Theatre and Other Aspects of Popular Culture* (Garden City, N.Y.: Doubleday, 1962), 27. The words were written in 1954.

22. Pauline Kael, "Movies, the Desperate Art," in *Film: An Anthology*, ed. Daniel Talbot (Berkeley: University of California Press, 1959), 64.

23. Pauline Kael, "Incredible Shrinking Hollywood," *Holiday*, March 1966, 86.

24. Dwight Macdonald, *On Movies* (Englewood Cliffs, N.J.: Prentice-Hall, 1969), 470.

CHRISTOPHER LASCH'S QUARREL WITH LIBERALISM

1. Christopher Lasch, *The American Liberals and the Russian Revolution* (New York: Columbia University Press, 1962), xvi.

2. Arthur M. Schlesinger, Jr., *The Vital Center: The Politics of Freedom* (New York: Houghton Mifflin, 1949), 256.

3. Daniel Bell, *The End of Ideology: On the Exhaustion of Political Ideas in the Fifties* (New York: Free Press, 1960), 370, 373.

4. Schlesinger, *The Vital Center*, 174.

5. Bell himself, in fact, criticized the messianic character of liberal anticommunism in the 1950s; see *The End of Ideology*, 108–12.

6. Christopher Lasch, *The Agony of the American Left* (New York: Knopf, 1969), 5.

7. Lasch, *The Agony of the American Left*, 10.

8. Lasch, *The Agony of the American Left*, 29.

9. Christopher Lasch, *Haven in a Heartless World: The Family Besieged* (New York: Basic Books, 1977), xv.

10. Lasch, *Haven in a Heartless World*, xxi.

11. Lasch, *Haven in a Heartless World*, 169.

12. Lasch, *Haven in a Heartless World*, 168.

13. See Christopher Lasch, "Life in the Therapeutic State," *New York Review of Books*, June 12, 1980, 24–32.

14. Christopher Lasch, *The Culture of Narcissism: American Life in an Age of Diminishing Expectations* (New York: Norton, 1979), 94.

15. Lasch, *The Culture of Narcissism*, 51.

16. Lasch, *The Culture of Narcissism*, 175.

17. Lasch, *The Culture of Narcissism*, 50.

18. Christopher Lasch, *The Minimal Self: Psychic Survival in Troubled Times* (New York: Norton, 1984), 19.

19. See Lasch's remarks on professional historians in "Consensus: An Academic Question?" *Journal of American History* 76 (1989): 457–59.

20. Christopher Lasch, "The Saving Remnant," *New Republic*, November 19, 1990, 33.

21. Lasch, *The Culture of Narcissism*, 42.

22. Lasch, *Haven in a Heartless World*, 183.

23. Lasch, "Life in the Therapeutic State," 27.

24. Christopher Lasch, "The Crime of Quality Time" (an interview), *New Perspectives Quarterly* 7 (Winter 1990): 48.

25. Lasch, *The Culture of Narcissism*, 99.

26. Christopher Lasch, *The True and Only Heaven: Progress and Its Critics* (New York: Norton, 1991), 82.

27. Lasch had written sympathetically about populist political movements before. See *The Agony of the American Left*, 3–31; and "Populism, Socialism, and McGovernism," *The World of Nations: Reflections on American History, Politics, and Culture* (New York: Knopf, 1973), 160–82.

28. See Christopher Lasch, "Herbert Croly's America," *New York Review of Books*, July 1, 1965, 18–19.

29. See Christopher Lasch, *The New Radicalism in America, 1889–1963: The Intellectual as a Social Type* (New York: Knopf, 1965), 299–303.

30. Lasch, *The True and Only Heaven*, 402.

31. Lasch, *The True and Only Heaven*, 526.

32. Lasch, *The True and Only Heaven*, 531.

33. Lasch, *The True and Only Heaven*, 305.

34. See Eugen Weber, *Action Française: Royalism and Reaction in Twentieth-Century France* (Stanford: Stanford University Press, 1962), 74; and Michael Curtis, *Three Against the Republic: Sorel, Barrès, and Maurras* (Princeton: Princeton University Press, 1959), 211–12.

35. Georges Valois, in *Le fascisme* (1927); quoted in Zeev Sternhell, *Neither Right nor Left: Fascist Ideology in France* (Berkeley: University of California Press, 1986), 9.

36. Lasch, *The True and Only Heaven*, 305.

37. Lasch, *The True and Only Heaven*, 56–57.

38. See Christopher Lasch, "Birth, Death, and Technology: The Limits of Cultural Laissez-Faire," *The World of Nations*, 294–307.

39. Christopher Lasch, "Who Owes What to Whom?" *Harper's*, February 1991, 49.

40. Lasch, *The New Radicalism in America*, xii.

LUST IN ACTION: JERRY FALWELL AND LARRY FLYNT

1. Scott Alexander and Larry Karaszewski, *The People vs. Larry Flynt: The Shooting Script* (New York: Newmarket Press, 1996), ix.

2. Frank Rich, "Larry Flynt, Patriot," *New York Times*, October 12, 1996, A23.

3. Hanna Rosin, "Hustler," *New Republic*, January 6, 1997, 20.

4. Larry Flynt, *An Unseemly Man: My Life as a Pornographer, Pundit, and Social Outcast* (Los Angeles: Dove Books, 1996), 134.

5. Flynt, *An Unseemly Man*, 232.

6. Adam Davidson, "Afterword: Talking with Milos Forman," in Alexander and Karaszewski, *The People vs. Larry Flynt*, 177.

7. *Hustler Magazine v. Falwell*, 485 U.S. 46, 53 (1987).

8. See Robert C. Post, "The Constitutional Concept of Public Discourse: Outrageous Opinion, Democratic Deliberation, and *Hustler Magazine v. Falwell*," *Constitutional Domains: Democracy, Community, Management* (Cambridge, Mass.: Harvard University Press, 1995), 119–78.

9. *Restatement (Second) of Torts* (1977); quoted in Post, *Constitutional Domains*, 132.

10. Reported in John Heidenry, *What Wild Ecstasy: The Rise and Fall of the Sexual Revolution* (New York: Simon and Schuster, 1997), 197.

11. See Frances Fitzgerald, *Cities on a Hill: A Journey through Contemporary American Cultures* (New York: Simon and Schuster, 1986), 154–55.

12. See Rodney A. Smolla, *Jerry Falwell v. Larry Flynt: The First Amendment on Trial* (New York: St. Martin's Press, 1988), 6–9. Smolla's book is an extremely thorough account of the entire case.

13. William F. Fore, quoted in Larry Mertz and Ginny Carroll, *Ministry of Greed: The Inside Story of the Televangelists and Their Holy Wars* (New York: Weidenfeld and Nicolson, 1988), 46.

14. Heidenry, *What Wild Ecstasy*, 330.

LAURIE ANDERSON'S *UNITED STATES*

1. On Anderson's life and career, see John Howell, *Laurie Anderson* (New York: Thunder's Mouth, 1992), which contains a long interview with Anderson; and Roselle Goldberg, *Laurie Anderson* (New York: Abrams, 2000). The recordings referred to are *Big Science* (Warner Bros., 1982) and *United States Live* (Warner Bros., 4 CDs, 1984). *Talk Normal: A Laurie Anderson Anthology* (Rhino, 2 CDs, 2000) is a selection of Anderson's recorded work.

2. Goldberg, *Laurie Anderson*, 53.

THE MIND OF AL GORE

1. This essay was published in the *New Yorker* on October 16, 1998. In September 1999, Tucker Carlson published a profile of George W. Bush, in *Talk*, which included the following passage: "Bush believes that his connection to his softer emotional side is part of the key to political success. He became further convinced of this after reading a profile of Al Gore by Louis Menand that ran in the *New Yorker* last year. Bush finished the piece convinced that Gore lacks the warmth and personal appeal necessary to win a presidential race." On January 31, 2000, Nicholas Lemann published another profile of Bush, in the *New Yorker*, in which he wrote, "People who know [Bush] say he's itching to take on Al Gore in the general election. When Bush talks about Gore, he does so in a way that makes it clear that he has him pegged as a member of the liberal-intellectual coterie that rose to power in the sixties, at Yale and elsewhere. He has been quoted more than once as saying that he realized Gore didn't have the right touch when he read an interview Gore gave to Louis Menand for the *New Yorker*, an interview in which Gore dropped the name Merleau-Ponty."

   Actually, in our interview, I think that *I* dropped the name Merleau-Ponty, though I did so because Gore had cited him in his book *Earth in the Balance*. Gore's interest in ideas is something to be admired, whether one finds his views persuasive or not. And so far as the "right touch" is concerned, it might be remembered that Gore received half a million more votes than Bush did in 2000. I have not revised or updated this essay in the interests of preserving its status as a tiny footnote in the story of that election.

THE RELUCTANT MEMORIALIST: MAYA LIN

1. This essay is based on interviews with Maya Lin conducted in the winter and spring of 2002; it was published in the *New Yorker* on July 1, 2002, before any designs for the World Trade Center site had been made public. The essay has not been updated.

   After it appeared, two of the leaders of the Vietnam Veterans Memorial Fund, John Wheeler and Robert Doubek, wrote to the *New Yorker* to object to, essentially, the statement that the veterans had "betrayed" Lin. Wheeler and Doubek played honorable roles in the construction of the memorial, and almost everyone (including Lin) agrees that without some compromise, Lin's wall would not have been built. But their letters reflected exactly the mentality about public art that was one of the themes of the essay: having paid for what they called the "concept," the veterans felt free to mix and match as they saw fit in order to accommodate various non-artists who had an interest in the site. They did not see adding a statue and a fifty-foot flagpole as emendations significant enough to require even notifying the original artist. When the compromise was announced, the president of the American Institute of Architects, Robert M. Lawrence, called it "a breach of faith . . . with the designer who won the competition" (see Paul Goldberger, "Vietnam Memorial: Questions of Architecture," *New York Times*, October 7, 1982, C25).

2. Maya Lin, *Boundaries* (New York: Simon and Schuster, 2000).

3. See Wilma Fairbanks, *Liang and Lin: Partners in Exploring China's Architectural Past* (Philadelphia: University of Pennsylvania Press, 1994); and Jonathan Spence, *The Gate of Heavenly Peace: The Chinese and Their Revolution, 1895–1980* (New York: Viking, 1981), 154–56, 161–65, 174, 207. Information about Julia Chang's family and her experiences is from my interview with Julia Lin, March 2002.

4. See Robert L. Thorp and Richard Ellis Vinograd, *Chinese Art and Culture* (New York: Abrams, 2001), 395.

5. See Tom Finkelpearl, *Dialogues in Public Art* (Cambridge, Mass.: MIT Press, 2000), 121.

6. In the documentary *Maya Lin: A Strong Clear Vision*, dir. Freida Lee Mock (American Film Foundation, 1995). On the Vietnam Veterans Memorial and the controversy over Lin's design, see Mock's film; Jan C. Scruggs and Joel L. Swerdlow, *To Heal a Wound: The Vietnam Veterans Memorial* (New York: Harper and Row, 1986); Mary Eleanor McCombie, "Art and Policy: The National Endowment for the Arts' Art in Public Places Program, 1967–1980" (dissertation, University of Texas, 1992), 230–40; Daniel Abramson, "Maya Lin and the 1960s: Monuments, Time Lines, and Minimalism," *Critical Inquiry* 22 (1996): 679–709; and Wilbur J. Scott, *The Politics of Readjustment: Vietnam Veterans Since the War* (New York: Aldine de Gruyter, 1993), 129–62.

7. Peter Tauber, "Monument Maker," *New York Times Magazine*, February 24, 1991, 54.

8. Charles Gandee, "The Other Side of Maya Lin," *Vogue*, April 1995, 403.